ALONE TOGETHER

WALLY MIARS

ALONE TOGETHER

My Adventure on the Appalachian Trail

TATE PUBLISHING
AND ENTERPRISES, LLC

Published by Tate Publishing & Enterprises, LLC
127 E. Trade Center Terrace | Mustang, Oklahoma 73064 USA
1.888.361.9473 | www.tatepublishing.com

Tate Publishing is committed to excellence in the publishing industry. The company reflects the philosophy established by the founders, based on Psalm 68:11,
"The Lord gave the word and great was the company of those who published it."

Published in the United States of America

ISBN: 978-1-62510-171-6
1. Biography & Autobiography / Adventurers & Explorers
2. Sports & Recreation / Hiking
13.08.05

CONTENTS

INTRODUCTION

It was midafternoon when I crossed the alpine peak and found a comfortable rock to sit on. I was extremely thirsty. It was a scorching hot day and the climb up Mount Bigelow had forced me to drink all of my water long before I reached the peak. I was usually good about rationing water when I was low, but not that day. It was the dry season and there was no water to be found on the way up. I was thirsty and out of water, but it did not bother me. The rest of the day would be mostly downhill, and I would soon be back in the shade. I knew from talking to hikers heading the opposite way that there was water within a couple of miles down the trail. I was going to take of advantage of the stunning vista before me. Water would have to wait. I had earned this view by climbing and walking all morning.

The majesty of the view inspired memories of the hike to date. Two thousand miles had been covered and the end was close. I was hiking by myself, but I lifted my empty water bottle to those who I had hiked with for so long. I wished they were there to take in the moment with me.

As I looked out over the Carrabassett Valley below, I knew what Lug would have said had he been there—"Glorious Rapture" would have been his cry. And it would have been heard on the next mountain. My thoughts were on the previous two thousand miles of the trail more than the little that was left. With the exception of problems with my knees and my little toe, my body had held up and I was in as good a shape as any man in his fifties would want to be.

There is something about walking up a mountain that makes the views more beautiful and the air sweeter. Not that anybody walks up Mount Bigelow—climbing is a more descriptive word. It was a clear day, which I seldom experienced on an Appalachian Trail mountaintop. I had crossed so many others that were so foggy or so cold and windy that there was no way to enjoy them. But that day I could see clearly, and it was a beautiful day. Flagstaff Lake was to my left and Sugarloaf Mountain was to my right.

Scout, Firefly, Zama, Lug, Spiritual Pilgrim and many others had finished the trail and had returned to their life. Of the backpackers that I hiked with, Feather, Braveheart, Tank, and others had not finished the trail. Their feet ended their hike. For the time we hiked together, this colorful and varied bunch had made the trail interesting, and there was a small amount of regret that it worked out the way it did. I would like to have finished the trail with them, but I also learned in my many years that time spent on regret is wasted time. Later that day I would meet my wife at the base of the mountain and spend the night in the comfort of a local Inn. I would go on to finish the trail that fall. It was an adventure that would be hard to top in five lifetimes, and I was thankful for my chance to be a part of the great journey.

The view of the Carrabassett Valley provoked remembrance of the strange and wonderful encounters I had during my hike. The little boy near Bear Mountain came to mind. He would never know how he touched me when we met. I am sure it was not memorable to him or his family. And then there was the couple from Vermont who gave me a lift. I had not yet decided if they were really angels. Meeting Slow and Steady in Gorham was not easily forgotten. And the hostel operators who poured their lives into the hikers were a part of that memory.

The hike had changed some of my opinions of my fellow man. I had seen people at their best, which is when they are helping other people. I started out thinking this was a hike through the mountains but found out it was much more than that. I also had to laugh at the thought of some of the strange people who I had met. For me, hiking the Appalachian Trail is not about walking, it is about people. By comparison to most of the hikers, I was ancient, but they made me feel welcome and maybe even young for a moment.

This book is in part a story of one of the great American adventures. It is about an experience many will only dream of. It is also a contrast between the first half of the hike and the last half. The first half of the hike was with some great friends who I met on the trail. They made the grueling experience a social event that I will never forget. Because of circumstances, the rest of the hike was a patchwork of hikes that was devoid of those friends and lacked any continuity. Mixed in the backdrop was some of the best hiking in this country. I had a new perspective on life, on the outdoors, and mostly a new perspective on my fellow man.

THE COURTING

On the third day of my hike, I met a couple of boys in their late teens at Neal's Gap, Georgia. They lived in Georgia but knew nothing about the trail until a few days earlier. They decided on the spur of the moment to tackle the entire trail and took off with no forethought, heading for Maine. I met them when they were staying overnight at the hostel with a couple dozen fellow hikers attempting a thru-hike. The two had very little knowledge about the trail and were, to say the least, ill prepared. Their gear was nothing like hiking gear. Their clothing was nothing like hiking clothes. They attracted considerable attention from the other hikers because of their demeanor. You would be hard-pressed to find a couple of guys more lighthearted. Some even suspected their mood was enhanced. Most of the hikers at the hostel were giving them much needed advice about what they would need to be successful on the trail. All were somewhat amused at these two. But the good advice added up to a lot of money they did not seem to have.

I was less supportive. I listened to the other hikers explain to the misguided pair what was ahead and what they needed. There counsel was aimed at educating, but there was also strong encouragement. After listening quietly long enough, I curtly asserted they should go home and start the trail when they had the proper gear, knowledge, and the finances to do the trail. I spoke to them as kindly as I could, but it seemed that the kindest thing to do was bring these young men down to reality. I think

11

there were a few of the hikers in the hostel that were taken back by my frankness. I get that reaction a lot. I believe some of the hikers there stepped up the encouragement as a counterweight to my cruelty. Others privately thanked me for my honesty toward these young men. By the time everyone took to the trail the next day, one of their mothers had picked them up. The word I got later from another hiker was that the mom was relieved they had changed their minds. How much my words helped to shock them into reality, I cannot say, and it is not important. I am sure they would have been a welcome addition to the hiking family that year had they been prepared. I am also sure they would have gone home within a few days without any help making that decision. If they had been caught in the blizzard we would go through, they would have been in big trouble. To this day, I hope that they prepare and educate themselves and attempt a thru-hike.

I tell that story to say this. Few people, if any, wake up one morning, decide to hike the Appalachian Trail, and then take off for Georgia. Anyone that would do that would most likely not last long. The trail must court you subtly for some time. It demands too much of a person to not allow the idea to become part of you. And any long distance hike, no matter what trail, calls for a counting of the costs. And there are significant costs. It takes money. It takes preparation. It takes time. It takes the right gear. Just sorting out the proper gear is an endeavor that takes months for most hikers. Furthermore, few people have the time and the resources to commit to a six-month endeavor that demands so much from the body and spirit.

Every year some estimated 3,000 men and women of varied backgrounds and ages attempt what is called a "thru-hike." It is starting and finishing the trail in one calendar year. That is 2,175 miles of backpacking that usually takes five to eight months. Most start at Springer Mountain, Georgia, and finish at the summit of Mount Katahdin, Maine. The trail passes through fourteen states. It has been estimated that the elevation changes are the equivalent of fourteen trips from sea level to the peak of Mount Everest and back to sea level. The trail is a footpath that is marked by frequent, vertical white blazes on the trees and rocks. It is not hard to follow, although most hikers at some point miss a turn and get off the trail briefly.

Not all start in Georgia. Some start in Maine, heading southbound to Georgia. Of those who start out in Georgia, a considerable number do not make it out of Georgia. The statistics are that about 10 percent finish the entire adventure in one year. For those hearty souls who can endure blisters, hunger, cold, heat stress, loneliness, exhaustion, boredom, and numerous other hardships, the reward is beyond description. Getting to the end usually burns off most body fat. To observe hikers at the end of this journey preparing to climb the last, tallest, and meanest mountain at Baxter Park in Maine, you would think they were a tour group from a concentration camp. The Appalachian Trail is a 2,175-mile long fat camp. Months of living on a calorie-deficit diet temporarily changes the profile of even the well-fed, middle-aged man.

On a beautiful day in March, I would join the young and old alike who take the adventure that most only dream about. I know how blessed I am that I had the opportunity.

There is no such thing as a typical thru-hiker. For most their lives are in transition. Many are college-bound or college graduates. Some would not even know how to spell college. There are considerable more men than women, but the ladies hold their own on the trial. Not all the hikers are young. I met a man in his mid sixties and a lady that I would estimate to be around sixty. Some, like me, were married, but most are not. Some were recently divorced. I met one couple hiking together that had recently retired. They come from all over the world. I personally met hikers from Germany, Australia, New Zealand, England, and Italy. They seem to share a common bond with one another that transcends all their differences. It is as if they are all on a team together and know how much they need to encourage one another. This kinship is obvious and immediately noticed. It is one of the truly amazing things that I noted while hiking the Appalachian Trail. People of totally different backgrounds and values see themselves as part of a great endeavor and work together.

Thru hikers are the minority on the trail. The largest in number are the day hikers. These may be local people who are just out for some fresh air and exercise. Sometimes the day hiker is a vacationer passing by and they just wanted to get a sense of what this famous footpath is all about. They park in any one of hundreds of trailhead parking lots and walk in for a while and then turn around and walk out, satisfied they now know about the trail. For some locals it is a frequent routine that is part of an exercise program.

There is also the weekender or short-term hiker. In the Smokies we ran into a lot of college kids hiking on spring break. I also met many families out for the weekend. They are usually easy to spot because they are not concerned about weight or bulk. For two days, I can carry anything, and I have carried some ridiculous stuff. The prospect of the waiting vehicle is of comfort and so they proudly load up their packs, and the heavier the pack the more the bragging rights. Thru hikers that start with the heavy pack soon learn an important lesson of the trail—"Less is more."

Another type of hiker on the trail is the section hiker. I love these people. They are mostly people who cannot get away for more that a week or two a year so they work at one section at a time with the ultimate goal to finish the entire trail. It must be tough for them because just about the time they start to get into shape they have to head home. I met one lady who had just finished her twenty-five year endeavor.

There are many section hikers on the trail at any one time and they add so much to the backpacking experience. I started out on my journey as a thru-hiker, but I ended up finishing it in two years and was technically a section hiker. Most of them move at a slower pace because their conditioning never gets to the level of thru-hikers. They add something special to the trail.

The trail is a busy place. Some areas are more popular, such as the Smokies, the White Mountains of New Hampshire, and the Long Trail portion in Vermont. Much of the trail is made up of parks or national forests. The Great Smoky Mountains gets nine million visits per year. Not all of them hike on trails, and there are many more trails in the Smokies than just the AT. With as many as there are hiking the trail, I am amazed that it is in as good of a condition as it is. That is due in part to a great effort by the AT conservancy, hiking clubs, and para-government organizations educating the public on trail ethics. Volunteers do an immense amount of work to maintain and improve the trail.

For me, the itch to hike the trail started out in the mountains of Montana in the summer of 2001. My wife Marilyn and I were at a guest ranch with our daughter Rachel and son-in-law Joel. We had enjoyed a week of horseback riding in the Bob Marshall Wilderness area as part of a guest ranch stay. Rachel challenged us to go with them the next summer for a week of backpacking on the Appalachian Trail. I had little interest in hiking the way they were talking about doing it. I had done my share of backpacking during hunts in Alaska and Canada. But the idea of walking around the woods without a gun seemed pointless. Nonetheless, to be polite, we agreed to consider it.

Over the next few months, the idea of hiking on the Appalachian Trail during a vacation together began to grow. We decided at some point to take them up on the challenge. As we looked at the map of the AT for the first time, I was shocked at how big the Appalachian Trail was. Using numerous criteria, we chose to hike somewhere in New England. In part because I do not do well in extreme heat, but also because some of the New England states seemed like a place we would like to explore. After some discussion, we settled on hiking in New Hampshire and then driving up to the Maine coast for a few days. The choice of New Hampshire was made with little knowledge about the trail in that state.

On the first day of the trail, we started at the north end of Mount Moosilauke, heading south. We did not get started until the middle of the afternoon. We had gone only a few feet down the trail when we came to a sign on a tree. The sign warned hikers that the trail ahead is not for beginners. It reminded me of a scene in the *Wizard of Oz*. The four travelers were approaching the witch's castle in a very spooky, wooded area and came across a sign that read: "If I were you I would go back." Like that foursome, we did not heed the sign. To make matters worse, it started to rain. And it would rain most of the rest of the day.

Not only was the trail we picked one of the greatest challenges on the entire trail, but we knew little about the efficiencies of long-distance backpacking. Like most short distance hikers, we cared little about how much our packs weighed. For instance, we took cookware from our kitchens. Our cooking stove was a propane setup that used canisters of propane. We took two containers of fuel to insure that we would not run out. I had the brilliant idea of taking Boy Scout hamburgers for the first night out. That was eight pounds of burgers, carrots, and potatoes wrapped in tin foil. Our packs, tents, sleeping bags, and other gear were not backpacking gear. It was the kind of gear that you could go into any sporting goods store and buy off the rack and then camp out of the trunk of your car. It is not the kind of gear that long distance hikers would even think of carrying because of the weight. When our packs were all loaded up, the weight was staggering and we were proud of it. I had to help Joel get his backpack on and the ladies had to help me get mine on. I was so top heavy my wife could have pushed me over with her little finger.

Mount Moosilauke heading south was unbelievable to us novice hikers. There were places where the climbing was so steep there were rebar handles set in the rocks to aid hikers. It was not hiking; it was mountain climbing. My wife is a kindergarten teacher. She is a lady. And she has never aspired to be an outdoorsman. But she dug in and worked hard all that afternoon to get to the shelter area two-thirds of the way up the mountain. I was impressed with her. But it was not all bad. The trail paralleled a roaring stream most of the way up, and when we could see north through the mist, the view of the mountains was breathtaking. The sprawling green mountains covered in mist was a sight that all of us shared in awe.

We arrived at the shelter area just about dark. The shelter was full and there were few spaces that would accommodate our tents. The best we could do were spaces that were less than ideal. The thing about Boy Scout hamburgers is you need a fire to cook them. By the time we arrived at the camping area, all the firewood was soaked. Joel and I spent the next hour or two trying to get enough of a fire to cook the eight pounds of food I had carried all the way up the mountain. We went to bed that night hungry, wet, and exhausted.

The rest of the hike was less eventful but still quite the challenge for us. We endured a severe thunderstorm, exhaustion, sleep deprivation, and all of the other typical inconveniences of backpacking. On the last night we met a hiker at the Fire Warden's Cabin on Smart Mountain. His Trail name was Red Fog. He was a man in his midforties from Michigan who was working on finishing a thru-hike. He had just completed a twenty-eight-mile day. I had known little about the thru-hike tradition, but Rachel was quite aware of it. Rachel asked most of the questions and seemed to know quite a bit about the AT. The meeting had little impact on me at the time, but that memory would return to me in various ways as the trail courted me.

❧ ❧

There would be more courting. I am a member of the local Rotary club. Every week there is a program as part of our gathering. Some time after our trip to New Hampshire there was a young college grad who was the speaker for the program. This young man capped his graduation with a thru-hike of the trail. He spent approximately twenty-five minutes telling the story of his adventure. I was mildly interested in the trail at that point, but I found his story fascinating.

The timeline is fuzzy, but there were a few other things that caused me to think about the trail. I had a conversation about the young hiker at Rotary with Joel and Rachel, and we had more discussion about other hikers. At some point it became an occasional topic of conversation among us. Rachel bought me a book about backpacking. Little by little I was being drawn into the idea of hiking the trail.

In 2003, I went on a Dall Sheep hunt in the Talketna Mountains of Alaska. It involved backpacking and camping in the mountains. It is a hunt touted by many as a strenuous hunt, but I found the backpacking and camping exhilarating. I had done a lot of hiking during my hunts in Alaska, British Columbia, and Quebec, but most of the hiking ended with a trip back to base camp at the end of the day. But the sheep hunt involved setting up a spike camp at the higher levels. I was surprised at how much I enjoyed the backpacking experience.

By late 2004 I had begun to talk about and consider a thru-hike. Rachel egged me on by buying me a book for Christmas about hiking the AT. The trail had begun to draw me in and I was not resisting. By the summer of 2005 I had begun to talk seriously about it with my wife. She was as supportive of the idea as she could, given the fact I was going to be away from her for several months. At no point did she use her veto. I dug around on the Internet and found trailjournals.com. It was an Internet site that hikers could use to organize a journal and post it for all to read. Many hours during the preparation phase were spent perusing that website. It was invaluable for the insight hikers passed on.

That summer I purchased a backpack and hiking stove and some other gear. Slowly the pieces were coming together, but I had not yet committed myself to the trail. My next step would be doing a test hike.

The backpack I purchased had all the bells and whistles you would want. It had a separate section just for the sleeping bag. It had numerous, smaller pockets that would be useful for stowing items that were used often. It was a beautiful green color and it fit me like a glove. I loaded it up with all of my other gear, some food, and my water filter I had purchased. When I was done, I weighed it and walked around in my field getting used to the load. The weight without food and water was just over thirty-five pounds. Once I had bought a backpacking tent, I was ready to head out for a test hike.

I searched around on the Internet and found out about a trail that is in my home state of Michigan. The North Country Trail is a well-kept secret in Michigan. The North Country trail starts at the border of Vermont and New York. It travels through New York, Pennsylvania, Ohio, Michigan, Wisconsin, and Minnesota and ends up in central North Dakota. It is 4,600 miles long. The part that runs through the Manistee National Forest is a beautiful wooded trail. It was there I would do my test hikes.

I made a couple of smaller hikes of twenty miles. The first one was a twenty-mile hike that included a loop called the Manistee River trail. It was without event, and I completed the trail in an evening and morning. My confidence soared. The second was a disaster. I had a trail guide that I had printed off the Internet, but when Marilyn let me off I forgot to take it. On the first day, I hiked till late in the day and enjoyed myself. On the second day I had planned a twenty-mile day. The first half of the day went well, but at the Manistee River I only took two quarts of water with me. Because I could not see ahead with the trail guide, I did not realize that I would not see any water for the rest of the day. It was extremely hot and arid that day and Michigan had been in a drought condition for some time. There was no water anywhere and by the time I got out of the woods at a road late that afternoon I was dangerously close to dehydration. Not knowing if water was ahead, I aborted the hike and called home for a pickup. The valuable lesson learned was to always know where I could get water.

The next experience was again in the Manistee National Forest. I had planned a fifty-mile hike in three days. I was well prepared that time and made it the entire fifty miles in just over forty-eight hours. The most valuable lesson learned was that I needed to get my pack weight down to a more reasonable level. It would take weight off my legs and would lower the overall amount of energy consumed. After twenty miles of hiking in one day, the weight was too much. The bottoms of my feet were extremely sore. But the confidence in my ability to go long miles with no problem was established, and I was closer to a decision to hike the entire trail.

I was also presented with a chance in the summer of 2005 to hike in the Steamboat Springs area of Colorado. Joel and Rachel made this trip with us. Steamboat Springs is just west of the Continental Divide and sits at an elevation of about 6,500 feet. From there we hiked up one of the trails in the area toward the Continental Divide. It was known as the Red Dirt Trail and it led to the Continental Divide Trail—a national scenic trail.

The terrain was a good test of my ability to hike in the mountains. Hiking in Michigan is not a good gauge of your ability to hike the trail. Aside from elevation sickness, the hike was a confidence booster. And the elevation was much greater than what I would face on the Appalachian Trail.

❧•❦

Back at home I went to work, getting my pack weight down. I went out to trailjournals.com and researched gear. I found that much of the gear I had previously bought was simply not meant for the long-distance hiker. The efficient long-distance hiker should have the lightest gear that he can find and still be functional. For instance, the stove I had bought to cook with was too heavy when you considered the gas canister that you had to carry. I bought a lightweight alcohol stove. I carried the fuel in a 20 oz pop bottle and it cut my weight down by almost a pound.

My handy backpack weighed just over six pounds. That was too much. I found a pack on the website that only weighed seventeen ounces. It was not as handy as my first pack, but the five pounds it lowered my overall weight made it worth the trouble. The pack was little more than a bag with straps and three large, external-netted pockets. I worked out a system to load and unload it. The straps were just as comfortable and it fit well on me. And the color was blue, which matches my eyes.

The sleeping bag I had was light, but I found a down-filled bag that saved valuable ounces. I had a five-dollar sporty water bottle that weighed a few ounces. I ended up using a sport drink bottle to carry water, which cut my base weight by a few ounces. Every piece of gear was given critical evaluation.

In addition to the gear I would carry, there was considerable thinking put into what I would and would not carry. The amount of clothing I carried was very little. Two spare pairs of socks were plenty. I had no spare pants, only one pair of convertible pants. I would end up wearing the same pants the entire trail. When I washed them in town, I would wear my rain pants. I bought a pack cover but ended up finding a poncho that was built with extra material in the back to hang over the pack and ended up leaving the pack cover at home. Instead of a watch, I carried a small clip-on clock that also served as a compass and thermometer. I had one short sleeve shirt and one long sleeve shirt. Both were made of synthetic material that would dry quickly and wick away moisture from my body. I would hike during the day with the short sleeve on and change at night into the long sleeve shirt for its warmth and dryness. I referred to it as my evening wear. I started out with a fleece jacket and then found a down jacket that was a full pound lighter. My cook set was titanium. The backpacking tent was only three pounds and I would buy one later that was only two pounds.

By the time I boarded the plane for Georgia my base weight was down to twenty five pounds without food and water. It would get lower as I switched from winter gear to summer, found new and lighter products, and sent home clothing I did not need. By summer, my base weight was about fifteen pounds. My underlying philosophy was the pound mile. It was a concept I read somewhere. For every pound you carry for one mile on the AT, it is like carrying 2,176 pounds one mile. So the difference between carrying my fleece jacket and my down jacket was the same as carrying my Tacoma pickup one mile. The weight difference for me meant that I could go farther every day and get home to my family sooner. I was constantly comparing notes with other hikers and looking for a way to shave off an ounce from my base weight.

For several months I had spent considerable time reading the journals of hikers. I especially noted the hikers who were in their fifties to get a feel for how they coped. I found the reading fascinating and would prefer reading journals to watching television. I noticed that the older hikers performed just fine and that increased my confidence. Some time in the fall of 2005, when I was sure my wife was on board, I committed to attempt a thru-hike in the spring of 2006.

The last bit of research before I left for the trail had to do with food. I had two concerns. The first was the cooking itself. I needed Marilyn's help with that. Up until then I knew how to make coffee and not much more. As I researched what was best for the trail, I soon discovered that most of the foods that I would end up eating were dried foods. So all I really had to do was expand on my ability to boil water and I was all set.

The other concern was what to eat. The average AT thru-hiker burns a lot of calories. I have read estimates as high as 7,000 per day, and I believe it. Weight is a critical factor in any food selection. Few long-distance hikers carry any food with water in it. Such meals as prepackage noodles, rice dishes, and dried soups were the preferred entrée. For lunch, nuts, dried fruits, peanut butter, and various cracker combinations were best. Breakfast consisted of oatmeal or pop tarts washed down with a dried instant breakfast. For long stints between resupplies, I would carry a box of cereal and dried milk.

I studied nutritional needs and weight-to-calorie ratios. If a food could provide 150 calories per ounce and had proper nutrition, it was preferred, providing I could tolerate the taste. If a particular food was necessary for good nutrition but had a lower ratio, it was at least considered. For instance, dried apricots were high in potassium, vitamin C, and fiber. So they were included even though they were not high in calories relative to their weight. The same goes for raisins. Meats and cheese were seldom carried because of the ratio. As an example, prepackaged chicken or tuna had about fifty calories per ounce. Cheese was even less. The one common element of most of the foods that I would carry was that I would be sick of them before I was done. To this day I cannot look at macaroni and cheese and was not able to bring myself to eat oatmeal for months. The most number of days that I would carry food in my pack was seven days in Virginia. There were also a few six-day outings.

For Christmas in 2005, I received a set of titanium hiking poles from the kids. I received the poles, much like all my trail related gifts, with great anticipation. During a training walk in the woods around my house, I used the poles. They seemed cumbersome and unnecessary. I tried to warm up to them a couple of times but could really see no need for the extra seventeen ounces added to my load. But they cost a lot of money and I knew there must have been a reason for hikers to use them. I would end up packing them for the trip to Georgia and give them a chance to prove their worth. I decided if they were not worth the weight, I would have them shipped home and add them to the collection of retired hiking paraphernalia. By the time I got to Neal's Gap, Georgia, I would have fought Mike Tyson for them.

In my real life, I am an electrical contractor. I have owned a small business in Charlotte, Michigan, for over fifteen years. I had trained my employees to perform most of the functions in the company that I had been doing. My last months would be spent preparing them for my absence. I had hired good people, which made it easy. There would still be issues that I had to be involved in as the estimator. I would have to leave the trail a couple of times to be involved in bidding a critical job.

By far, the most difficult part of the trail would be the separation from my wife. Marilyn is a kindergarten teacher. That would give her about three months of freedom to come and visit on the trail. We also hoped to find some other opportunities that would allow us to get together.

Before leaving, I decided on a trail name. It is traditional to have your trail name developed on the trail by others. Those names are not very complimentary. They usually reflect some weak moment, stupid mistake, or noticeable body feature. I was not going to let that happen to me. I chose the name Silver Streak. I would be the old man on the trail most of the time and my black hair had long turned silver. Silver was taken as a trail name by someone else, so I added Streak as a reflection of the speed I was known to hike, at least by my family. I would come to figure out that most hikers on the trail made me look like Silver Slug. Nonetheless, I was satisfied with the name. Most who knew me would just refer to me as Silver, which worked.

A week before I left, I went to our family doctor for my annual physical. The results of the blood test were not in yet but the doctor gave me a green light to go. He was excited that I was going on this trip and so I was leaving with his blessing. The nurse called me with the lab results the day before I was to leave. She informed me that my cholesterol was okay but my triglycerides were just a little high. She suggested that I start doing more walking. I had to chuckle to myself and assured her that I would do just that.

So at 3:12 in the morning of March 1, 2006, my alarm went off. I left my wife of thirty- three years behind and placed the remote control in her hands for safe keeping until I returned. Within minutes, my son Garrett was driving me to Detroit to catch a plane to Georgia. It was a modest adventure by some standards and an extreme adventure by others. To me it was both. That day I woke up in Michigan as Wally Miars and would go to sleep at Hawk Mountain Shelter as Silver Streak.

THE BEGINNING

Springer Mountain, Georgia, to Fontana Dam
Miles traveled: 176 miles
Days hiking: 13 days

Anyone can walk the AT. A blind man has done it. An eighty-two-year-old lady named Grandma Gates has done it. She walked the entire trail with a sack draped over her shoulder and tennis shoes on her feet. A five-year-old walked it with his grandfather. I met Needles on the trail. He was a brittle diabetic, which can be a challenge for normal activity. Some have walked the trail numerous times. The most I am aware of is eight times. The first one to thru-hike the AT was Earl Shafer. He walked it three times, including once when he was seventy-five. It does not take an athlete to trek the fourteen states and 2,176 miles, but it does take time. I talked to Sticker at the Nantahala Outdoor Center in North Carolina. He was checked into the North Carolina hostel for the evening. He was walking it for the third time, and he was in his sixties. I know that he made it as far as New Hampshire, and I am confident that he made the entire journey.

Only about 10 percent of those who attempt it end up completing a thru-hike. Some go home because of physical problems. It can wear on you! Knees, severe blisters, or just plain exhaustion can send you home. Some go home because of boredom. It does get boring. I was with Wrong Way when he decided that it was no longer fun for him. Others end the trail because of personal or business matters. The commitment takes you away from all that is important. Scout said it all when she said that most of the challenge is mental. While I was away, I missed three funerals of friends that I should have been at. Aborting a hike is nothing to be ashamed of.

I remember sitting at the terminal gate not believing that I was really about to get on a plane to begin this crazy journey. But there was no lack of resolve to make this journey.

I had contacted Dave, who was a listed shuttle driver, to take me to the top of the mountain. Dave took me to a parking lot and walked with me the one mile up the trail.

At the famous beginning point I met an older man with a long, perfectly formed, stiff beard that was pure white. The beard and his attire reminded me that I was in the southern mountains. Many Sleeps was his trail name. One of the roles of Many Sleeps was that of preacher. His job was to sell hikers on the virtue of "leave no trace." The philosophy is "take only pictures, leave only footprints." It is a practice that is essential to the health of any trail, but especially one as heavily traveled as the Appalachian Trail. He was preaching to the choir. Trail ethics are not a problem with most that travel the trail, and I was impressed with the extent to which most go to preserve the condition of the trail. Many Sleeps was one of thousands who work as volunteers to enhance and maintain the trail. They remind me of the spectators at a marathon cheering loudly people they do not know.

At the top of Springer Mountain is a rock with a brass emblem. Near that rock is the book that thru-hikers' names are entered. Many Sleeps officially entered my trail name without ceremony. It was surreal to finally get to that point. At the same time, he entered two other hikers who must have been in their early twenties. They were a married couple named Hit and Miss. They had bandannas wrapped on their head and they looked the part of the long-distance hiker. They were slim and stout with gear that looked as though it had been on the trail for quite some time—used but not worn out. They took off ahead of me and as they disappeared into the trees, I instinctively knew that was the last I would see of them. I would read about them in the shelter registers for a while and then after a while I stopped reading back that far.

Dave was a class act. He had accompanied me up to the peak and back. I bid myself *adieu* at the parking lot, and I was off on my new adventure. When I awoke in the morning in Michigan, I had set a goal to get to Hawk Mountain Shelter. It felt good to finally be walking with leaves under me, and I knew that my goal was attainable. The walk was mostly downhill for that day's segment. I walked the entire 7.6 miles to the shelter without seeing anyone. However, once to the shelter, I was shocked at the number of people there. The shelter was full and there were numerous tents of differing sizes, shapes, and colors. I pitched my small one-man tent, fixed my first hot trail meal, and was ready for sleep. I went to bed that night exhausted. I was amazed at how far I had gone and what I had accomplished thus far. I went to sleep that night with confidence in my abilities. I felt good.

$$\Rightarrow \cdot \Leftarrow$$

On day two I awoke to a twenty-eight degree temperature. Once out of the sack I had to move quickly to keep from getting too cold. One of the hikers who had pitched his tent close by was very informative about the terrain ahead for the day. It would be some of the steep uphills and downhills that the trail is famous for. I was not in Michigan anymore. The newness of this experience would take much of the edge off the demands of the day. So his word did little to assuage my excitement. Actually, I was quite aware of the challenges of terrain that day because I was carrying an official AT map that included a profile of the elevation changes.

Breakfast would mostly be oatmeal for the next few weeks until I would get sick of it. Once I had eaten and packed up I headed out, but not before talking with a couple of young hikers. One was from my home state of Michigan. His name was Superman and his buddy was a hiker from Atlanta named the Jolly Green Giant.

Jolly Green was indeed a stout and large man in his early twenties and looked like he would not have any trouble on the trail. I would see a lot of them for the next few days. Superman and I talked briefly while they were packing. It was nice to meet someone from my home state.

I excused myself and scurried down the trail, eager to put in the first full day of hiking. As I walked, I wondered what my wife would be doing at that time and if all was okay at the office. Those thoughts would be a constant on the trail.

❯•❮

Most of the trail is just a path through the woods that is pretty much like any trail. I have always been amazed at the condition of the trail given the number of people who pass over it each year. In some places you are still walking on leaves. Now it was only March 2nd and by May it would be different. The spots on the trail in Georgia that were leaf covered would be worked up mud in a few weeks. Because it was my first day, I expected a lot of people on the trail. The crowd would thin out soon enough. The trail would inflict its yearly attrition soon. I would never see most of the people that I met at Hawk Mountain Shelter again. I would pass them much like Hit and Miss passed me. What happened to them I do not know to this day. That is the way the trail goes. You only know for sure what is going on with the people who are ahead of you. That information is easily gathered from the registers at the shelters. The registers are simple notebooks that are placed there by volunteers. Hikers enter small corny comments in them for those who follow. Each hiker tries to outdo the other with clever comments, poetry, or artwork. Some of the entries are very good and quite entertaining. For the most part they are clean and uplifting. One was rather scary. It read: "I came up here from the road to kill and rape, but there was no one here. Maybe I'll come back some other night." I convinced myself that this was just a silly hiker.

⋙•⋘

When I arrived at the Gouch Mountain Shelter, some were already there and others would continue to come. One of the noisier ones was Compass. His excitement had not worn off and he had not walked enough to wear down his energy so he was celebrating like a Packer fan at Lambeau Field when the Vikings were getting beat. Compass's trail name was interesting. When he started the trail, he started at the parking lot near the top of Springer Mountain like I did. Only he went the wrong way from the parking lot and started down the mountain instead of up. What made it worse was that he had his family with him and they were going to escort him to the beginning. They went down the mountain a considerable distance before they realized what had happened and turned around. His trail name would follow him for the rest of his hike. Trail names that are derived while on the trail are seldom complimentary.

I met Turtle D and Turtle M at the shelter. They were a retired couple from New Hampshire. He was retired from the forest service in New Hampshire. Like so many others, I would not see them again. But it was great to meet someone on the trail that was close to my age. I also met a young man from Massachusetts named Rick. In a few days I would have a part in assigning him a trail name that would stick. He told me of trail magic that he had experienced at lunchtime—grilled cheese and orange juice! For the next few days, all I could think about was that grilled cheese sandwich that I had missed. I would see Rick again down the trail and do some more hiking with him. Jolly Green was also there, and many others who I do not remember.

This would be my first real experience with shelter life. The shelter experience is the most interesting part of hiking the trail. Moose, bear, deer, and other woodland animals do not even come close to being as interesting as people. Quite often I have been

31

asked by those who are curious about my hike, "Did you see any interesting animals?" My usual reply is about the moose I saw in Maine and then I leave it at that. But what I do not tell them is that the humans were the interesting story. For me a trip to the mall is more interesting than a trip to the zoo. I sometimes watch cable channels that show the amusing things that animals do— and there are some pretty amusing things that animals do in the wild. To me, sitting at the mall watching people is comical.

There are plenty of places to camp on the trail that are not connected to any shelter. It is referred to by hikers as "stealth camping." Few do much of that because the shelters are in fact the best part of hiking the AT. Seldom do hikers choose tenting over sleeping in a shelter. Only a few times did I stealth camp by myself; but that night would be one of them. I was not at all affected by the tough terrain, so I decided to push on past the shelter. I announced my intention to those at the shelter and gave them time to consider joining me, but there were no takers. After loading up on water, I said my good-byes to the Turtles and the others and was off by myself. The newness of the experience was still keeping my pace and my spirits up.

The rest of the day's hiking was like most days on the trail— uneventful. That night, however, would be an exception. I finished out the day with a late push, desperate to get to water. I arrived at a stream that had a small campsite near a bridge that crossed the stream. But there was an area large enough to get my tent up and so I pitched it using the last few minutes of daylight. I fixed some macaroni and cheese and added some tuna. I topped it off with some hot chocolate and Snickers for dessert. Once supper was over, I opted for the safest campsite by hanging my food bag. Finding a limb in the dark that fits all the criteria was a bit of a challenge. I managed to find one that would work and was quite pleased with myself when the job was done.

With supper eaten and the dishes washed, I crawled into my one-man-tent and was just settling down. I had no sooner settled into my bag when I heard an unbelievable amount of rustling from the wooded area above the stream and away from the trail. It was getting closer and was coming right at me. Whatever it was, it was large. I had rehearsed in my mind a hundred times what I would do when a bear approached my tent and now the test would come. I had decided long before that I would not go down without a fight. I was not about to lie in my sleeping bag and let some bear haul me off in my sleeping bag like a very big burrito. As quick as I could, I got out of the tent and flashed my headlamp in the direction of the noise. Relief washed over my body when I discovered the noise was human—at least close to it. It was two Rangers with their night vision goggles on. They looked twice as big as any human, but on closer inspection they had a pack on that made my pack look like a daypack.

The trail passes near a military base where the famed Army Rangers train. These Rangers were out on night maneuvers. They moved past me and over the bridge without saying a word as if I were not there and melted into the dark on the other side of the stream. Within the next hour several more would pass by. My emotions went from fear to a feeling of pride in one moment. I was sharing the woods with some of the bravest and hardest working men in our military. Part of their training was to carry their partner on their back for a considerable distance. If they cannot carry their partner, they are not fit to be Rangers because one of the tenants of the Rangers is that you never leave a man behind. My nephew trained as a Ranger and was required to jump out of a helicopter with all of his gear and a heavy machine gun. I have always admired all the men and women who give so much of themselves to protect our freedom and the freedom of others. The Special Forces even more so because of the rigorous training that is necessary. Their missions are some of the most dangerous. I have always been proud of my nephew who trained as a Ranger and now I was out in the woods with Rangers.

After my brief scare, I returned to my bag to work on my daily journal. I had committed myself to keeping a record of the trail for my friends and family to read. This journal was posted on the Internet occasionally, which allowed my family to follow my adventures on the trail. Day two was a rousing success. I had traveled about seventeen miles on my first full day of hiking the AT. I barely noticed the exhaustion from all of the excitement of the trail. My plan when I started the afternoon before was to get to Neels Gap by the end of day three. Not only did that seem likely, but with about seven miles to go I felt I could push on past Neels Gap. I went to sleep that night pleased and feeling quite good physically. Blood Mountain would take care of that cockiness.

⋙•⋘

The next morning came early and cold. I began the morning by affirming that I would simply push on past Neel's Gap and camp somewhere past the famous hostel. An urgent call to nature had me scrambling to get the recommended two hundred feet away from the trail and stream. In my haste I had not noticed a house nearby. Once done with my business and the evidence buried, I discovered I had been practically in some person's backyard. The expensive house was all windows in the back, and I wonder to this day if I had put on a show for some family while they ate breakfast before going off to work. I imagined all day I was the topic at the water cooler of some office, or that some housewife might need to visit her therapist.

Once packed up, I was bouncing down the trail by myself. The quietness of the woods on day three was punctuated by gunfire off in the distance. The Ranger base was not far away and the would-be-rangers were working on their small arms fire. It served as a reminder to me that as quiet and peaceful as it is in the woods, there is always trouble in the world and that it is not all well and good elsewhere. But for that day it was another world altogether. Nothing was going to interfere with that. I did feel honored that I was sharing the woods with our brave young men.

The climb up the mountain took some of the starch out of me. The walk down did me in. Anyone who does any amount of hiking in the mountains will tell you that the hardest part is the downhill. The climb up is hard on the lungs, but they soon recover. The downhill is murder on the knees and lasts longer. The knees are what end up forcing many people off the trail.

By the time I was at the bottom of Blood Mountain and at Neels Gap, I was ready for my first experience in a hostel. I had read enough journals on the worldwide web to know that there was a good chance the hostel operator would take all of the hikers into town to an all-you-can-eat restaurant. I could not help wondering if they would have any grilled cheese sandwiches. I would write in my journal that night that I was the hanging curve ball and Blood Mountain was the bat.

For twenty dollars I received a shower and a soft warm bed at the Walasi Yi center. Not a bad deal. By nightfall, the place would be packed and there would be people tenting outside. Once I was checked in and showered, I visited with the hikers there. Among the hikers there was a lady from Kentucky by the name of Bluebell. She seemed to be the leader of the pack. She was a married woman who was about my age. There was also a hiker there who had blisters the size of a quarter. They were actually past being blisters. He was not going far. Foot care is crucial to successful hiking. No backpack should be without foot care items. I would never see most of those people at the hostel again, but I met Scout there. I would end up hiking over eleven hundred miles with her, as well as others we would meet in the next few days. Scout was a middle-aged woman from Seattle, although she was raised in North Carolina and had family there.

While there, I bought some souvenirs for home and sent home a couple of clothing items that I felt I was not going to need. It is cold in early March in the mountains, which I had prepared for. But during the day you generate enough body heat to keep warm. During my entire hike, I seldom hiked with more than a short-sleeved T-shirt that my daughter had bought me for Father's Day. I ended up hiking the entire AT with that shirt and retired it when I finished. At night I needed enough warm clothing to get me through supper. After that I would crawl into my bag to keep warm. So I ended up sending home my fleece pants and body armor. Aside from that, I was very content with my pack contents.

The hostel owner operates an outfitters' store and has a scale there. He has made a fortune on those hikers who had not properly prepared for their hike. The store weighs the packs, consults with the hikers, and ends up selling them gear—new gear. In exchange for a loaded up VISA, the store sends your excess gear home at no cost. I left Walasi Yi pleased with myself for having the good sense to prepare for my adventure ahead of time. I could not have hiked the seventeen miles on day two with a pack that weighed fifty pounds, which is what some of the hikers carried from Springer Mountain to Neel's Gap.

That night I got my first taste of what an AT hostel was like. Sleep was difficult because of the human sounds. I can only describe it as a symphony of snoring and farting. The buzz was too much for me. I have been in crowded Caribou hunting camps before and should have expected it, but it caught me by surprise. I expect old, overweight men to snore, but I did not know young people snored with such gusto, and I certainly did not expect the ladies to contribute so much. As I lay in bed that night struggling to go to sleep, I promised myself to get some sleep aid and earplugs when I could get to a town.

⋙•⋘

The next morning I left early and headed down the trail, hoping for a good night's sleep at the end of the day. I passed Bluebell and some others within minutes. I would find out later from her website journal that her knees became inflamed and she got off the trail before she got out of Georgia. She seemed like a lot of fun, and I would have enjoyed hiking with her. I have never met anyone from Kentucky that I did not like.

Later that day, Scout, Cedar Moe, and Rick caught up with me and we formed a convoy for the day. Some time after that we met Mickey One Sock heading south. He gave us some history on some of the mountains around us to add a little color to our day.

That night, the four of us set up a stealth camp and settled in for the night. Cedar Moe is one of the more interesting hikers that I met on the trail. He was from North Carolina or Tennessee. He carried a cedar walking stick about six feet long, and it must have weighed five pounds. Because it was a soft wood it slowly wore down. He was a Christian and made every effort to get to a church, any church, every Sunday. He made good miles and could have left us all in the dust. Instead he chose to travel with us for a while. His Christian spirit was an inspiration to me.

That night, after we had set up our tents and eaten, we visited for a while. Rick had a set of miniature Yahtzee dice and a score pad.

"Anyone care to play Yahtzee?"

After a quick glance at the game, Scout said, "The dice and pad are not too small for me, what about you, Silver?"

After looking over the game, I said, "I would get a headache just trying to play with that little of a set. My eyes are too old and I am too tired."

After an extended effort to find an opponent he gave up, but Scout had more to say about it.

"You must play that a lot to bring it along."

"You have to have something to do besides hike."

Scout stopped what she was doing. "I think Yahtzee would be a great trail name for you, Rick. What do you guys think?

"I am in. What about you, Silver?" Cedar Moe said.

"Yahtzee it is," I chimed in.

Rick did not veto the name and so it was that Rick became Yahtzee, and I think he was proud of it.

Cedar Moe had tuna from a can with his macaroni and cheese. That would play a part in the night's events. I do not sleep very soundly when on the trail. Maybe it is the surroundings or the hard ground. Quite often I wake up in the night. That night I awoke around midnight. Cedar Moe's tent was about ten feet from mine and there was a lot of commotion around his tent. I listened as he sniffed continuously to the point that it was annoying. I considered telling him to blow his nose. At some point, he began to rattle through his pans and other gear, and I would have said something but I did not want to wake the others should they be sleeping through his little circus. He did not seem to me to be that rude, and I did not remember him having the sniffles that night. As I lay there listening, I had a call to nature that would not go away. It was early in March in the mountains and it was cold. I fought off the demands of my bladder for as long as I could. But as I lay there, I thought maybe I would go ahead and take care of it and bop Cedar on the head while I was at it.

Once the decision was made to get up, I took a couple of minutes dreading the cold and planning my moves. The plan was to move fast so that I did not get too much of a chill. With one quick motion I unzipped my bag, unzipped the tent, put on my boots, and scrambled out. I was able to get out with haste and move away from camp for some relief. Once I had accomplished my task, I returned to my tent and decided not to address Cedar Moe about the noise and commotion. Having settled into my sleeping bag, I had reorganized my sleeping area and was able to get to sleep.

Ignorance surely is bliss. That night a bear had entered our little bivouac and was sniffing around Cedar Moe's tent, drawn by the smell of the tuna. The noise I had made getting out of my bag and tent had spooked the bear. The others had been watching the bear, but I was totally unaware of our visitor. Their tents opened up to the middle of our camp, but mine was facing away so I could not see in the Georgia moon that a bear was going through the remains of Mo's supper, sniffing for the rest of the tuna Moe had earlier. Had I known that I had spooked a bear, I may have had trouble going back to sleep. I was glad that we had taken the time to hang our food bags from a nearby tree before retiring for the day.

There are a lot of misconceptions about bears. For the most part they are afraid of humans and avoid us. I have hunted bear with bow and arrow and observed them over the years while hunting them. It is hard to hunt them because they are so weary of humans. There have been a total of fifty-two people killed by black bears between 1990 and 2003 in all of North America. However, within a month of when I passed through Tennessee on the trail, six-year-old Elora Petrasek was killed by a black bear. Her mother and two-year-old brother were also injured in the attack. The Rangers later caught and destroyed the bear. The experts believed that the bear was diseased and that it affected his behavior. There was no provocation by the family that was attacked. They were simply in the wrong place at the wrong time. Such attacks are rare but when they do happen, they serve to remind us that wild animals can be dangerous.

If you are with other people, running could be an option unless you are the slowest runner. Quite often I am asked about the dangers of the trail, especially bears and snakes. I have no scientific statistics to back it up, but I can tell you that I felt safer on the trail than I do driving the highways. You are more likely to have a disaster on the highway with a drunk driver than a crazed bear in the woods. Most everything we do has a risk attached to it. Maybe the greater risk is to sit around doing nothing and die an early death caused by a heart attack or other health issues from lack of exercise. I felt safe on the Appalachian Trail.

❧ ⚜

While the four of us were packing up, Jolly Green Giant and Superman came by and we joined in to bring our little convoy to six. We would all hike together for about a week. But Scout and I knew we were going to lag behind eventually. We were middle-aged hikers walking with kids in their prime. I was hiking with kids who had never heard Ricky Nelson sing or knew who Hoss Cartwright was. But for the time being I enjoyed their enthusiasm and kept up as best as I could. Soon I would find some more hikers that hiked at our pace, and I would hike with them for quite some time.

The six of us stopped for lunch at the side of a mountain road and decided to combine some sun, food, relaxation, and silliness into a very memorable break. While we were resting, Stumpknocker came by. I recognized him from journals I had read on the Internet. Stumpknocker was a trail legend, and it was a pleasure to meet him after reading so much about him. He lives near the trail in Georgia and was just out for a small hike. He had planned on starting another thru-hike in a couple of weeks.

Later on that day I received my first trail magic. A family of three was waiting for hikers in a parking lot with some treats. They had a little girl of about four who took a shine to me. I think I just have the look of a nice old grandpa. Her name was Meredith, and her trail name was "Miracle Baby." She was born prematurely and was not expected to live. I enjoyed her excitement. She had the job of dispensing the goodies and did it proudly. We enjoyed some cold pop and some treats, took some pictures, visited with the family for a while, and we were off. I made sure I posted a hello to Miracle Baby in my journal—I am sure that pleased her.

Later that day we met a huge young man named Thomas. Thomas was from Connecticut. He was carrying a pair of snowshoes that must have weighed close to ten pounds. He carried a pack that must have weighed over fifty pounds. Stumpknocker had warned us of him and that we should not let him send the snowshoes home. His theory was that it would then snow for sure. We picked up on that and it became a part of the shelter discussion for the next three weeks. Everyone implored him not to send them home, and it seemed like a joke then. Time would soon tell that Stumpknocker's superstitious prediction would be all too fitting.

That night I arrived at Tray Mountain Shelter and decided to stay in the shelter so I could get out early to claim a spot at the Blueberry Patch Hostel. Most of the shelters on the AT are three-sided lean-tos with a roof. Some have a shelf to cook on and some have picnic tables. All are infested with mice. The shelters are the center of the social life on the AT. They average about eight miles apart, although in places they are almost twenty miles apart. Most have a privy nearby and they all have a water source that ranges from a stream to springs that have a pipe tapped into the side of the mountain. In addition to sleeping at the shelters, they are nice for having lunch or taking a break. When they fill up, there are usually plenty of tent sites available around the shelter. Sleep is critical to someone who backpacks twenty miles and so they need quiet around bedtime. Most of the problems with noisy guests at the shelter were from hikers who were just out for a couple of days. The long-distance hiker knows when it is time to go to bed and that time came early for the thru-hikers.

That night some of the guys at the shelter collaborated to name Thomas "Tank." The name fit and it stuck. In addition, Scout dubbed Yahtzee, Superman, Jolly Green Giant, and Cedar Moe collectively as the "Super Friends." The group would not last though because each hiker had different plans for the trail and they soon split up.

I had read about the Blueberry Patch from trail journals on the Internet. I sold the Super Friends on making a push to get to the Blueberry Patch early and go to town for an AYCE (all you can eat) restaurant. So we hit the trail early. Scout had a cousin in the area that was going to pick her up at the road and host her for the night, so it was just the Super Friends and the old man. I had trouble keeping up with the younger guys and ended up at the road by myself. For the first time in my life I hitchhiked. It is common for thru-hikers to hitch into town. Twenty-two hundred miles is enough to walk in the mountains, and so thumbing it into town is a common practice that is tolerated by the law and accepted by the local residents. Within minutes I had a ride to the hostel from a local builder.

I was greeted at the hostel by Linny. She had an empty laundry basket and instructed me to surrender my clothes to her and she would take care of cleaning them. I gleefully obliged. Other than my "evening wear" long sleeve shirt, two changes of sock liners, and a change of underwear, I had no change of clothes. That is part of the lightweight backpacking philosophy. However, I did have a pair of rain pants. So I put on my rain pants and my long sleeve shirt and turned over the clothes for wash. They now had six days of dirt and body ash on them and were quite raunchy. I showered to complete the ablution. The rest of the guys had waited for me so we could go into town.

A ride into town was made possible by a local hiker who stopped by. We were on our way to town for the first time, and we were all excited to get some town food. It was midafternoon so there were not many people in the restaurant. I made a pig of myself, as did the other guys. The trail burns up more calories than you can carry and consume and by the time you get to town, your body is depleted. I left refreshed and ready for some relaxation back at the hostel. I had sent a mail drop of food to the hostel, so a trip to the grocery store was not necessary.

Back at the hostel I was able to slip into some of my clean clothes, work on my journal, take a nap, and just relax. Most hostels on the AT are garages or barns that have been converted into makeshift bunkhouses. They have wooden bunks two or three high. They range from four to thirty beds. Some have full kitchens; some have just a hot plate. Most have some kind of heating system; some have a wood-burning stove. If you are lucky there will be a table to sit at. Some have a laundry; most do not. Almost all have the most important thing: a shower. There are two things that consume your thoughts on the trail—food and showers.

That day was a tough day for me. It was the first Monday away from home. On Mondays, I watched my grandson Elijah. It was the first Monday in a long time that I had not watched him and I missed him. I had a lot of fun with him, and it would be hard not seeing him every week. The separation from family would be my greatest struggle throughout the trail.

Gary and Linny Poteat operate the Blueberry Patch Hostel. In addition to laundry, showers, and a warm, dry place to sleep, they serve a top-notch breakfast. Once the breakfast is over they return you to the trail. The hostel is their Christian ministry. As Gary put it, they are offering a cup of cold water in Jesus's name. Anyone who washes hiker's dirty underwear deserves a special crown. Their ministry is supported by the voluntary donations of the hikers. I really enjoyed their Christian spirit and found the stay very refreshing.

❖•❖

We were back at the trail by nine that morning. Blueberry pancakes and a good night's rest energized us. We were able to scramble out of Dick's Gap with ease. However, some of my planning was breaking down. I had planned on consuming all the food I carried from Springer Mountain by the time I reached Neels Gap. At Neels Gap my food drop would get me to the Blueberry Patch were I would have a food package waiting for me. The problem was that I had lost my appetite. It is common for hikers to lose their appetite for a couple of weeks and I expected that. But I had been picking up more food in the mail than I was eating. For that reason I was carrying more food than I had planned.

The young men forged on ahead of me and I was left by myself. Scout caught up with me later that morning. I ended up ahead of her again later in the day but stopped when I got to the border of Georgia and North Carolina to celebrate the first state erased from the list. We took turns taking pictures for one another at the sign and then moved on to the greeting that North Carolina had for us. Two of the worst peaks so far were just across the border. Scout and I needed a break at Muskrat Creek Shelter before moving on in an effort to catch up with the Super Friends. Along the way we saw our first snow on the north side of the mountain. Although it was just a dusting, it caught my attention.

❖ ❖

We arrived at the Standing Indian Shelter with just enough light to pitch our tents and fix a quick supper. There was quite the party going on at the shelter. There were four young girls from Illinois Wesleyan there and they had the young bucks acting goofy. Their presence was cause for a fire and some frivolity. I let it slip discretely that I was working for one of the girl's father to keep an eye on his daughter. Word got around and I was looked at suspiciously after that. Fortunately, all were able to settle down and get some sleep.

At Standing Indian Gap I met Bluebird and Abandon. They were a young couple from New York. Bluebird was an engineer and Abandon was a teacher on leave. We would play leapfrog with them for the next three weeks before they finally got too far ahead of us. I also met D Rock while I was there. He was from Baltimore. Of all the people on the trail, D Rock was the champion at snoring. He had a snore that actually scared me.

❖ ❖

Our first challenge the next day was to go up and over Standing Indian Mountain. It was the first time we were above 5,000 feet. On the way down certain muscles surrounding my knees began to bother me. It was not my joints, which was good. The pain got worse as the day wore on. The pain would dog me for the next few days before going away.

About midday, I met up with a jovial work crew clearing the trail. They had two-man handsaws and were cutting a section of a large tree that had been blown down the year before. According to them the effects of Hurricane Katrina had reached as far as northern Georgia. There were numerous blow-downs lying across the trail and they were opening the trail up by cutting a section of the trees out. Many of them were two feet in diameter. The men were all volunteers who worked to keep the trail free for hikers. As I walked away, I could not help but feel a warm sense of appreciation for their labor.

That night I caught up with Scout at Big Spring Shelter and Tank showed up later. There was a note from the Super Friends that they were going on to the town of Franklin, North Carolina. I would see the four again, but our days of hiking together were over. It was fun hiking with them. I fed off of their energy and their lighthearted ways were a great distraction. Soon I would meet other friends along the way who would fill that void.

⇛•⇚

The next day was a short one. I needed some town food and a shower and Franklin was just the ticket. Tank and I agreed to split the price of a room. Scout would meet her niece in Franklin and stay with her. On the way, we crossed another milestone of sorts—our first one hundred miles was completed near Glassmine Gap. Pictures were taken and our water bottles were raised in honor of the event. I have learned the value of celebrating small victories.

The woods lacked leaves and thus color. Most of the mountains were varying shades of brown and black, but the scenes were still spectacular. I took a lot of pictures but there is no way to capture the beauty of the mountains. The euphoria is beyond description when you take in such scenery, knowing you walked up that mountain on your own two legs. The ridges, valleys, and peaks combine to form infinite combinations of beauty regardless of color.

With plenty of daylight we arrived in Franklin. I called my personal trainer that night to discuss my leg. It only bothered me going downhill. My personal trainer is my daughter Rachel. Rachel has a four-year degree in exercise science. I described my pain and how it only bothered me on the downhill portions of the day. By the end of the day it was unbearable. She confirmed that is was most likely just my body reacting to the strain. I fought through it and the pain melted away as I got stronger.

That night there was a severe thunderstorm, and we were all glad to be out of the weather. As for food, I still had enough food to get me to the last of the mail drops I had sent and so I did not need to get to a store. Also, my appetite had not yet returned. I had to make myself eat trail food. Town food did not seem to be a problem, but trail food was already getting old.

From Franklin, I estimated that I was four days away from the Smokies. There were challenges that awaited us. We were hearing some reports of deep snow along the ridge we would be hiking and it added to the drama and gave us something to chew on in the shelters. The hotel operator, Jim, took us out that morning. As he was driving he gave us some breaking news.

"You guys know who Stumpknocker is?"

"We met him during lunch a few days ago and talked to him," I said.

"Well I got word three days ago he broke his arm in a bad fall."

"That must have been just about when we met up with him," I responded, shocked.

"Well according to him it will delay his thru hike until he can get the cast off. You guys need to be careful, especially in the Smokies. I heard a few days ago there was three feet of snow in places up there. But then the information was a little dated."

His words were not all that comforting to us because we already had developed a phobia for the Smokies.

⇒•⇐

That morning we went up and over a couple of beautiful balds. Tank walked slowly, so I was alone most of the day. I met up later with Scout, we waited for Tank, and we all had lunch together in the sun near one of the mountaintops. The days were rather warm and the nights were very cold. That day the sun felt great and we took a long lunch before separating. During all my hiking on the AT, I very seldom hiked with anyone during the day. Usually people walk alone even if they are with someone.

In the afternoon the sun baked the water right out of me and I was running low on water. Somewhere on the trail Scout and I met up and we worried together about where to get water. The map did not show any water sources ahead and we were both out. The water that was reported to be at the previous shelter was nonexistent. We walked together and we both looked for anything that resembled water. It was late in the day when we found a small spring coming out of the ground. It was slow enough that it took us ten minutes to get enough water. We rehydrated, had a snack, loaded up with water, and were off with renewed vigor. We both had planned to get to the Cold Springs Shelter and was sure Tank would make it also.

There were a couple of hours of daylight left when I came to a clearing. As I approached the clearing I saw what looked through the trees like a pole barn. When I cleared the trees I saw it was a large tent. Hanging off the tent was a six-foot green flag that said "AT ANGEL." I headed in that direction and as I got closer I made out Bluebird, Abandon, and Scout. Bluebird and Abandon were scarfing down hot dogs and Scout was grinning and laughing like a giddy schoolgirl. Trail magic! It does bring a smile to a hiker's face. Trail angels are near rock star status on the AT. They are a great source of joy and their kindness is burned in the memory of the hiker. It is another AT phenomenon.

Manning the tent was Apple. He was a jovial fellow. His tent had all the things that you would need to live out in the mountains in comfort. At the entrance of the tent was a grill and cooler. Comfortable lawn chairs were provided. The smell could not have been more welcome if it was a rack of ribs. I ordered up a hot dog and ate candy bars while I waited. The four of us were caught up in the jubilation of trail magic. I usually do not get excited about ground up cattle genitals and orange soda, but that day it was like filet mignon and cabernet.

I decided I needed to know more about our benefactor. "So, Apple, where are you from?"

With typical Texas pride, he proclaimed, "Austin, Texas!"

"And how long are you here?"

"Altogether I will be here a week, go home for a month, and will be back in April to start my own thru hike."

"And you are just here for trail magic?"

"Yep. I have a cot, plenty of food, and all the comforts of home right here in the tent. Except that I am almost out of hot dogs. Sorry I can only give you one."

"That's all right. I usually limit myself to one a year anyway, but I have no limit on peanut butter cups and snickers bars. Do you have any fruit?"

"You betcha. Why would a guy named Apple be wandering around in the woods without a big bag of them? Take all you want!"

I had lived in Texas for a few years and so we talked about West Texas, football, and all the other important topics. Apple is a fond memory of mine.

⇛•⇚

After a good night's sleep, our day would include 3,000 feet more of downhill than uphill. The muscles around my knees were so bad by the end of the day that I was in severe pain. Thankfully it was a short day. Only sixteen miles, but the last few miles were descents into the Nantahala River Valley.

At the Nantahala River, we stayed at the Nantahala Outdoor Center. There is a hostel there that houses not only hikers but also river rafters and bicyclers. The center organizes rafting trips and cycling trips as well. It was a bustling place. The hikers only make up a small percentage of the guests. There is a store and a restaurant that are quite well stocked. We were able to do laundry and take showers. We met Sticker there as well as some other hikers, but Sticker is the one I remember most. He was of my generation, and that meant something to me. He had many stories of the trail and we talked for a long time.

Soft beds with sheets, showers, clean clothes, and a hot breakfast were welcome. So far I had not been out on the trail more than three days continually. There would be a much longer stretch soon enough. For now we were enjoying the hostels and were thankful for them. In the morning it was a plate of bacon and eggs with coffee. I would be sorry later that day for all the bacon I ate—heartburn. But I started up out of the valley energized and now excited that I was headed for the Smokies.

The trail is old. It has a lot of hikers on it each year. As a result, some erosion takes places. Not a lot, but one place where it becomes a problem is around tree roots. Some of the tree roots are exposed and standing up. In places there is a network of them that can be quite tricky to walk over. You must actually walk on them balancing yourself so as not to catch your feet in them. It is one of the trail hazards that you get used to. That day there were a lot of them and it slowed us down.

In the morning we came upon a college-age kid who had broken his ankle by getting it caught in the roots. He was sitting on the trail in a tangled mass of roots with a pale and pained look on his face. His ankle and lower leg were severely swollen. His friend was by his side looking as if he was waiting for him to die. Scout and I stopped to see what we could do to help. Another one of their friends had called for help with his cell phone and had gone to meet the rescue team. When we were sure that we were not needed, we excused ourselves and moved on.

About an hour later, we met one of the rescue team members coming up from a side trail. He had told us that they would have been there already but all the rescue workers were in church and they had to be rounded up and their gear marshaled to the mountain. Apparently rescues in the mountains are quite common. We found out two days later when we were at Fontana Dam that they had gotten him off the mountain at about four that afternoon. Word travels up and down the mountains like a series of echoes.

Later we came upon a young man leaning up against a tree, pale and sickly looking.

"Are you okay?" Scout asked, concerned.

"I would be except I am extremely dehydrated," he replied.

"I am sure we an afford to give some water. Silver, can you spare half a quart and I can give him half a quart?"

"Sure, I have fresh quart in my backpack. No backwash. Will one quart even be enough?"

That young man was no doubt embarrassed and tried to refuse the water. "My buddy just left to go find some and bring it back to me."

Scout was quite insistent. "We have plenty and your buddy may not be back for a while so just take it. We will be just fine. Most of our hike is downhill for a while. You need to get water in you as soon as you can."

Once we had fixed him up and was sure he was going to be okay, we left him.

Later that day at the shelter, we met Firefly for the first time. He was a college-age kid from Alabama. As with most hikers, his trail name reflected one of his lesser moments. While hiking the AT in Maine the year before, he lit himself on fire with his alcohol stove. It was bad but not bad enough for the fellow hikers to forget it. They assigned him the name and it stuck. Firefly would provide much of the entertainment for the next few weeks and meeting him added to my hike immensely. D Rock, the snoring champion, was also there.

The morning temperature was a balmy fifty-five degrees. For most mornings the temperature was in the twenties or thirties. The warm temperature made getting out of the sack and on the trail easier. The opportunity was not missed. I was packed up and on the trail at the crack of dawn. The pattern had been set. Tank first and me second, and Scout was usually the last one out of camp.

The drop down to the Little Tennessee River was a steep descent of about 3,000 feet. My legs tolerated the downhill much better than before and I could tell my legs were getting stronger. I was grateful. The hike was uneventful and by two o'clock, Scout and I were at Fontana Dam. The dam backs up the Little Tennessee River and forms Fontana Lake. It is the dividing line between Tennessee and North Carolina as well as the entrance to the Great Smoky Mountain National Park.

Fontana Dam is part of the Tennessee Valley Authority. It is an impressive sight. The TVA, as it is known, covers seven states and has twenty-nine hydroelectric dams. They provide power to millions of homes and much industry in the southeast. We would pass by or walk over other TVA dams. The TVA work was a brilliant effort to provide electric power and jobs. Roosevelt founded it during the Great Depression. Fontana Dam is the tallest dam in the eastern United States and was built during World War II. Nearby Fontana village was first established as a housing area for those who built the dam.

From the dam, I called the Hiker's Inn for a pickup. I had planned on staying there so that I would have a place to send a mail drop. The package that was waiting for me there was the food I would need for going through the Smokies. I had sent it to myself before I had left Michigan and before I knew what foods I would be sick of by then. That package was the last food drop that I would have for a while.

That night I was taken to Robbinsville for some pizza and a salad. I am not much of a drinker, but I found it interesting that I was in a dry county. I was not aware that there were such places anymore. That night I reassessed my gear and sent some things home. All told, I had rid myself of about six ounces of gear. I would continue to evaluate my pack for the next month and make adjustments.

Later that night I called the office. My office manager informed me that a bid for a Walmart store was due and I was needed at the office to put it together. I called my wife and we talked about options. The decision was for her to meet me at the East end of the Smokies. Marilyn would drive down and meet me there and we would drive home together. It was a long drive for her, but she seemed up to it. I was excited to get to see her, and getting off the trail for a couple of days seemed like a good idea. The plan would mean that Marilyn would have to drive down on a Saturday and pick me up that night. For my part, I would have to get through the Smokies in five days. That was only about fifteen miles per day, which did not seem unreasonable if the weather was good.

The weather is always the X factor in the Smokies. The weather can sour quickly. During my year of research on the trail, I had read trail journals about the Smokies and seen pictures of knee-deep snow drifts and was concerned about getting caught in a bad snowstorm. It happens often. For that reason, I felt that the faster I got through the Smokies the better.

There is a road at Newfound Gap that offers an escape at the halfway mark if the weather is too bad. I would hike to Newfound Gap and check on the weather. If the prospects were bad I would go into Gatlinburg and wait. So I went to bed that night excited about a trip home and nervous about the weather.

A PROMISE KEPT

Fontana Dam to Standing Bear Farm
Miles Hiked: 78
Days Hiked: 5

In 1971, while in the air force, I flew over the Smokies. They were beautiful from 10,000 feet. It was clear why they were called the Great Smoky Mountains.

They are not all that high compared to the Continental Divide or the Pacific Crest Trails. The highest point on the Appalachian Trail is at Clingman's Dome, which is near the middle of the Smokies. The elevation there is 6,643 feet. But the weather caused by the elevation is quite phenomenal. When I flew over the area, it was early morning and the fog had formed in the valleys. It was beautiful. At one point the ridges jutted up through the clouds in the valley like a huge shark fin out of the water. It was a combination of green ridges with heavy clouds settling below. I decided then that I was going to have to go there and said it out loud. So thirty-five years later I would cross Fontana Dam and keep that promise to myself.

March is the most unpredictable month for weather in the Smokies. It can go from clear and warm to blizzard conditions in a very short time. The snow can be deep and the winds harsh. Backpackers must always be prepared for the worst weather should they get caught in it. The ridge that we would walk on in the Smokies is the dividing line between North Carolina and

Tennessee. In places, it is almost scary how narrow the ridge is and how steep the sides are. The trail is a few feet wide on the knife-edge ridges in places and then the mountainside drops off at a spectacular angle. On those ridges a northbound hiker on the trail has his left foot in Tennessee and his right foot in North Carolina. Or as I like to say, I can turn to my left and pee in Tennessee or turn to my right and pee in North Carolina.

It had taken me thirteen days to go the 165 miles to get to Fontana Dam. That was not the pace that I needed to get through the trail in five and a half months, but that was okay because I was still getting into trail shape and my body was starting to respond to the daily abuse. My legs were stronger, I had begun to shed weight, and my lungs no longer ached as much going up the steep southern mountains. It takes four to six weeks to reach optimum hiking shape. So in four more weeks I would be a lean, mean, hiking machine.

⇛•⇚

Jeff drove Bluebird, Abandon, and me to the bridge. He gave us the weather report and it was encouraging. For the next three days it would be clear. After that there were no guarantees. By all accounts, there are never any reliable weather reports for the Smokies past three days and even then do not bet your life on any forecast for the Smokies.

I did not know where Scout, Tank, and Firefly were but predicted that I would cross paths with them soon enough. The walk across the top of Fontana Dam was cold and windy and so I moved at a stiff pace to get to tree cover. The rest of the day was uphill. It was clear, but it was also very cold and windy. Staying warm though was not a problem. The walk all day was uphill and even with the temperature in the thirties, I was sweating in my T-shirt.

At about noon I found a place out of the wind but still in the sun and celebrated the Smokies with some peanut butter, Ritz crackers, and a Snickers bar. Coconut Monkey joined me and we talked about our homes.

Coconut Monkey got his name because his companion on the trail was a coconut crafted into a monkey. It was a souvenir from the Caribbean.

I hiked most of the day without seeing any thru-hikers. What I did see were a lot of college kids on spring break. They travel in small packs. After a cordial greeting they would ask, "Where are you headed?" What they were asking is what shelter you have reserved for the night. In the Smokies you need to make reservations for a spot in the lean-to's and everyone knows where they are going. But the thru-hiker does not usually make reservations. That is because each shelter has four spaces reserved for thru-hikers. Since thru-hikers do not make reservations, they go as far as they can before stopping off at a shelter. I enjoyed the question because they would ask where I was headed and I would say with emphasis "MAINE!" They got quite a kick out of that and it would usually result in some cheering, shouting, and high fives. It does not take much to trigger a response like that from college kids.

For the most part the kids on spring break were well behaved. I was impressed that they were spending their spring break hiking instead of heading to some nasty old beach. A guy can only take so much sun, sand, relaxation, and pretty girls in bikinis. The college kids certainly added to the experience through the Smokies, and I was mostly glad they were there. There would be one exception.

In part I was glad they were there because I love walking and think everyone should walk more. We live in a society that has all but abandoned the use of their legs. I am amazed at what expense and effort we go to in order to "save" our legs. I watch as people sit with their cars idling in the parking lot at Walmart, waiting for a parking space that is one hundred feet closer to the store entrance. I have seen young, healthy men jump in their trucks and roar down their long driveways to get the mail. Instead of wheelbarrows we buy tractors with trailers to move items around our house. Even small yards are now mowed with riding lawn mowers instead of push mowers. What amazes me even more is the popularity of the drive-through.

I need go no further than my own hometown to see this. I have driven by McDonalds in the morning and have seen the cars wrapped all the way around the restaurant and out into the street to the point that it becomes a traffic hazard. Our society is absurdly lazy. I sometimes let myself imagine that some fast-food chain is working hard on a drive-through restroom. Then one will never have to get out of their cars. Once one of them develops the idea, the other chains will have to follow.

❧•❦

At the end of the first day in the park, I checked into the Russell Field Shelter. The wind was howling and it was cold, but it was not raining or snowing and I was glad for that. I was met as I approached the shelter by a young lady who was out walking around in a puffy pink coat. You do not see pink anything on the trail very much, so she stood out. Her trail name was Zama and she was traveling with Lug. Zama was of Spanish heritage and the name meant dawn, which was her real name. Lug was assigned his name because he did most of the heavy lifting. They would become great traveling partners for the next three weeks.

Firefly was at the shelter, and Scout would make it there close to dark. Tank would not make it, and we would not see him again for some time. We were all hoping he was still carrying his snowshoes. I also met Applesauce and Cruise. They were cousins hiking the trail together. I would see a lot of them for the next three weeks and then never see them again. Most of the rest at the shelter were college kids.

That night the wind blew so hard it shook the shelter. I lay in bed hoping that it was not snowing, but too afraid to look out of my sleeping bag.

As with many mornings in the month of March, getting out of the sleeping bag was dreaded. It was fifteen degrees in the shelter. I was up and on the trail first. The first mountain I climbed that day was Rocky Top. I remembered the bluegrass song Good Old Rocky Top sung by the Osborne Brothers. I did not see much to sing about at the time.

At the top there was a pile of rocks and not much else, and I was freezing. When I topped the peak, the wind was blowing at about twenty-five miles per hour and my thermometer said it was nineteen degrees. I had on gloves but still my hands were numb. There was nothing good about Old Rocky Top. I scurried past and got down into the good ole trees as quick as I could so as to get out of the wind. It was bitter cold, but the only part of me that was cold was my hands. That tells you how much energy is used up backpacking. And I was only wearing my T-shirt.

All that day the wind played havoc on my ability to regulate my body temperature. When I was in the wind and shaded on more level ground, I would be cold and would bundle up. Then the trail would switch to the other side of the ridge and I would be in the sun and out of the wind. Several times I had to stop and adjust my clothing to fit the circumstances. That happens some all along the trail, but it was a real problem all through the Smokies.

It is essential to stay dry when hiking. Regulating your body temperature to avoid sweating is important. To that end, clothing selection is important. There are fabrics that wick moisture away from the body and dry quickly. By contrast, cotton fabric holds its moisture and holds it close to the body. The common saying is "Cotton kills." Keeping dry is essential to safe hiking and the key is the proper clothing.

⟩•⟨

Most of the day was a typical lonely walk, but I had lunch at a shelter with Applesauce, Cruise, Zama, Lug, and Scout. That night the same group, along with Firefly, ended up at the Double Spring Gap Shelter.

At the shelter was a group of about ten college kids who were working on the trail. They were forestry students who worked as volunteers under an agreement with the park to keep the trail in good repair. It is great practical experience and they can pad their resumes. The group was led by a well-organized young lady who commanded their attention and respect. They were required to sleep in tents so as not to take up space in the shelter. Most of us were quite impressed with the group and especially the leader.

That night was the one exception to the spring break crowd's polite and respectful ways. Two of the guys from Wisconsin were up all night talking about their sexual conquests and other male exploits of manhood. I guessed to myself that most of it was fiction. It was a case when the first liar does not stand a chance. It was hard to listen to, and they were told by me and Scout to take it outside, which they did. But we could still hear them. The measuring contest went on for quite some time and it got more ridiculous with each minute. I did not see any sign of alcohol, but I was sure there was some involved, because sober people just do not make such fools of themselves. Somewhere during the disgusting exchange, I went to sleep.

The next morning Scout made sure to fire up her stove as early as possible to bother their sleep. Her stove sounded like a Lear Jet taking off. We generally attempted to make as much noise as possible.

Later that day Scout caught up to me and we topped Clingman's Dome together. At the top of Clingman's Dome is a tower with a spiraling ramp going up to an observation deck. What little view we could see to the south was beautiful. The statistics are that you can only see from Clingman's Dome forty-six days out of the year. What we saw to the north made us nervous—heavy, black, rolling clouds churning toward us. We took some pictures and got off the mountain as fast as we could. The trail had frozen ice standing on it and it started to snow while we were on our way down.

Once we were at a lower elevation, the sun came out and it was warm again. Scout, Firefly, and I sat with a group of four from Indiana and ate lunch. We were amazed that two hours before we were afraid of the weather and then we were sitting in the sun with all our outer gear off, sunning and relaxing. Such is the fickle weather of the Smoky Mountains. Our conversation with the Hoosiers included their questions about trail food. They thought they were doing something wrong because the food they were eating lacked personality. I assured them that they had missed nothing.

After lunch, we pushed on to Newfound Gap. There is a north-south road that crosses at the low point on the ridge. It is a tourist stopping point that resembles an elaborate rest stop on an interstate. There were maybe fifty cars and lots of people there. The parking area affords a view of the valley below the area and there were actually some vistas to behold through the occasional mist. There are placards along the wall that explain the area and about the trail. One of the placards tells of the thru-hikers that pass through on the way to Maine. Some of the tourists had questions for us about the trail and, as always, Scout and I were glad to answer them. We were all proud of what we were doing.

That parking lot was my opportunity to get off the trail if bad weather threatened. I made a half-hearted attempt at getting a weather report, but no one knew what the weather was going to be like. I was feeling confident enough that weather was not going to keep me off the trail so I pushed on.

When I arrived at the Icy Springs Shelter, a man and his son of about eight met us. The dad and his son were out on a hike and the little boy was giddy with excitement. We visited with them for a while and it was fun to see the child's excitement bubbling over. There was a fireplace in the shelter and he was busy rounding up firewood so there would be a fire. I am not usually much for fires in camp, but the little boy was excited about it so I joined in.

Firefly showed up later and then Zama and Lug. Firefly was in his usual silly mood and he provided the nightly entertainment as he always did. I was glad the five of us were together.

That night, Firefly made an unusual request, "Silver, is there any chance I can become your son-in-law?"

"Not very likely, Firefly. I only have two daughters and both of them are married. And you are too old and ugly to be adopted. I could offer you a job when we are done with the trail, but there would be no special privileges except an invitation to the annual Christmas party."

"But if you ever discovered you had a daughter from the days when you were young and crazy, you would let me know, right?"

"Two things, Firefly: I was never young and I was never crazy. I will leave those up to you"

Scout had to jump in at that point. "Silver, I can believe you were never young, but crazy is a stretch."

It would not be the last time he brought it up.

About dark, six well-fed men showed up to claim their reservation. They were quite put out by the number of people that were there. The shelters sleep ten and the park makes reservations for six, and the other four spaces are for the first four thru-hikers at the shelter. Either there was a mix-up in the booking or someone was not where he was assigned to be. Shelters always have room, especially when it is cold outside, but these men were not at all gracious about the situation. They claimed their rightful spots in the shelter and were very rude about the whole thing. Zama and Lug volunteered to pitch a tent outside to make room. They claimed they wanted to tent anyway and were just waiting for the shelter to fill up. The rule is you cannot stay in a tent in the Smokies if there is space in the shelter.

The men from Mississippi were by far the worst people I met on the trail. They were also comical. One hiker had his pillow from home with him and it had a paisley cover on it. They all had new gear, including price tags hanging on a couple of pieces of gear. A couple of them had huge blow-up air mattresses. It was obvious that these men were not experienced hikers. I entered into a conversation with one of them and found out their story. They were from southern Mississippi and were getting away from the mess of Hurricane Katrina. One of them told me they wanted to get away because their neighborhoods were still a mess with all the debris scattered in their yards. They were quite put out because FEMA had not yet cleaned up their yards and they were sick of looking at the mess. In Michigan when a tree blows down on our property, we get a chain saw and cut it up. We do not wait around for the government to come and clean up messes.

They had no sense of humor either. Hikers mostly refer to themselves by their trail name. They were mystified by these strange people who used such names, and mocked us. Apparently they knew nothing about thru-hikers and did not want to learn anything about us. That night I slept next to one of the men and he scared me. He was as wide as he was tall and I was afraid that if he rolled over on me I would be dead. He also snored loudly and continuously. I noticed in the morning that he was wearing a breathing strip. It did not say much for the product.

The best part about this bad experience is that it was the exception to my experience on the trail. Most all of the hikers I encountered on the AT were courteous and respectful.

⤜•⤛

Day four in the Smokies would be my first twenty-mile day. It would also be the first time I got off the trail by missing a turn. It would not be the last. I was off ahead of everyone and hiked hard all morning. The wind was blowing hard across the trail, and fog kept the visibility to 100 feet, but there was still no snow on the ground, for which I was grateful. I was wishing I could see more of the Smokies than the fog was allowing.

In the early afternoon, Scout, Firefly, and I met at Tricorners Shelter. While we ate we talked each other into going to the next shelter. Once the decision was made, we hurriedly packed up and were off. The difficulty in the decision was not the miles but the amount of daylight left. From our experience we knew we would have to push hard to make it to the Cosby Knob Shelter in time to fix supper. Firefly led the way and I took up the rear. In the mist I lost sight of Scout.

Soon after we were on the trail, a hiker coming toward me passed on info about the shelter ahead. He told me there was no shelter; that it had been torn down. There were only campsites. That was fine with me because I like to tent when it is cold. You can stay a little warmer on the ground in a tent. But the bad information would lead to confusion later in the day.

That afternoon I came to a group of signs. I did not study all of them. Instead I saw the sign for Crosby Knob Campground to the right, followed the sign, and was off. I had lost sight of Scout in the mist, so I picked up the pace and was moving rather rapidly. The trail was going down a steep hill. When you are going down steep hills you have to watch your step. Because of the speed and because it was downhill, I was not paying attention to the white blazes. After I had gone down about a mile and a half, I started to check for blazes but there were none. I went about another 200 yards checking for blazes but found none. I then turned and headed uphill looking for blazes but was mostly resigned to the belief that I was off the trail. The climb up was frustrating.

When I arrived back at the cluster of signs I noticed that there was a Cosby Knob Campground and a Cosby Knob Shelter. Because of the news I had received, I was expecting a campground. Once I had figured out which direction, I took off in a hurry. I do not like hiking at night in the Smokies. You are not allowed to stealth camp. So the rest of the day was a blur as I pushed on hard. I arrived at the shelter by using the last minutes of daylight. Apparently the shelter had been demolished and rebuilt. I figure

I had walked the twenty trail miles and an additional three miles on the side trail; but I was going to be reunited with my wife the next day and so my spirits were high.

In the shelter that night was a husband, wife, and three teenage daughters. The family seemed to enjoy one another and the experience. Of all the encounters on the trail with other hikers, the families were the most enjoyable to me. There is something about families sharing the outdoors in these primitive conditions that strengthens families and creates memories. That night one of the teenage girls in the family was having a long conversation with her boyfriend. It seems even in the most primitive conditions the cell phone is a necessity.

The confusion of the day before was behind me. It was encouraging that I was able to hike twenty-three miles and get up ready to go. I was truly getting into trail shape.

It was now March 18th. By the end of the day it would be eighteen days on the trail and 235 miles. Scout, Firefly, Zama, Lug, and the many other hikers on the trail had kept it interesting and I was pleased at the way I was handling all the issues on the trail that would normally have bothered me. Aside from missing my family, I was enjoying the experience. The pain in my leg was gone, I had no blisters, and I was picking up the pace. Most of all I had survived the Smokies and every day we were getting closer to the time when we would no longer have to concern ourselves with dangerously heavy snow. So Scout, Firefly, and I lined up like a small town parade and proudly headed victoriously down the trail and out of the Smokies, wondering where Tank was, how he was doing, and, most importantly, hoping he still had his snow shoes. I know I was relieved to be leaving the Smokies.

Going the last few miles out of the Smokies, we walked together on the trail, and what a beautiful day it was. The air was brisk with a temperature of twenty-nine degrees, but there was no wind or mist, such as what we had experienced the last four days. The clear weather gave us a view of the frosted mountain that was astounding. Scout was beside herself over the setting we were enjoying. The wind the night before had formed Rime Ice on the trees. I have lived in the flat lands of the North most of my life but have never seen such a sight. Rime Ice is not like snow, because snow easily falls of the branches and limbs. This white ice formation coats the limbs and must either be melted off or the wind shakes the tree enough that it breaks off and falls. The surrounding mountains were all various shades of white. It was a great shot for a post card.

Half way down, Scout, Firefly, and I stopped for quite some time at a little knob with a vantage point over the valley. The view was spectacular. The white of the higher elevations transitioned to the forest colors in the valley. I was reminded of Frost's poem, "Stopping by the Woods on a Snowy Evening." The peaceful surroundings were such that no one could speak for a while, even Firefly.

Our plan was to stop at Standing Bear Farm where my wife would meet me. Scout and Firefly planned on staying there that night and then move on without me. The rest of the hike over to Standing Bear Farm was through a burned out forest. It looked as though a forest fire had swept through within the last two years.

Standing Bear Farm is a great way to end the Smokies. It is a great hostel, but it is not much of a farm. I think I saw a small garden. It is operated by a man named Curtis and his wife Maria. Curtis could serve as a double for Tommy Lee Jones. He looks like him, sounds like him, and even acts a little like him. I am still not sure he was not the famous actor. We arrived at the farm about noon, where we celebrated our first showers in five days, caught a ride down the road to a restaurant, and made pigs of ourselves on BBQ and then relaxed at the hostel. Scout did her and Firefly's laundry and we all sat around in the sun and talked.

I had not sent anything to myself at Standing Bear Farm and was not expecting any mail, but I happened to walk by the pile of packages awaiting hikers and noticed a familiar return address label. It caught my eye because the return address label was adorned with cats. It was from my mother. She had anticipated my arrival at the "farm" from my postings on the Internet and sent me a package there. In the package was my mom's famous fudge. Her fudge is to die for. I broke out the package and the three of us ate some. I left the rest of it for Firefly and Scout to share. It was a fitting way to say good-bye.

Later that night Tommy Lee and his friends had a fire, roasted marshmallows, and passed around a mason jar with some kind of clear liquid in it. I knew for sure I was in Tennessee.

When Marilyn arrived later that night, I introduced her to Firefly and Scout and we talked briefly. I said good-byes to them thinking I would never see them again. I was going to be off the trail for three or four days and it would be hard to catch up to them because they did not plan on taking off much time hiking in the next few weeks. I had no way of knowing we would be brought back together by a blizzard. With good-byes said, Marilyn and I were off to a hotel.

THE BLIZZARD

Standing Bear Farm to Damascus, VA
Miles traveled: 220 miles
Hiking days: 13

For whatever reason, leaving the comforts of home to return to the trail was no problem at all. I was told by Curtis's wife that I would not make it back to the trail. Instead I was eager to get back to the task at hand. I was pleased with the way my body had responded to the rigorous demands of the trail. I was particularly elated that my knees had held up and amazed that I had no problems with blisters. In three short weeks I had gained a lot and was not about to lose that.

While I was home, my daughter Rachel came to the house and we worked on a plan for her and Marilyn to visit me on spring break. Marilyn is a teacher and the first week of April is spring break for her. So Marilyn, Rachel, and my grandson Elijah planned to come down and visit me and do some hiking while they were there. That was exciting to me. I studied the maps and figured I could get to Damascus, Virginia, by the time they arrived. That would be the perfect place for them to come and visit. I now had a timetable—get to Damascus by April 4th. That goal seemed reasonable at the time, but there would be problems ahead.

I left the trail on Saturday night and was in at the office Monday morning. For the next two days I worked in the office and spent some time with my family. On Tuesday, I left home in the evening in a one-way car rental and drove late into the night. By now everyone I had hiked with was well ahead of me. Still, my spirits were high and I was well rested. Curtis informed me that I had missed a blizzard in the Smokies that had stranded hikers there for a couple of days. I felt vindicated for all the worry and fuss I invested into my crossing of the Smokies.

I was on the trail heading north by eleven o'clock in the morning. The day's hike was uneventful. It took me over Max Bald. Max Bald is a peak with a grassy surface of about one thousand acres. There are several such balds in the south. There was a beautiful view of the snow covered Smokies from Max Bald, but the cold winds quickly drove me off the mountain and down into the woods. During my entire time on the trail, there were very few mountain peaks that I could enjoy a view from.

I felt pretty good that I could get an late start and still get in seventeen miles that day. I arrived at the Roaring Fork Shelter just as it was getting dark. There were four army soldiers at the shelter. They were out for a few days of hiking. I fixed Ramen noodles and they shared some of their food with me. Later we swapped military lies until we all fell asleep. The next morning I made sure that I thanked them for their service to our country and was on my way.

⤜•⤛

My first major trail town would be Hot Springs. It is one of those towns that the trail goes through. AT emblems are set into the concrete sidewalks. It is a typical trail town that has welcomed hikers and made them part of the background. When I arrived in Hot Springs I checked into a hostel called Elmer's. The hostel was one of the better ones I stayed in. I slept on a real bed—a bed with sheets and a pillow. The hostel had an optional meal that was all vegetarian. I am a devout carnivore and so I passed on the optional meals and instead visited a restaurant that serves one-pound burgers fit for a hiker.

Between Standing Bear Farm and Hot Springs I had met Hetaeras Jack, who was just out of the navy. I also met a father and son hiking together named Sourdough and Sidewinder. I saw both of them again at the hostel in Hot Springs. Sourdough and Sidewinder had been forced to stay in Hot Springs and wait for their dog to be delivered from the kennel. They had left their dog with a kennel before they entered the Smokies. The park does not allow dogs.

There are businesses that kennel dogs at one end of the park and deliver them to the hikers at the other end. Over the course of the trail I met several hikers who took their dogs with them on the trail. That is the only stretch of the trail where dogs are not allowed. Interesting though, the Smokies are the only place on the trail where horses are allowed.

I also ran into D-Rock, who I had not seen since before the Smokies. If I heard it right, D-Rock stayed in Hot Springs to work and I do not believe he finished the trail. He would try again the next year and that fell through as well. I would not see Sourdough and Sidewinder again until northern Maine in September when they were a little more that one hundred miles from finishing.

While in Hot Springs, I visited the local outfitter. At the outfitters store I checked my email and the salesman looked up the weather forecast for me. The forecast called for one day of rain and cold weather at the lower elevations and possibly snow at the higher elevations. After that it was supposed to get warmer. I have never had much confidence in weather predictions and this particular forecast would do nothing to change that. I have never been superstitious, but at about the same time I was eating my sixteen-ounce burger, Tank was at the post office shipping home his snowshoes. Had I known what was going on, I would have carried them myself.

At the post office, I picked up my bounce box. A bounce box is a box containing items that I need occasionally, such as my large bottle of vitamins, battery charger, and maps. I usually send the bounce box two weeks ahead of me. When I pick it up, I use whatever I need from it and then ship it ahead again.

In the morning I was out of the hostel early and climbed up the cliffs overlooking Hot Springs in a fairly heavy rain. I paused at the top of the cliffs and looked out over the valley below, unaware of what I was getting myself into. I had no sooner lost sight of the town then the rain turned to snow. With each tenth of a mile, the snow was falling harder. I was amazed at how fast the snow had accumulated as I hiked up into the mountains. The temperature had dropped to ten degrees within hours of leaving town. Because I was climbing uphill through snow, I was generating a lot of heat and so I was still hiking with only my T-shirt under my poncho, and I had no hat on and yet I was sweating.

By about two o'clock in the afternoon, I arrived at a shelter where I met four hikers who had settled into the shelter. Three of them were already in their sleeping bags and the other one was fixing a hot meal. They could not believe I was hiking in just a T-shirt and no hat. I could not believe they were in their sleeping bags with five hours of hiking left in the day. I had just stopped in to eat lunch in a dry place and they were insisting I stay there rather than go on in the storm. I learned they were from Kentucky and were out for two days of hiking. They had been let off at the north side of the mountain and were heading south as far as Hot Springs. I was a little puzzled because they could hike downhill into Hot Springs before dark. They had started the day about six miles from where they were and had just hiked up to the top of the mountain. I said my good-byes and was off to the next shelter.

As I walked away from the four guys, I was reviewing in my mind what they had done. They drove several hours to get to Hot Springs, paid someone to drive them out to a point on the trail, hiked up the mountain, and camped on a mountaintop in the middle of a snowstorm and frigid conditions and were going to bed at two o'clock in the afternoon. I thought they were rather silly. Then I began to think some more. I left my business in the hands of my employees, left a nice home and beautiful wife, ate peanut butter and Ramen noodles instead of my wife's cooking, and was going to hike twenty miles in a blinding snowstorm. Maybe those guys were the normal ones. Or maybe all hikers are just off in the head. I thought about what I would be doing at home. On a day like that, I would be sitting in my living room drinking coffee and watching the snow from my couch. Truth is stranger than fiction.

By late afternoon the snow had accumulated to about five inches and the temperature had leveled off at ten degrees. I was glad the wind was not blowing hard. The day's hike called for me to hike up the mountain and drop down to a gap and then back up to the shelter that I had in mind. When I arrived in the gap below, there was a notice for a hostel just down the road. I was tempted but decided to pass on it.

There was something very peaceful about walking through the snow that day. The flakes were huge and because there was no wind, the snow was settling on branches to a depth I had never seen before. The snow seemed to muffle all sound and there was a stillness that was inescapable. Had it not been for my boots getting wet and heavy, I would have been enjoying the snow. It was uphill for the next couple of hours and at about five o'clock I arrived at the Little Laurel Gap Shelter, which completed a twenty-mile day.

At the shelter, Frank was already there and in his sleeping bag staying warm. He had been there most of the day. To conserve my core temperature, I fixed a hot supper as quickly as I could and ate it while lying in my sleeping bag. I was wearing my evening wear—my fleece jacket and rain pants to keep me warm. I cuddled up and watched the snow accumulate on a picnic table. I could not help wonder two things: where was Scout and Firefly in all this mess, and if Tank had shipped home his snowshoes. My guess at the time was that he had mailed them home. Frank and I agreed on one thing for sure; we were glad for the volunteers who had built the shelter.

>—•—<

The next morning was worse. It had continued to snow all night and there was about nine inches of snow on the picnic table. To make matters worse, the wind had begun to blow. Still the sun would peek out occasionally and give us hope, only to slip back behind the clouds and the snow would resume. Frank was content to ride it out in the shelter and I agreed for at least a while. After some time though, I started getting an itch to get going. The sun came out for about an hour, the wind died down some, and it was a balmy fifteen degrees, so I was convinced that I could move on. The one thing I was not going to do was go out alone in such severe weather, so I turned on the influence and talked Frank into making a push for the next shelter. It was named Jerry's Cabin. We wondered if it could be a cabin? And maybe there would be a fireplace? So at about ten o'clock Frank reluctantly gave in and we got out of our bags to get ready. My plan was for us to play leapfrog so that neither of us would have to break up all the snow. All of this discussion took place within the warmth of our sleeping bags.

Once out of the bag, it was time to get moving quickly. I carried a garbage bag inside of my backpack to keep everything dry. I mentioned that my boots got wet the day before. And so were my socks. When I got out of the boots, I put my spare pair of dry socks on to keep my feet warm in the sleeping bag and hung my wet socks up to "dry." If I wanted to have dry socks that night I would have to change into my wet socks and store my dry ones in my backpack. So I packed away the dry socks and pulled my frozen socks over my feet forcefully. My science teacher in college, Mrs. Bland, taught us that the majority of our heat is lost through our scalp. Apparently she had never put on a pair of frozen socks. I thought I was going to go into shock.

With my socks on, it was now time to put my boots on. The wet boots from the day before were now frozen boots. After I took them off, they froze in the form that they were in when I took them off. Someone needs to explain to me why it is that wet books shrink once they're off your feet. It took considerable force to get my feet to reform the boots by breaking the ice. As if putting warm feet into a frozen boot is not enough, I had to stand up in the boots and forcefully push hard to reform the boots so my feet could get in the frozen mold. The whole process of putting on my socks and boots had taken a toll on my spirits. My feet were in extreme pain and I was sure both of my feet were severely bruised. The only thing that would help was to get down the trail. Frank was not ready yet, but I needed to generate heat quickly so I started off after admonishing him to hurry up.

By now the wind had picked back up, snow was falling again, the sun was gone, and so was Frank. I walked as slow as I dared and still generated some heat, and finally Frank showed up. I slowed down so he could catch up, but the more I slowed the more he slowed. It was pretty obvious that he was going to lag back and let me break up the snow all day. Still I was glad I was not walking alone. We had gone about a mile and the wind picked up to a scary strength and visibility was practically zero. I began to reassess my situation. I was hiking in the mountains miles from help with a guy whose heart was not in it. It was seven miles to go to the next shelter and I was concerned about getting lost in blizzard-like conditions. I felt as though I was alone in this effort and that caused a great deal of concern. I needed someone I could depend on, so with a little over a mile traveled I turned around and Frank was all for returning to the shelter. I imagined myself getting lost and freezing to death only to have mushroom hunters find my remains in the spring.

Back at the shelter I was perplexed. The last thing I wanted to do was to lie around in a shelter all day curled up in my sleeping bag, but I needed someone who could work with me to get safely to the next shelter. With the boots and socks off, I crawled back into the sleeping bag and lay there evaluating all my options over and over again. I also could not help wondering what other hikers were doing in this mess. That day was one of the worse days on the trail for me, not because of the snow, but because it seemed as though I was doomed to lay around the shelter all day struggling to stay warm when I had planned on covering a lot of miles.

At about noon a hiker arrived. "How long have you guys been up here? "

Ashamedly I admitted, "I arrived here last night, and Frank has been here since the night before. We tried to make it earlier but we kept getting whiteout conditions and turned back. Have you seen anyone else out in this mess?"

"No. The word I got from my shuttle was that everyone is holed up in hostels and hotels. I just got on the trail back at the road. I had taken a couple days off and was itching to get back to the trail."

"What are your plans?"

"I am here to get some peanut butter and jelly and then I am back at it. I hope to make the next shelter before dark."

"Want some company? It will take me a few minutes to get ready, but we could take turns opening up a path in the snow."

"You would need to hurry! I do not want to get cold so I will be leaving in a few minutes."

Curious about Frank, I asked, "What about you?"

"Yeah I guess so, but I will need a few minutes."

"I am Silver Streak. And you?"

"I am Big Foot."

"Big Foot? Where did you get that name?"

"I wear a size 15W shoe."

"That will work pretty good for breaking up the snow. Do you know anything about the next shelter? The map says it is Jerry's Cabin. Any chance it is really a cabin?"

"I have no idea, but I am going to find out soon."

I hastily packed away all of my sleeping gear and was back in the boots that had refrozen. By now my feet were very tender from getting jammed into the boots twice. In my haste, I made a little mistake that would have consequences for another month. I had been drying my gloves in the sleeping bag with my body heat and I forgot and left them in there. I did not realize it until I was heading down the trail, but I did not want to lose sight of Big Foot, and it would take quite some time to dig all the way into the bottom of my backpack and into my sleeping bag. I decided to push on and do my best without them.

The weather was intermittent. One minute it would be snowing and blowing and the next minute it would be calm. But the real dilemma was that there was enough snow built up in places that you could not be sure where the trail was. It was made even worse by the crust of snow that had been forcibly packed onto the trees by the swirling winds, thus covering up the blazes. On more than one occasion we were not sure if we were still on the trail and had to backtrack until we found a blaze. We had never wandered off the trail, but we were not going to take any chances. I believe all together we reversed our direction three times for a total of about a half-mile of backtracking.

Frank now had two people doing the work and he stayed closer to Big Foot and me as we took turns leading the way and breaking up snow. Big Foot figured out what Frank was up to and confronted him about taking his turn up front. Several times that day the wind picked up to the point that we had white out conditions. We were in close formation and even then there were times when we could not see each other. At those times we all had agreed to stop in our tracks and wait for it to blow over lest we lose one another and the trail.

The southern mountainsides are covered with Rhododendrons. They grow low over the trail and there are a lot of them. Even with the high winds, the leaves are formed in such a way that they hold a lot of snow. That snow had weighed down the branches so low that in places they formed an archway. We had to duck and crawl to get past them. As we went under them lots of snow would be knocked off and fall on us. With my gloves down in the bottom of my backpack, my hands were exposed to the snow that would fall on them. Normally I would have just packed away my hiking poles and tucked my hands under my poncho, but the footing was treacherous in places and at times the wind so strong that I needed the poles to keep me from being blown over. So my hands were constantly getting snow dumped on them and more than once I had to stop long enough to thaw them out. But I dared not stop for long because I would have gotten separated from the guys. My hands were so badly frozen that I would have decreased feeling in my thumb and forefinger for about a month.

At some point in the day we came to a sign that marked a bad weather detour marked with a blue blaze. Big Foot turned to me and said, "I am guessing we should take the blue blaze."

I pulled out my map and quickly researched the trail ahead. "I believe it is an exposed ridge of rocks covered with snow. It could be treacherous. Breaking a leg on that ridge in this weather could ruin your whole day. What do you think, Frank?"

"I think we should take the regular trail, we would just have to go slow."

My feelings were obvious and I responded emphatically, "If this is not bad weather then there is no such a thing. There is a reason for the blue blaze, which is only the second one I have seen on the trail and we have been over some pretty tough terrain." We had to shout to even hear each other over the howling wind.

Big Foot sealed the deal. "I don't want to depend on anyone to haul me out in this weather. I say we take the blue blaze and if they call us sissies so be it."

I was perplexed that the only one that felt we should stay on the main trail was Frank. With about an hour until dark, we came over the top of a hill and were on our way down when Big Foot first smelled smoke and then we all did. It was Jerry's Cabin

Shelter. We all celebrated out loud and I was thankful that Big Foot had come along.

Grizzly and Tank were at the shelter. I was glad to see Tank again. It was then that I found out what I had suspected all day— Tank had sent home his snowshoes. They had been there all day riding out the storm and taking turns fetching firewood. The cabin was merely a shelter with a fireplace and it had a tarp in front of it to block the wind. The guys had a fire going when we arrived. Also at the shelter when we arrived was a couple who were out for a few days of hiking. They were locals who seemed to not be bothered by the blizzard. We had not been there long when they left the shelter with the plans to pitch a tent somewhere down the trail. Once gone we had fun guessing why they wanted push on.

The fire in the shelter was small, but it was large enough that we could dry out our socks and take the edge off the bitter cold.

At an appropriate time, I explained to those in the shelter about Tank and the snowshoes and laid the blame for the storm at his feet. All in good humor of course, and Tank took quite a ribbing that night. The move to get to Jerry's Cabin Shelter was a good one, and I was glad that I had made it there. There is comfort in numbers at times like that. The talk in the shelter centered on the question of moving on, and we agreed to go the next day unless it was worse in the morning. I wondered what they thought was worse. We would be crossing roads in the morning and the worse case would be to hitch a ride out of the mountains.

That night I awoke wishing I had a larger bladder. In the end I was brave, but I did not venture far from the shelter to take care of business.

❧·❦

The morning brought no sunshine. By now the snow was close to twelve inches, but at least the wind had died down. We planned to travel as a group of five and take turns at the front. It was a good plan, but it did not work out. Tank took off early. Grizzly and I took off together and never saw Frank or Big Foot the rest of the day. On the map we would cross Big Butt Mountain about late morning. I wondered about the name until we came across a rock at the top about thirty feet tall with a rather distinctive crack in it. Grizzly and I took turns getting our picture taken in the crack, had a good laugh, and were on our way. Besides passing Tank later on, we saw only one other hiker at the next shelter. He was planning on staying put until the weather settled down.

The snow was deep everywhere, but at the mountaintops it had drifted in places to over two feet. Grizzly and I studied the maps and were imagining that the balds on the other side of Highway 26 would be extremely difficult for the next few days. That would slow me down enough that I would be out of food before I arrived at Erwin. We both decided to try to get to Highway 26 before dark. From there we could call Miss Janet and have her come and get us.

Highway 26 is an interstate highway and hitchhiking is illegal so all hinged on getting out by dark and being able to call Miss Janet. I liked the plan because it would get me out of the mountains and into a town that had a Pizza Hut. There would be better days to cross bald mountain than when it had two or three feet of snow. It helped that Grizzly had a cell phone. So after a quick lunch at the shelter we were off. The rest of the day was mostly slipping and sliding up and down the hills.

Late in the day we had to make a 1,600 foot climb. I had thirty years on Grizzly and had to push for all I was worth to keep up with him. To make matters worse, once we passed Tank we were blazing a trail through the snow by ourselves. That suggested to me that no hikers had been caught in the storm, or they had been able to get out before it got bad. About an hour before dark, we made it out to the highway where Miss Janet picked us up and took us to the Pizza Hut in Erwin, Tennessee. I ordered a large pizza and ate most of it.

Once Grizzly and I had filled up, he left with his friend he had called. I would never see him again, but I read on his posted journal that he finished the trail in mid-August by climbing up Katahdin with his father.

I have never seen the formal definition of a blizzard and do not care to. To me that was a blizzard, at least in the mountains. Bristol, Tennessee, was only about forty miles from where we got off the trail at Sam's Gap. The race that weekend will be remembered by NASCAR fans as the one at which the race crews had snowball fights, and the race would be delayed while they cleared snow off the track.

In the final analysis, I am glad I went through that experience. An old man walked twenty miles, eight miles, and seventeen miles while stomping through deep snow and sub-zero windchill factors in a T-shirt. I will have something to tell my grandchildren.

The snow had stopped, but the trail would be covered with melting snow that would leave its own set of difficulties for the next few days. I was thankful that my legs had gotten me through it—nothing beats a great pair of legs.

⋙•⋘

Miss Janet is a legend on the trail among thru-hikers. Few hostel operators enjoy more fame than her, and for good reason. She loves hikers and treats them well. Her house has been converted into a hostel that houses upward of fifteen hikers. She feeds them a big breakfast. And she makes you feel at home. She offers everything you could ask for in a hostel—showers, laundry, Internet access, and a warm place to sleep. Among the luxuries were boot driers. She also offers shuttles to various trail/road crossings for day hikes. That would come in handy for the next few days.

When I walked into the hostel, I was met by Firefly. I was so glad to see him. He was there with Jolly Green Giant and Superman. Scout was at the Holiday Inn Express with her parents, who had come to visit her. Jolly Green Giant had an amusing story. He had been picked up by some Baptists on the way to a church potluck dinner. The way Jolly told it, he had been kidnapped, but he got an AYCE experience free and was treated like the guest of honor.

Firefly informed me that Cedar Moe had been bitten by a Brown Recluse Spider and got off the trail at Hot Springs for medical attention.

The Brown Recluse Spider is a common insect in the shelters. They are not aggressive, but when they do bite you the consequences are profound. Brown Recluses have been found in 41 percent of our homes, but conflicts with humans are rare because of the habits of the spider. Thus few people are aware of their existence or the problems they pose. They live in dark corners of our homes and come out at night only to retreat to their secret places during the day. Hikers hang their gear and clothing up on hooks in the shelters and the hikers quite often are dressing in the early morning hours. The risks of hikers on the AT being bit by the spider are not high, but it does happen. I ran into another hiker in Pennsylvania who may have been bit by one.

The spider is about half an inch in length, brown, and has a marking on the main body in the shape of a violin. Its bite begins as a raised and inflamed area red in color. The swelling soon hardens. The victim experiences nausea, fever, shivering, and vomiting. The bite area later develops into an ulcer with a dry bottom and blue and gray borders. In some cases the tissue around the bite needs to be removed. That was what Cedar Moe went through. Scout saw Cedar Moe in Hot Springs when he was at his worst. She described his leg as swollen to the point that it looked like elephantiasis. Cedar Moe had surgery to remove the tissue around the bite area and they pumped him full of antibiotics. His youth and conditioning were in his favor and he was able to bounce back.

Over the next three days at Miss Janet's Hostel, I met several hikers for the first time. Some of them I would see again and some I would never see again. Among the new friends was Mrs. Gorp. She was walking the trail for the third time. Also, there was Juliana and her dog, Thoreau. Juliana was from Chicago and had no trail name. There would be several attempts to attach a trail name to her, but she vetoed every one of them. Pinky was a small college age girl who I would see on the trail occasionally up until the Delaware Water Gap. Wayfarer was about my age and was an electrician, the same as me. There was also Little Red, who was a teacher from Tennessee. She was using her spring break for some section hiking. And there was a hiker from Germany there named Bruno, who was fighting some leg problems.

In 1998, my family went on a white-water rafting trip in West Virginia down the Gauley River. In a freak accident, I tore my right knee out of the socket and had to pop it back in place while floating in the icy cold waters. Since then I occasionally have trouble with my knee rotating out of position. The result is a swelling of the meniscus and severe discomfort. Over the last couple of days it had gotten bad enough that there was a knot on my knee the size and hardness of a walnut. I used one of my short days in Erwin to visit a chiropractor to get it back in place. This would happen two other times on the trail. It is a chronic problem but not something that was going to keep me from hiking. After three times, I figured out how it was happening and made some corrections to the way I hiked. Throughout the day, I turned to my right to look behind me for blazes if I couldn't see any ahead because I wanted to make sure I was not off the trail. That rotation may have been what was causing my leg to rotate out of position. By simply teaching myself to look around to my left, I was able to avoid that problem.

The snow accumulation had begun to melt. That made for some interesting hiking, especially on the downhill portions.

Scout's parents picked her and me up and took us up to a point twenty miles from Erwin and we hiked back. On the way down to Erwin, we met up with Bluebird, Abandon, and Yahtzee. I had not seen Yahtzee since the Georgia/North Carolina border.

They were heading north and those of us on the day hike were heading south. The hiking was difficult enough and we had a late start so we only made it eleven miles that day.

On that first day of hiking we came across the carcass of a freshly killed wild hog. This hog must have weighed over 300 pounds. Their feeding and rooting habits have caused problems in the parks and forests of Tennessee. They root in the ground for food and thus cause damage to many of the plants and trees. The problem is so severe that the Rangers roam the hills at night with rifles equipped with night scopes. The campaign realistically is not to eradicate them. Their best hope is to keep them in check.

On the second day several of us finished the last nine miles into Erwin. On the third day we went up to Roan Mountain and hiked back to Carvers Gap. We now had completed thirty-four miles in the three days while we were at Miss Janet's. It was a good opportunity to get rested up some. The storm had taken its toll on our bodies and psyche.

⊰⊱•⊰

After three days, Scout, Mrs. Gorp, and I left together heading north, ready to resume logging some big miles. The stay at Miss Janet's was an enjoyable break, but we were ready to get back to serious hiking. In order to hike with the people I knew I would have to bypass a twenty-six-mile stretch. I would hike that later.

By that time, all the snow had melted and the hiking was just us against the mountains again. And by the time hikers get past Erwin, their muscle development is close to its peak. The hiker's blood is richer in red corpuscles, which helps in the absorption of oxygen. And their legs are rock solid. They have shed lots of excess weight. We were lean, mean, hiking machines. To reach that point of training makes hiking much more fun. There were good times ahead for us and some big challenges. At that point I was on pace to hike the trail in five months. That thrilled me.

The first day away from Miss Janet, we were able to stay at a hostel at Highway 19E. I hiked that day with Juliana, Scout,

Mrs. Gorp, and Wayfarer. It was great to hike in the sunlight on dry ground. That night when we arrived at the hostel, Superman and Firefly had arrived ahead of us. The hostel operator offered to make a pizza run. That night Juliana and I split a pizza and I had a salad. Juliana was leaving the trail after that day for medical reasons and I would never see her again or know how things worked out for her.

➤•◄

The next morning I was the first person on the trail and stayed on task all day. Scout and Mrs. Gorp had announced that they were only going as far as Moreland Gap Shelter. My goal was to get to the Kinkora Hostel. That would make it a twenty-four-mile day. I was beginning to look at every day as a possible twenty-plus day. I had some help though. For the first time I was hiking with my IPOD. I marched most of the day to "Thank God I'm a Country Boy" and other favorite tunes. My day was broken up some by a short trip down a side trail to Jones Falls. I had a snack there and lingered and enjoyed the falls. It was a worthy detour. The roar of the falls was both deafening and hypnotic, and the mist cooled me off. It was hard to pull myself away from the falls.

Part of that stretch of trail is along the Elk River. As I walked along the Elk River, I imagined how great it would be for my sons and me to fish the river. They love to fish and I was missing them. I imagined us catching our limit of trout and cooking them over a fire while hatching lies. There is a lot of good trout fishing in the southern mountains and that day I vowed to return to the area to do some fishing. *I need to stop promising myself things.* It was a long day, but I was able to make it to Kinkora just ahead of a downpour.

At Kinkora, I found out that Zama and Lug were there, along with Cruise and Applesauce. I had not seen them since the Smokies. Cruise's family had visited them and brought some chili and fruit. We had some great food that night. Bluebird and

Abandon were there as well. There were others that I would never see again moving at the pace I was on.

Long after dark, Mrs. Gorp and Scout came in from a downpour. The entire hostel stayed up late that night visiting with one another like it was a family reunion. At some point in the night, Bob, the owner, showed up. Bob is known among AT hikers for his volunteer work on the trail and his generosity to hikers—and the hostel itself is quite a contribution. For four dollars you get a shower, soft bed, the use of a kitchen, and a shuttle for resupply. The stay at Kinkora was the fifth day in a row we had stayed at a hostel. I was getting spoiled and loving it. There would be plenty of time for hardships.

❧•❧

Morning meant breakfast compliments of Zama and Lug. They had availed themselves of the opportunity to get to a store and had bought eggs and bacon. We had a full breakfast similar to what you would get in the best southern restaurants. It would not be the last time they provided a great meal for the entire hostel. Zama was a great cook, which is how she made her living before the trail. Lug did his part to help her. Of the two, Zama was the leader but together they provided great conversation, an occasional laugh, and fresh insight to our daily travels. At some point in the morning, Lug let out his famous "Glorious Rapture!" Once breakfast was out of the way, I was on my way to Damascus. Scout's plan was to stop at Watauga Lake for lunch with another of her cousins and Mrs. Gorp was planning on slowing down. Firefly was still in the hostel when I left and was not sure what he was going to do. I decided that I would go as far as I could that day and see where it took me.

I hiked most of the day knowing I was pretty much on my own. I also stopped at the Laurel Fork Falls and watched some teenagers playing. The roar was deafening and their play was entertaining. I also met a couple of locals out for a small hike along the river. One of them approached with obvious curiosity when one of them asked me, "Are you one of those hikers doing the entire trail?"

"Yes, I am," I said, making no attempt to hide my pride.

"How long you been on the trail?

"I started March 1st."

"How far do you walk every day?"

"It depends. A full day of hiking usually is at least twenty miles, maybe more. Sometimes when I get into a town in the middle of the day I only end up with a few miles."

"We go for a walk every day but not for anything like that. I am walking to get my strength up." He pulled up his shirt to show his fresh zipper. He was recovering from heart surgery.

"I am walking to avoid mine, or at least delay it for many years."

"Good for you. I wish I had done more of it. Where are you from?"

"I am from Michigan"

"Don't let any of these southerners give you any flack about being a Yankee."

I assured him I had been treated with genuine southern hospitality. After a few minutes of friendly conversation I was off, delighted to have met them.

⇒•⇐

That night I had Applesauce and Cruise all to myself in the shelter. They were from Damascus and were not far from home, so they were in good spirits. I was also in good spirits because I was going to be with some of my family.

My departure in the morning was early. As with most days I have a pretty good idea where I am going to end up at night. It was a pretty spring day and as I neared roads I could hear the motorcycles roaring up the hills. I pushed hard and ended up at the Abington Gap Shelter.

The night at Abingdon Gap was one of the scarier ones. I was by myself and did not know where everyone was. I knew most were behind me, but I did not know where Firefly was and thought it would be nice to have him there. Soon after I got to sleep, I was awakened by earth-shaking thunder and lightning that lit up the woods in flashes that I thought for sure would start a fire. The swirling winds blew so hard the shelter shook and loose items on the floor of the shelter rolled around. The rain came down in sheets and some of it was driven back into the shelter, forcing me to retreat to the very back wall. I would find out the later that Firefly was caught out in the storm and was soaked. I was fortunate to be at a shelter. The eastern side of the state of Tennessee was hit by numerous tornadoes that night and there was a lot of damage to homes. As I sat and watched the storm, I was thankful for the people who had built the shelters on the AT.

The morning would involve just a ten-mile hike gently downhill into Damascus, Virginia. The crossing of the border into Virginia was punctuated with a brief celebration, albeit a lonely one. Unfortunately, I was not able to check Tennessee or North Carolina off the list of states because I had the thirty miles south of Erwin to finish. It would be quite some time before I could check off Tennessee or North Carolina. I walked with great reflection that day because Damascus is one of those milestones of any thru-hike. What I had been through and how I had progressed was worth reflection. It was hard to believe that I had been out just over a month and had done almost one-fourth of the trail. I coasted into Damascus midday.

GOD'S THUMBPRINT

Damascus to Pearisburg
Total miles: 163
Days hiked: 10

Damascus is one of the great towns on the trail. Every year on the weekend after Mother's Day they hold Trail Days. I have yet to go but hope to soon. There is a parade and other events for the hikers. It is like a homecoming for AT hikers. The town is also a major cycling center. More people come to Damascus for cycling than hiking. There is an old railroad bed that has been turned into a bike trail called the Virginia Creeper. The Creeper is an old train track converted to a cinder trail that runs from Abington, Virginia, to Damascus. The total length is thirty-four miles. The AT and the Virginia Creeper both pass directly through town. There are hostels and bed-and-breakfasts to cater to the hiker and cyclist in town.

Once in town, I checked into a small hostel and settled in for one night; after that night I had reservations at the Fox Inn B&B for the next few nights. Superman had already hiked into town and had settled into the hostel. After a shower, I got wind of free food. Cruise and Applesauce's family owned a cycle shop in town and had turned the store into a big potluck dinner. All the hikers were invited to come and eat up. Everyone who was on the trail that I knew of showed up and we ate, visited, and had a good time.

Later that night Scout showed up after a day of hiking nearly thirty miles. She checked into the hostel with Superman and me. Scout was a small middle-aged woman. For a person with short legs she could hike with amazing speed. Most hikers carry two hiking poles, but she only carried one. At first she only used a stick she had found on the trail, and it was not until she was at Erwin, Tennessee, that she carried a man-made hiking pole. I believe her parents bought it for her. Her sister had hiked the entire AT the year before. Most hikers also use alcohol stoves, but Scout used a gas-operated stove. I am sure it added almost a full pound to her gear. The stove was called the Whisper Jet, but I thought Lear Jet was more appropriate. She was always up early making breakfast and when she started her stove it sounded as if a jet was on a runway close by.

Scout would sneak off somewhere every morning to do Yoga in the privacy of the woods. She was always the last to get on the trail but would soon pass up the rest of us. And at night she worked long hours on her journal, keeping it up regularly. Her sense of humor was much needed on the trail and she was the glue that held together our little group. So it did not surprise me when she would push herself to catch up to her "brood" once she fell behind, which was not often.

❧•❦

With Rachel and Marilyn in town we had planned to do some hiking while we visited. The plan would call for Marilyn to drive Rachel and me up to Elk Pass. From there we would hike back toward Damascus and meet Marilyn at a point halfway to town. From there Marilyn would join me and Rachel would take over the chore of watching Elijah. When Marilyn dropped us off we left a large sack of fruit for the hikers.

On the way back to town Rachel and I saw Mrs. Gorp heading north and I introduced Rachel to her. It would be the last time I saw Mrs. Gorp.

Hiking with Rachel was great. She runs marathons and hiked for her honeymoon and does well at it all. We had a chance to talk and had a good time hiking that day. When we got to our pre-assigned meeting place late, we decided to forgo the last few miles into town and go get some food.

The plan for day two of their visit was changed due to weather. It was the last day of good weather and we wanted to do something together that all would enjoy. There is a place on the trail in the Mount Rogers National Park Recreational Area where there are wild ponies, so we drove up to that portion of the trail and hiked out to the trail and found some ponies. We fed them apples and Elijah had the opportunity to pet some of the ponies, which, it turns out, are not really all that wild.

On the way back we stopped and dropped off the leftover apples at a place on the trail that I thought Scout and Firefly would be coming through. I would find out later that they did get the apples. Marilyn and I then finished the portion that we had passed up the day before. That night we felt we deserved a trip to an AYCE and so it was.

❧ • ☙

The following day Rachel and I went back to Elk Pass and hiked north. A rendezvous time and location was agreed upon and Rachel and I were off. Marilyn spent the day shopping and entertaining Elijah. That day the wind blew so hard that we had to use our hiking poles sideways to hold ourselves up. It was nice to have Marilyn and Rachel to hike with. Because they had Elijah along, I could not hike with both of them, but I would have been disappointed if they had not brought Elijah along.

Rachel had been preparing for a marathon and so she was in great shape and we both were able to move at the same pace all day without a problem. Throughout the day we saw no hikers, but we did see more of the wild ponies. At the end of that day, Marilyn arrived at her assigned place at the same time we did. We took Elijah to the trail and let him walk a little. He was just twenty months old and had his first experience hiking on the Appalachian Trail, but it would not be his last. Since then we have taken him on the AT twice and the North Country Trail once and he loved it. I hope to instill in him a love for hiking and walking that will last a lifetime.

⇒•⇐

The next morning I went into Damascus to the post office while Rachel and Marilyn got ready to depart. At the post office was Cedar Moe, who was back on the trail. The Brown Recluse Spider bite had forced him off the trail for a few days, and he was just now getting into Damascus. It was amazing how quickly he rebounded from the spider bite and caught up with us. I visited with him a few minutes and left him.

Rachel, Marilyn, and Elijah were ready when I returned, and they took me out to the point on the trail that they had picked Rachel and me up the day before. It was there I said good-bye to them all and they drove off. Of course, Elijah just waved good-bye like he was going to see me again later, not knowing it would be a long time. But I knew, and it was hard to say good-bye.

⇒•⇐

Now I was alone again. I was alone in a river of people. And it was raining quite hard. I had not had any contact with Scout, Zama, Lug, Firefly, or any other hiker for a couple of days, but I knew them. I knew how much they could and would go in a day and my reckoning had it that if I pushed hard the rest of the day I would catch up with them. So I did just that. I was fresh from some easy days of day hiking and walked hard without much of a break, except to stop at a shelter and eat lunch. At the shelter I met Bronco Billy. Bronco Billy was holed up for the day because of the rain. He had a policy of not hiking in the rain. A quick visit with him and I was off, arriving at Trimpi Shelter late in the day. I was disappointed when I arrived at the shelter and no one was there. So I settled in and made a hot supper of soup and crackers.

I was a little down that I had left my real family and did not know where my trail family was. But a few minutes before dark Zama showed up.

"Zama! It is good to see you. Where are the rest?"

"The rest are right behind me"

I asked curiously, "Who are the rest?"

"Lug, Scout, Firefly, and Tank."

"Tank! I have not seen him since the blizzard."

"Where did you come from today?"

"I stayed in Abington last night and my family dropped me off back at the road. Did you meet Bronco Billy back at the last shelter? He told me he does not hike when it is raining."

"He told us that. I wonder if he is a mailman?"

"I loved those bridges over the streams today, and that waterfall was awesome.'

"Did you see Mrs. Gorp, Silver?"

"No, I think she is out in front of us somewhere. She did not stop in Damascus and seemed to be moving fast, but I have not seen her entries in the shelters."

"I think we should celebrate our reunion with a fire. I will start gathering firewood."

"Let me finish my supper and I will help."

That night we all caught up on the last week's events. And Tank was unusually talkative that night as he filled us in on his exploits.

➤•⬅

The next day we all moved out and onto the trail in quick fashion, and there was a reason for it. The partnership shelter was one of the nicest shelters on the trail, but we were not going to stay there overnight. That would have made for a very short day. The real reason for the excitement was that the shelter was adjacent to the headquarters of the Mount Rogers Recreational Park, which was located at the road. At the headquarters was a phone, and there were menus available to order pizza. The menus were from a pizza place that delivered to the shelter. There were two shelters on the trail where you could have pizza delivered to the trail at the shelter. The other one was in Pennsylvania.

By noon we were all gathered, decisions were made, and the phone call was placed. I ordered both a pizza and a sub. The sub was to be saved for supper. While we waited we all used the phone and our phone cards to make calls. I was not carrying my cell phone at the time but I was able to check on Marilyn and Rachel to make sure they had gotten home all right, which they did.

It was a beautiful sunny day and we spent our time sunning on the concrete patio at the headquarters and talking. Once the pizza arrived, the only noises made were chewing and moaning. There are two pizzas that vie for the top of my all-time favorite pizzas. One is Davis Brothers Pizza in East Peoria, Illinois. I have loved their pizza for most of my life. However, my number one favorite is my wife's thin crust pizza.

It would be a while before our group would even think about strapping on our packs and heading down the trail. The warmth of the sun and the greasy fare that lay in our bellies set us up for a brief nap and some lazy contemplation. For a couple of hours we felt human. It was decided amongst ourselves that there should be more of this kind of shelter. But in reality most shelters are far removed from the roads or other civilized access for good reason- safety and serenity. There are shelters along the trail that are too close to a road access and the local teenager riff-raff tends to ruin them with parties and general mayhem.

Having packed up, we were crossing the parking lot at the headquarters when a car pulled up and disgorged three hikers. Among them were Braveheart and Messenger, along with Braveheart's father, Wise Panther. They had stayed at the shelter the night before and caught a ride to church and ate lunch with the people who picked them up. We would see Braveheart and Messenger for a couple more weeks. Like all of those who passed in and out of my hiking experience, they added a certain flavor to the hike.

➤·❦

The hike that day was mostly along a ridge overlooking a valley. In that valley ran Highway 81. From southern Virginia to western Pennsylvania the trail parallels that highway and crosses it several times. As I hiked it occurred to me that the NASCAR race was at night and that if I could get to the hotel where the trail crosses the highway, I could watch the race. My oldest son Garrett frequently comes over to the house and we watch races together, and I thought if I could watch the race it would be like I was home. So I picked up the pace and got to the next shelter to eat my sub sandwich. There I informed Firefly and Scout I would be going into the hotel. Zama and Lug were planning on pushing on past the shelter and pitching a tent. I invited Scout and Firefly to stop at the hotel and use the shower in the morning, and so with those arrangements made I was off on the last three miles of the day.

When I got to the hotel I found out I was wrong about the race being a night race. I was sorely disappointed. I made a call home and watched some bad TV and was off to a good night sleep.

➤·❦

It was April 10th and I had traveled 523 miles. I was really feeling good about the pace that I was hiking. Twenty-mile days were common, almost expected. Anything less and I felt like I was loafing. And Scout, Firefly, Zama, Lug, and I seemed to be hiking at the same pace and staying together. It was the best of times on the trail. Even the weather was playing its part in the harmony. Aside from the blizzard we had all been caught in, the weather had been extraordinary.

With the exception of the four-day excursion back to Michigan and the two days I took off at Damascus when Marilyn and Rachel visited, I had not taken a day off to just relax. That was about to change. I estimated that I would be in Pearisburg late on Good Friday and so I had planned to take the Saturday off and go to church on Easter Sunday. The thought of a day off just to relax appealed to me, and I was sure I could find a good church to attend.

Scout and Firefly showered at the hotel and we went to a restaurant. Day 41 on the trail was without event, save the creative idea Scout came up with. She went to a local truck stop near the hotel I stayed in and bought some bread dough in a can and some cheese. Her plan was to have a fire that night and roast the bread and cheese on a stick. She enlisted me to carry the cheese all day up and down the mountains. She carried the dough. Zama and Lug had to get to a mail drop in town and so we were only hoping they would make it to the same shelter we were aiming for.

The hike that day guided us across active cattle pastures that were privately owned. There are several such places on the AT. The government and the trail organizers negotiate the easements through private property, and I applaud the parties involved for the great cooperation. The pastures are fenced in and stiles are placed to cross the fences. The stiles are steps that go up over the fence and back down again, making the fence crossing easy for humans and there is no risk of cattle getting out and causing trouble.

We crossed several ridges that day and ended up at Knot Maul Shelter. Zama and Lug had ended up there along with Tank. That night we made a fire and roasted our bread and cheese. It was a simple little treat, but it rounded out an excellent day with class. All agreed Scout had a great idea. Lug was dealing with a scalded conscience that night because he was a vegetarian. That day the knats were so thick he believed he had swallowed enough of them to violate his meatless oath. We consoled him as best we could.

In the morning I was out of camp first and made good time down into a valley and up onto the next ridge we would be hiking. It was a very cold morning and I had to walk fast to generate heat. Once on the ridge I got confused because there were no blazes and twice I had to backtrack to make sure I had not gotten off the trail. I think the trail workers must have run out of white paint in that part of Virginia. But once at the shelter, where we were to meet for lunch, I was taken back by the view from the shelter. The valley below was called Burkes Gardens. It is known locally as God's Thumbprint. The valley stands out from an aerial view as a thumbprint on the middle of the parallel ridges. I went to the Internet and looked at the view from an Internet map service and it is a distinct looking thumbprint. The farmer's tilling methods created a patchwork of different shades of green that was stunning. The flat land with its fence rows and crops is completely surrounded by neatly folded green ridges that extend up to the main ridges circling the valley. In the nineteenth century the Vanderbilt family attempted to buy the entire valley but the locals would have nothing of it. I took pictures, but I am not a photographer who can do justice to such sights.

The shelter was a stone structure with four sides and a roof. There was also a fireplace. By that time of the day the sun was out and the morning chill was replaced with a sundrenched heat. The six of us lay in the sun like a herd of seals and took naps. When it was time to leave Tank announced he was going to stay. The relaxation and the view were such that he could not stand to move on. Everyone understood that. So after a two-hour respite the five of us moved on and left Tank with the warning that he may be invaded by Team Australia.

Team Australia was a name given by Scout to a group that had been hiking around us, moving about the same speed as our group. The team was named such because the leader of the group was an Australian by the trail name of Captain Kangaroo. I would estimate the Captain at about thirty years old. He had developed a following of young college age kids, including a nice young girl named Pinky. They had an interesting ritual that included the Captain reading bedtime stories from Earl Schafer's book about his first thru-hike of the AT. To say they were a fun-loving troupe would embrace the art of understating. They could be quite noisy and tended some times to get carried away, or at least more than we were used to. I spent some time in conversation with some of them individually, and they were much different individually. It was the group dynamics that transformed them into entirely different people. I have often thought that sociologists and psychologists could do their thesis by traveling the Appalachian Trail and observing the people and how they behave on the trail. The Captain seemed to keep them reined in enough that they were bearable.

Team Australia seemed to have formed sometime after Damascus in late March, or at least that is when we started noticing them as a group. I would see them as late as the Wednesday before Memorial Day in eastern Pennsylvania. We would play leapfrog with them for the next two months until I left the trail around Memorial Day. Our group tended to avoid them as much as we could because our older demeanor did not mesh with their younger exuberance. More importantly, their group was large enough that most of the time it crowded the shelters when we were all there. Having warned Tank about the impending invasion, Scout, Firefly, Zama, Lug, and I watered up and were off to finish out our day.

The rest of the day was scorching hot and dry. In Virginia most of the trail is on the ridges. The hiking is relatively flat, but there is no water on the ridges. The trees had yet to leaf out and so most of the sun was getting through the trees, and on really hot sunny days it affected us. On this day the heat and direct sunlight worked to bake the moisture out of us, and we all were running low on water. I slowed up and let Firefly and Scout catch up to see if they had any water/ "How are you guys doing on water?"

Firefly replied, "I have been out for a long time and could use a drink myself. Scout is right behind and may have some in her camel pouch."

When Scout caught up, I repeated the question and she answered back, "I am out and am desperate for a drink."

"My map shows no water for about eight miles"

Firefly was trying to put the best spin on it. "Well, at least we do not have to carry as much weight."

I summed it up with my own calming influence. "We have been through this before and we will be all right. We just need to push on to the stream miles down the trail."

Firefly was less positive. "It is a long way to that stream. I am not sure how, but we need water bad."

Within minutes we met up with a group who were obviously not hikers. One of the girls was an absolutely gorgeous young girl, or at least that is the way Firefly described her. I do not notice that sort of thing. And she had what I had mistaken for an Australian accent. It was in fact a New Zealand accent and she was quite put out by my bad guess.

All together it was a group of several locals who were taking the girl from New Zealand for an afternoon excursion. Firefly asked if they knew where there was water and they offered to take us to their car for some liquid refreshments. They were parked about a half-mile down the trail and so we followed them to their car were they had coolers full of iced pop, water, and beer. Scout, Firefly, and I rehydrated. Once we got the fluids down and had our wits about us again, we visited with them. The girl was visiting as part of a Rotary youth exchange and the rest of the group was the Rotary hosts. I am a member of Rotary and so we made that connection and talked for some time about what they were doing. We talked for about a half hour like we were long-lost cousins.

The rest of the day was spent in a sense of relief that I was not going to die from dehydration. There never was a time on the trail when I felt I was in trouble, but partly because a lot of care was taken to plan for water.

We arrived at the Jenkins' Shelter late in the day. The shelter was located along a noisy stream that was music to my ears. There were a few shelters located along streams on the trail and they were usually my favorite. The sound of the rushing water had a hypnotic effect. Another reason I like streams at the shelter is more practical. At the end of the day, I like to take my shirt off and rinse it in the stream and wash off. No soap, just water. On particularly hot days there is so much sweat that there would be salt stains on the shirt. I vowed to make this the only shirt I would hike with on the trail so taking care of it was a priority.

We arrived at the shelter in time to enjoy a long supper. It was at the shelters that we most enjoyed the antics of Firefly. He was the Johnny Carson of the AT. After a supper that included peanut butter sandwiches with jelly, Firefly decided he wanted some extra dessert so he tipped his head back and squeezed jelly out of his container into his mouth. I saw him do this on more than one occasion. There were only the five of us at the shelter.

❧◦❧

An early wakeup was in order because there was a planned stop for all of us. Zama and Lug had a mail drop in Bastien. They were being supplied by many of their customers back home. Zama and Lug worked at a bar and grill in Seattle. Their regular customers and some fellow workers were excited enough about the undertaking that they organized an effort to send them provisions. Zama spent a lot of time communicating with their friends back home to keep them informed on what they needed and where they needed it. The logistics were difficult, but the connection to home was a source of encouragement for them.

The guidebook was helpful in letting Scout, Firefly, and I know that Bastien had no store or restaurant and I was low on food. I needed a little more to get me to Pearisburg. So the rest of us planned on going to Bland for a quick supply stop.

The five of us hiked together that day and went our separate ways at the road. Zama and Lug went left to Bastien and Scout, Firefly, and I hitched a ride the seven miles to Bland where we found a gas station/restaurant. I had a burger and a giant order of fries and Scout had a steak sandwich; Firefly had the rest of the menu. For some strange reason, I had been craving a lemon meringue pie. I asked the cook for a piece and she broke the bad news to me that there was none. I was crestfallen. She felt so bad she whipped up a batch of some kind of crispy fried sweet bread that was on the house. It had a short life once it was put on our table. Southern hospitality!

We still had enough daylight to go the four miles to Helvay Mills Shelter. On arrival, we discovered that Team Australia had already started to show up and they were going to be there in force. And there were already several other hikers who had set up tents. There was still about an hour and half of daylight left, and we had only hiked about thirteen miles so it was unanimous that we move on and stealth camp down the trail. The water at the shelter was down a steep hill so we opted to find water farther down the trail. That was not a good idea. We pressed on and walked the ridge till just before dark and found no water. We ended up pitching our tent and eating some fruit we bought in town because we had no water to cook with. We resolved to get up early and walk to the next shelter a few miles down the trail to eat breakfast. The early departure would mean less sunlight to bake the water out of us. There was no real worry about water except the fact that we could not cook any food.

The next day would be long, over twenty-one miles, and that would make the following day into Pearisburg manageable. One thing that was bothering me was pain in my feet that seemed like tendonitis. I have a problem with that sometimes and when I do it takes a while to get rid of it. If I can tell it is coming and cut back a little then the problem can be mitigated. I decided that a couple of days off in Pearisburg would be just what I needed. It would allow me to get to Easter service, and I needed to get to the post office Saturday. My summer sleeping bag, rated at 45 degrees, was waiting there and I would send home my winter sleeping bag. That would drop my pack weight by another pound. My pack weight was getting down much like my body weight was.

❧ ❦

The next morning we got off early because we needed to get to water to fix breakfast. We made Jenny's Knob Shelter in about two hours. Once we were fed and rehydrated, I busted out ahead of the others and in an hour I was crossing Lickskillet Gap.

The second half of the day was an easy hike. Most of Virginia's trail follows the ridge tops, but that afternoon's section of the trail followed the valley. There was a fast moving stream flowing through the valley that was therapeutic to a tired and weary hiker. The trail crossed the stream several times and never got more than a few feet from it. The day ended at the Wapiti Shelter, which was still within earshot of the stream.

At the Wapiti Shelter, the only hikers from our group were Scout and I. Firefly had shot on ahead of us and I am not even sure why. It was quite often that way with him. And we knew Tank was somewhere behind us. I had the feeling that he and Firefly could only take so much of Scout, Zama, and Lug. We were the older generation and it seems a steady diet of our generation is too hard to take. When they had their fill of us, they had to get away, and they did.

But we had company. It was Team Australia.

That night I witnessed firsthand an interesting event. Captain Kangaroo read a bedtime story to his groupies. I remember when I was in kindergarten, we had mats and were expected to lay down on them at nap time and the teacher would read to us. For most of the kids it was like a lullaby and we were all soon sleeping. The Captain's followers were enraptured by the story of Earl Shafer's hike on the AT. They were reverently quiet and attentive. When the story was over, the book put away, and an acceptable period of reverence was observed, they reverted to the youngsters they were and the noise and tomfoolery returned.

※•※

In the morning I snuck out early leaving the snoring Team Australia. They and Scout would pass me when I stopped for an early lunch. Later that day the trail led up to a ridge. By 3:00 p.m. the clouds moved in, the sky was black, and it grew dark as night. The winds picked up and close lightning and thunder was shaking the ground. I started looking for shelter. I can walk in the rain, and did many times on the trail, but when I am hiking on the top of a mountain ridge with metal poles in my hand I get just a little uncomfortable when lightning starts to hit the ground. So I worked my way down off the ridge and found a large rock jutting out and got under it

As I sat under the rock, it dawned on me that it was Good Friday and much like the day Christ was crucified the skies had turned black in the middle of the day and the earth shook. It was a great reminder to me of the meaning of that day—quite fitting.

Once the sky cleared enough, I was off to Pearisburg. I was going to get almost a forty-eight-hour respite from hiking. And I needed it. I was having trouble with my little toe on my right foot. On the inside of the toe, there seemed to be developing a blister or sore of some kind. Little did I know the significance of that development, but it would play into much of my hike.

Team Australia was planning on moving on past Pearisburg with little rest, and I took comfort that their much larger group would be well ahead of us. The biggest significance of separation from them was there would be less congestion at the shelters, not to mention less noise.

I was also getting excited about my change in sleeping bags.. I had exchanged cold weather items for much lighter items. The fleece pants sent home early in my hike, the boots were exchanged for much lighter hiking shoes at Damascus, and Marilyn took home a couple of items with her. My base weight without food and water had dropped to less than twenty pounds. I could fly now. The lesson on the trail is that "less is more."

❧•❧

The ridge I was walking on that day ends rather abruptly, overlooking Pearisburg. Because of the steepness of the mountain, the trail was a switchback pattern that seemed to go on forever. Halfway down, the sound of cars and dogs and mothers hollering at their children and husbands assured me that civilization awaited.

Team Australia had passed me earlier that day and they had congregated near a hotel parking lot with one of their group member's family. Scout was there also. They had come to pick up their son and had been kind enough to bring food and drink for all. I craved fresh fruit when I was on the trail and so I opted for an apple.

Scout and I visited with our trail angels for a few minutes and then accepted a ride to our destinations. I had decided to take a break from all my trail family and check into a local flee bag for the night. Scout went on to the hostel operated by the Catholic Church. I punctuated the long day with a trip to a pizza house.

Later that night, I took advantage of the one thing the hostel did not have, a television. I wanted to get the latest news on what politician was caught in his folly and what baseball player was getting in trouble.

On the way home from the pizza place, I met a local with long hair and a wild look in his eye. He was muttering all kinds of condemnations and loosely quoting Scripture. From what I could gather he lived in the hills and came down infrequently because of all the reprobates in town. He latched onto me because I had a sympathetic ear. My guess is that the whole town had learned to avoid him but now he had a new set of ears to annoy. I am an expert at escape and evasion and still I had trouble shaking this guy. Walking faster did not work and being rude did not work. I tried to correct his scriptural quote and that only enraged him. Finally I did what I do best, I ignored him and it worked. He finally tailed off, ranting to himself and looking for a new audience.

FOOT TROUBLE

Pearisburg to Waynesboro
Miles: 226
Days hiking: 13

After checking out of the hotel, I walked over to the hostel—a walk of about two miles. There I found Scout, Tank, Firefly, Zama, and Lug. Also, I met a new hiker at the hostel. Her name was Feather. Feather had started the AT the year before but was forced off the trail by foot problems. She was starting where she left the trail the year before. Feather was in her early twenties, about the age of my youngest son. We immediately become friends.

There was also a man who went by the name Charlie. He was not a hiker but was staying at the hostel on a work-for-stay basis. I think his understanding was that he would be a supervise-the-work-for-stay tenant. Apparently his expertise as supervisor was invaluable. Firefly did most of the work and he provided the technical support. More than once I ran into trail bums who hang around hostels freeloading. Most of them are harmless but they do not fit into the mold of the hikers and it is obvious.

⇛•⇚

The mood that weekend was festive. Everyone was in an exceptionally great mood. Firefly was unusually silly, even for him. Zama was in her element when she was in the kitchen. She had been there the night before and had put together some great dishes. I did my part by crossing a large grass field to the Super

Walmart and buying fruit enough for everyone and a gallon of ice cream. Zama pledged a "brecky pie" for Sunday morning and a complete menu was arranged for a sunrise breakfast.

Six weeks before, I had not met any of these people and now we were celebrating together as though we were good family. Such is the necessity of life on the trail. Humans are truly social beings and I was beginning to figure out I was human.

The one downer to the weekend was Tank's news. Apparently he had what sounded like planter fasciitis. Planter fasciitis is a tearing of the tendons in the bottom of the foot. The cure is a combination of rest, anti-inflammatory medicine, and icing down the area. It does not go away easily and in the worse cases it requires surgery. Sometimes different shoes can help. The podiatrist would be Tank's first visit after the weekend to get a diagnosis. Tank took the dilemma with his usual stoic demeanor.

❧·❦

The next morning the breakfast table was set, complete with flowers that Scout had found and picked. At breakfast I questioned Charlie about all the commotion in the night. "Charlie, last night you seemed to have been having a bad dream. You were carrying on for several minutes."

"What was I saying?"

"I could not understand it. It was like no language I had heard before."

"I may be getting a new vision?"

"New Vision? What is that?"

"I am an American Indian. I have been seeking a new vision for my life and last night may be a sign I am getting the new vision."

Scout had be following the conversation and chimed in, "How long has it been since you had a vision?"

"Several years."

I was a little more skeptical than scout. I doubted he was Indian. I was thinking he needed his medication. Or maybe he had too much.

While in Pearisburg, I had met two eccentric characters in one weekend. I needed to get on the trail. Sometime during that weekend I began to draw a significant comparison to the book Tom Sawyer. In his journey down the river, Tom met some strange people and got into some interesting exchanges. It was as if I was living that book.

After breakfast I caught a ride with the caretaker of the hostel to a small Baptist Church. Zama and lug were staying behind to receive their prearranged care package, and Tank was contemplating a course of action that had no hiking in the near future.

Firefly, Scout, and I would head out, and we invited Feather to join our merry band. She gladly accepted and fit in immediately. I would never see Tank again and suspected as much when I left so I made sure I left with a proper farewell. We had hiked with him from early on in Georgia and although he was quiet and unassuming he was apart of the gang.

❧•❧

After the Easter service I caught a ride back to the trail and was off. That morning I would spot a morel mushroom just off the trail, which made me homesick. I hunt them every spring and it is no small event in Michigan. There are towns in northern Michigan that have mushroom festivals in the spring. I know of people who take a week's vacation to hunt mushrooms. The spring ritual would have to wait for another year. I was rested and I was on my way to Katahdin.

It was a short day of hiking because of the late start. I arrived at the Rice Field Shelter and found that Scout and Feather had already settled in. With a pretty young girl traveling with us, I was quite sure that Firefly would stick closer to us. Sure enough, he showed up at the shelter later and kept closer to everyone over the next couple of weeks. While we did manage to get Team Australia in front of us, one of the more subdued members had lagged behind and we enjoyed his company for a couple of days. We were all in for something a little different that night.

Scout announced she would camp under the stars in an open field near the shelter. If our group had a leader it was Scout. Firefly, Feather, and I also ventured out from the security of the shelter. We set up for the night and watched a dazzling sunset go down over the West Virginia mountains. There were several shades of red spread out over the sky in streaks no artist could duplicate. The mountainous horizon was so strong that everything around us took on a pink tint. And the crisp cool air carried a sweet smell of flowers. There were no bugs and no rain. It was nirvana.

We were all in an open field on an exposed ridge and thought nothing of it. I noticed on the trail that very little attention is paid to weather reports. Weather reports were just not important. Some time in the middle of the night the wind picked up to a violent level and thunder and lighting was everywhere. The peaceful sunset had hid a violent thunderstorm brewing. We all scrambled to pull down our tents and get to the shelter. I was the last one to the shelter and had just got the last of my gear under the roof when the sky unloaded a deluge. In the excitement, we discovered that Braveheart and Messenger had arrived in the middle of the night and they ended up sleeping through the commotion.

The next morning would be the first time I hiked with Feather. She amazed me! She moved along the trail with her long legs in a way that challenged me to pick up my pace. I had been on the trail for over a month and was in great shape, but Feather matched me step for step. Maybe it is because she was my daughter's age, but Feather and I struck up a friendship. It injected a new energy into my hike. Her temperament also melded well with Scout and together they became a team. She was intelligent, thoughtful, and had a great sense of humor. Braveheart and Messenger would also be with us for the next couple of weeks, which added to the personality of our group.

On my second day out of Pearisburg I contacted my wife by cell phone. We decided she would use some air miles to visit me when I got close to DC. After doing some projections, we decided that Waynesboro would be the perfect time and place for the meeting. She would fly down on Friday and go back Sunday. That weekend would be NFL draft weekend so I would get to watch the draft and Marilyn would relax.

The period was short-lived, but I enjoyed their company. Our little group was constantly changing and that made it more interesting.

On that day, we experienced fairly heavy rain and keeping dry was impossible. Added to that was a cold snap. The wet and cold kept us moving to keep from getting chilled and when we finally settled in at the Bailey's Gap Shelter we had traveled sixteen miles. That had become a light day by our standard. Wet wood was gathered for a fire and we left it to Braveheart to build it.

One thing that every hiker must do is keep one set of dry clothes in his backpack for nighttime. Once I was unpacked and dressed, I crawled into the bag with my dry clothes to get warm. The wet clothes were hung up in a futile attempt to dry them. There were three nights that I would be sorry I sent home my cold weather bag, and that was one of them. I fought all night to stay warm enough to sleep. According to my thermometer the temperature dropped to thirty-six that night, and, with all my clothes, my hat, and my bag, I still struggled to get some sleep.

Later that night Braveheart was able to get a modest fire going to dry out our clothes and boots. It had stopped raining soon after we arrived at the shelter but the temperature was dropping. Scout had Braveheart work on drying her boots while he played with the fire. Breaveheart did not watch them closely enough and part of Scout's heel was burnt. That would create a serious problem down the road for Scout. The smell of the fire was medicinal and the flickering light put a peaceful end to a very stressful day. But it did little for the cold.

In response to my remark about my sleeping bag, Braveheart posed a question about it. "I am not sure how they rate these sleeping bags. If I am in a sleeping bag rated for 20 and it is 20 degrees I am usually freezing to death."

Firefly threw in his two cents. "It is the Chinese who make the bags. They are all back in Hong Kong laughing, knowing American campers are over here freezing. They make their claims, we buy their bags, they get rich, and we freeze."

"We may have a class action lawsuit!" Braveheart added.

I suggested, "If you file a suit it will be both the Chinese and the lawyers that get rich and we will still be poor and cold."

"I read somewhere that it is based on the average person being comfortable in the bag for one hour at that temperature," Messenger said.

"So we should plan on sleeping no more than an hour at a time?" I said.

"I think I will write a song about sleeping bag ratings," Scout said.

The conversation only went downhill from there and we were soon off to sleep.

Most conversations at the shelter were innocuous. Subjects that are enlightening, inspirational, entertaining, etc., are acceptable. Political conversations are avoided for the most part. Camaraderie is essential and politics does not foster it among such a varied group. It would be tacky.

Day three out of Pearisburg was tough because I was struggling with a fairly sleepless night. To add to it, there were lots of boulder fields to cross. Boulder fields are stretches of trail covered by large boulders. You must hop from boulder to boulder and each hop must be planned. They slow you down and wear you out. The stretches in some places were over one hundred yards. In Maine that kind of terrain can go on for miles. Despite the difficulties of the trail, we were able to log twenty-one miles and end up at Sarver's Hollow Shelter.

During the evening rituals at Sarver's Hollow, Firefly again expressed his desire to be my son-in-law. I am not sure if he liked me or he thought I had lots of money. I explained to him that both my daughters were married but said within earshot of Feather that I was still lacking one daughter-in-law. I would not have minded Feather being my daughter-in-law.

That night, Feather informed us that the shelter we were in was one of several haunted shelters, but the only one that was bothered by it was her. To add to her discomfort was an unexplained light that could be seen through the trees. We assured her there should not be light down there and acted extremely puzzled by the light. Firefly made childish remarks to further spook her.

The shelter was just a few miles away from the campus of Virginia Tech. A year later a crazed gunman went on a rampage and killed thirty-two people and wounded many others before killing himself. I thought of that haunted shelter and the campus when it happened. How serene the setting in the mountains was and how horrendous that event must have been. What a contrast. The anger and hate that cause a young man to lash out so violently in contrast to the solidarity enjoyed by thru-hikers. As I have said before, I will take the risk of a bear or rattle snake confrontation over the dangers of meeting the wrong man at the wrong time. The Psalmist said it best: "Better to meet a she bear robbed of her cubs than a fool caught in his folly."

>>·<<

Day four out of Pearisburg was one of my favorite on the trail. I served in the military and have always been enamored by America's heroes. And there was none greater than Audie Murphy. Audie Murphy was the most decorated soldier of World War II, maybe of all time. After the war he became a movie star, playing the lead roll in mostly B movies. I grew up watching his movies on TV and remember most the movie *To Hell and Back.*

In that movie, he starred himself and the story of his battlefield exploits. When visiting Arlington a few years before, I made sure I visited his grave as part of my tour. I found out later that the number of people who visit his site is second only to JFK. He is better known for his acts on the battlefield than his fights after leaving the service. He devoted much of his hero status to fighting for better recognition of those men who suffered Post-Traumatic Stress Disorder. That is a battle that always needs a champion. The things that men experience in battle leave lasting scars and Audie Murphy made this his cause. Who knew better than him?

He died in a plane crash in 1971 on Brush Mountain, Virginia. Veterans from VFW post 5311 in Christiansburg, Virginia, later raised the money for a memorial and placed it on that ridge where he died—and the trail goes right by it. It is a fitting memorial to remind us of not only of him but all the men who sacrificed to keep men free around the world. I remember the day he died. I was stationed in Biloxi, Mississippi, and our sergeant announced at roll call that Audie Murphy had died.

Knowing ahead of time that the memorial was coming up, I was looking forward to visiting it. Even knowing about it, I almost walked by it because it is set off the trail about 100 yards. I hope one day to take my grandchildren hiking in Virginia and take them to that spot. We must always remember that freedom is not free. I am grateful to the men of the Christiansburg VFW for placing the memorial there. It serves as a reminder to the hikers who pass by.

We were hiking in a free country because of all the past heroes, many who never got the recognition. Some of our service men took lives and have to live with it the rest of their lives. Others carry with them wounds that they suffer with all their lives. For others it is the memory of a fallen comrade. And then there are the mothers, fathers, and wives who had to answer that knock at the door. All who serve devote their time at the age when they have so many other interests they could pursue. The sacrifices of our military are a large part of who we are as free Americans. That day I walked with the song by Lee Greenwood in my head—"I'm Proud to be an American, where at least I know I'm free, and I won't forget the men who died to give that right to me." Several times I sung it aloud as I walked.

❧•❧

Scout had added some variety to the evening shelter experience. She had been working on a song about the trail. Each night she added new verses or revised the old ones. She was putting her musical talent to use by characterizing the hiking experience in song. The song she was working on had drawn mild interest up until that night. On that night she introduced the latest revision that included boobies. That newest development revived the interest in her song. A female body part seems to add interest where there might otherwise be none. She continued to revise it for a while and it seemed to die either from a lack of interest or lack of quality. I cannot say which. However, her banjo playing experience would come in handy later down the trail for one of the better highlights of my trail experience.

❧•❧

That night at the shelter Braveheart, Messenger, and I discussed the possibility of reaching the Lambert's Meadow Shelter the next day. We had been traveling together as a group and Braveheart injected into the conversation that not only could we do it, but we must. Braveheart declared rather assertively that the next day we should do it because we were real men, and he declared it to be "Man Day." The plan was that we would leave the women behind and bust out the twenty-three miles so that we could be in Troutville by noon the following day to get the pizza lunch buffet at Pizza Hut that is right by the trail. I accepted the idea on principle. The principle being that I could get all the pizza I

111

could eat for a small sum. But I did not commit to it because I also knew of another restaurant in Catawba that was legendary. If we stopped there we might not have the time to make it by dark, but I left my options open. That was not well received by Braveheart, who wanted Man Day as if he desired it to be a national holiday. The other reason I was not too sure about Man Day was I liked our little group. Firefly was not in the conversation because he had camped up on the trail so he could get an early start on finding food the next day. He was out. They were sure he would be interested. I was not so sure.

≫•≪

Man Day started off with a warm commitment to the principle, at least by me, but the climb up and over Dragon's Tooth cooled that further. Dragon's Tooth slowed me down because it was a lot of climbing and was quite a challenge. I was also distracted by the report in my trail guide that there was a small store with a deli a half-mile off the trail. When I arrived at VA624 I turned off the trail and went down the road to the store. Just as I had expected, I found Firefly at the store. He was sitting on the sidewalk in front of the store and he was involved with a couple of hot dogs. His enthusiasm was contagious and I soon found myself wolfing down one, followed by some ice cream.

Sometime during our little store-side picnic Scout showed up and joined in the party. By the time the celebration in food was over, I was quite sure that Man Day was out of the question. With our hunger abated we returned to the trail.

The trail dropped off a ridge and crossed a large open pasture complete with cattle. It was a hot sunny day and we were in open fields. The streams that we crossed in the valley had cattle tracks all around them and thus I was not interested in any of that water. By noon I was out of water. When midafternoon came, I had been out of water for quite some time and was extremely thirsty and desperate for water. Around 5:00 p.m. I reached a parking lot at VA 311 where I found Feather. She was as desperate as

I was for water. While we were both talking about our water problem, a local lady drove in the parking lot and offered to take us anywhere we needed to go. I asked her for a ride to a local store to get water for all of us and instructed Feather to wait for Scout while I went after the water. Soon I returned with water enough for all of us. By that time Scout and Firefly had showed up. I took a survey and Scout and Feather were the only ones interested in going for the restaurant. Firefly was going on to the shelter and I was sure Braveheart would stick to the Man Day decree. What was left of our troupe headed for the restaurant.

The restaurant was a very classy family style place with cloth napkins and tablecloths. The girls at the door assigned a place to stow our packs and assured us they would be safe. That night we ate all the chicken and ham we could hold and drank pitchers of lemonade. Our bodies were still parched from the dehydration we had experienced that day.

⇒•⇐

Before going on to the shelter we stopped at McAfee Knob, a famous rock outcropping. We took pictures and moved on. That night I decided to cowboy, preferring a bed of leaves to the hard shelter floor. The Campbell Shelter is on a ridge that looks out over the valley below to the town of Roanoke. The trees shrouded the view, but I could tell the airport was just below. The lights and sounds were of civilization. I was just about lulled to sleep by the sounds when the first drops of rain drove me back to the shelter.

Troutville meant resupply, laundry, and pizza. My plans called for me to go at least twenty miles per day for the seven days after Troutville to get to Waynesboro to meet Marilyn. By now I was quite hardened and the schedule did not seem impossible, but my little toe on my right foot was growing more troublesome every day. I was not sure what was going on with it.

The seventeen miles into Troutville was an easy hike that I made by myself. Firefly had gotten an early start to catch up with Braveheart and Messenger. I pushed hard with the hopes that I would make it in time for the lunch buffet at Pizza Hut. I had spent a lot of money on that chain before and this would be my chance to get some of that back

The trail was easy into Troutville and I pushed hard not knowing what the times were for the lunch buffet, but assuming I was going to make it in time. At Troutville the trail comes out of the woods between two businesses onto a busy commercial four-lane road. Across the street is the pizza place. I hastily made it over only to find out that this particular store did not have a lunch buffet! Nonetheless I was going to have pizza and I did. I invited myself to sit with Tom. He was about my age and was moving so quickly that he was traveling by himself and had never picked up a trail name. I had seen him only once on the trail. I ordered a large pizza with sausage.

From there I went to the grocery store and found one of the most comical sights I had seen on the trail. In the deli area of the store Firefly and Wrong Way, a new hiker to us, were at a table. They had been taking items from the deli and eating them and saving the wrappers for check out. On the floor was a pile of wrappers that astonished me. It was going to cost them a fortune to get out of the store. They both seemed to be enjoying themselves immensely when I sat down with them. They laughed at the quizzical look on my face. In sympathy, or maybe for the amusement, I offered them the rest of my pizza and with little coaxing they accepted. It was sucked up with gusto. After getting to know Wrong Way, I purchased the food I would need for the seven days to Waynesboro. It would be the largest food supply I would leave town with on the whole trail, and my pack was bulging.

With resupply accomplished, I checked into a fair hotel and split a room with Firefly. At the end of the day I felt good about how far I had come in the last few days, but the challenge now was to go the one hundred thirty-nine miles to Waynesboro in seven days. I was confident it was not going to be a problem.

It rained all that night and well into the morning. Because of the heavy rain, I delayed my departure. I was quite anxious because I had to do laundry and was getting a late start. I walked over to a truck stop close by and did laundry and ate a nice plate of bacon and eggs.

From there I walked down the road and got on the trail. I had gone about two miles and came to a road crossing where I met a local who had been walking for exercise. We talked for a few minutes. He had a lot of questions about the trail, and I was only too glad to answer.

One thing he was curious about was how I cooked. His question caused me to realize I had not bought any alcohol fuel for my stove. He was heading into town to pick up some pizza and offered to give me a ride to the outfitter for fuel. He went to the pizza place I ate at the day before. While there, he ran into an old friend he needed to talk to so he gave me his keys and told me to go get my fuel. Within minutes he had me back on the trail with a full bottle of fuel. Where else would a person give their keys to a person going by an assumed name? I only remember him by the first name Charlie, but we acted as if we were old buddies. By the time he took me back to the trail it was later than I liked.

I was tired from a lack of sleep that night and was carrying a heavier load than I was accustomed to. To further the morning grief, the rain the night before had swollen the streams I was to cross. The streams were roaring and crossing them was a challenge. Most of the day was hiked with my feet soaked. The one upside to the wet feet was that I discovered I got some relief from the pain on my little toe. That would be helpful to know, because I would not know the real cause and cure of the toe for a long time.

Early that morning Scout announced that she was going to start out later that day. She planned to go to the first shelter out of town, or about ten miles. Feather was nowhere to be seen. It was always hard to know where Firefly was. And I had seen

Braveheart and Messenger when I had returned to get fuel, so I was sure they were far behind me. I was in a funk all day and saw no one that could cheer me up. The mood would remain with me until I reached the Blue Ridge Parkway.

The Parkway is a road that connects the Shenandoah National Park with the Great Smoky Mountains. Not including Skyline Drive, it is 469 miles long. It is a scenic rural road that winds through some of the most beautiful vistas on the East Coast. It is not a road you would take to get from point A to point B. The rise and fall, the curves, and the speed limit (maximum is forty-five) are an impediment to those in a hurry. It is the kind of road that a person would drive on for a leisurely Sunday drive in the mountains. It is popular with motorcyclists.

On the road there are numerous rest stops and parks. It was started in 1930 as a Depression Era work project and took fifty years to complete. The trail rises up to the Parkway and crosses it several times, and parallels it part of the time. What was so rewarding about it was the views. Most of the AT is in woodland cover. Views are few and far between. But the parkway gives you an opportunity to see some spectacular views of the valleys below.

The parkway lifted me out of my despair. I found a spot with a view a few hundred feet off the trail and took lunch and a nap.

I had hoped to go seventeen miles to Bobblet's Gap Shelter by the end of the day. It did not work that way. The late start, the trip back to town for fuel, and now the nap had cost me. I pushed on till dark and pitched a stealth camp about two miles short of the shelter. I was satisfied with the recovery I had made on the day and would make up for it the next day. Other than Charlie, I had not seen anyone all day.

⋟•⋞

The next morning I was off to an early start. I stopped at Bobblet's Gap Shelter and found that Firefly was there with Feather and Wrong Way. Feather had gotten out ahead of the rest of us but had started to miss Firefly, Scout, and I, so she purposely slowed up to wait for us. She was excited to see me and was hoping that Scout would catch up so we could have our gang back together. Wrong Way would hike with us for a few days. Scout did as she had promised and made the day before a short day. We had no idea where she was.

Wrong Way was from New York. He had been on the trail moving fast and it had become quite unfulfilling so he slowed down and was looking for a group he could fit into. There is something to that. I started the trail hiking by myself with no intention of settling into a group. My expectations were that I would just be hiking by myself as hard as I could. But the value in hiking with the same people cannot be underestimated. While in Maine, I ran across a group of trail angels who had hiked the entire trail in 2003. They had started out each one on their own and soon established themselves as a group. Every year they go to Maine and serve trail magic as a group. Their friendship has lasted. George Strait sings a song, "Let's Fall to Pieces Together," that says, "Alone is much better together." How appropriate for the trail.

Feather noted a campground just past a shelter that was about twenty-one miles out. The trail guide was usually quite reliable. Feather asserted her interest in staying at that camp. That would make my day a twenty-three-mile day. It was settled and we started out with Feather setting a grueling pace. Around lunchtime we arrived at the Bryant Ridge Shelter. A long lunch was not going to keep us from our goal for the day. So we spent a considerable amount of time relaxing and visiting. The shelter was one of the better ones on the trail.

The campsite was laughable. There was no campsite and barely enough level areas for all of us to pitch our tents. We had a lot of fun ribbing Feather about her selection. It was not her fault because the guidebook she was using stated there was a tent area there. But that did not keep us from giving her a hard time. That night was quite enjoyable and, as usual, Firefly entertained.

The next morning was an arduous hike up Thunder Mountain. At the top was a radar site that was once part of the NORAD defense system. No longer needed for that role, it was used by Dulles Airport. Firefly and Feather stopped there for a break and Wrong Way and I pressed on with the goal of stopping at a shelter for a planned lunch with all of us. Wrong Way was in the lead and I was following. I hike with a subconscious habit of keeping track of the white blazes that mark the trail. After some time, I figured out that I had not seen one for a while and convinced Wrong Way we were off the trail. We backtracked about half a mile and discovered our error. Wrong Way lived up to his name that day.

Once back on track, we arrived at a shelter for lunch just ahead of Firefly and Feather and they had Scout in tow. She had to hike an extra six miles to catch up to us, and it was going to make her day rough.

While eating lunch we were talking about our home and when I came to a point in the conversation where I was about to mention the name of my home town, I drew a blank and must have had a noticeably confused look on my face.

Feather let out an uncontrolled laugh and when she finally was able to contain herself she said, "It is called trail dumb." Then she turned to Firefly and said, "Silver has trail dumb."

Firefly could not resist. "Are you sure we should blame it on the trail?"

Scout, not wanting to be as cruel as Firefly, added, "I have heard a lot about it and have experienced it myself. It is a phenomenon that long-distance hikers experience. We use up so much energy with mindless walking and use up all of our blood sugar that works our brain."

Not wanting to let the opportunity pass, Firefly said, "But still, your own home. Maybe that was a combination."

I decided to rein Firefly in a bit. I said, "You know, my son-in-laws would give me the benefit of the doubt."

"Yeah, but back in…hmm…" Firefly was now mocking me, but my senses were recovering.

I helped him out—"Alabama."

"Thank you, Blue."

Feather and Scout were laughing hard by now.

After lunch, Wrong Way pushed out ahead of us so he could hitch a ride to a store. We stopped at the bridge over the James River. The river is traversed by way of a wide 625-foot long bridge built just for AT hikers. The cost is rumored to have cost one million dollars. I believe that cost seemed low. Most major rivers along the trail use auto bridges to get across them. There were several local teenagers at the bridge diving off it into the river and Firefly joined them. Scout, Feather, and I watched with amusement for about half an hour. I had no energy or interest in joining them.

We finished crossing the bridge and headed back up onto the next ridge and the shelter we were going for. By now Scout was in such bad shape she was moaning from the pain of a long day. She attempted to sway us into stopping along a stream to camp rather than going the rest of the way. Because we were not sure if Wrong Way had gotten back on the trail while we stopped at the bridge, we were not going to stop. Within a half-mile of the shelter Wrong Way passed us flying, slowing only long enough to announce he had ice cream. Suddenly all of us, including Scout, found new energy and the pace quickened.

Once at the shelter, we got our cook kits out and divided up the treats. First we ate the ice cream and then we ate the Cheerios and fresh milk he bought. It had been a very hot day and the ice cream for dessert, followed by the main course of cereal, was a proper end to a grueling day.

Even though Scout had participated in the excellent feed, she was in great pain. She had walked the extra six miles to catch up to us for a total of twenty-seven miles. Even the ice cream was not enough to comfort her. She asked for and received some Tylenol p.m.from me and crashed for the night, moaning herself to sleep. It was nice to have Wrong Way with us, but we were still missing Zama and Lug.

The next morning we had to finish climbing to the top of the ridge. At the top Feather and I stopped at a viewpoint to enjoy the scenery and philosophize. From where we were, we could see the old NORAD radar site we had passed by the day before. I looked like a golf ball sitting on a fairway. That gave us a whole new perspective on how far we were traveling in a day. The radar site was less than a day's travel and yet it was almost indistinguishable. Feather and I were enjoying the vista when the rest of the gang arrived and joined in the celebration. Soon they all went on and I stayed to make an important phone call to the office.

Around lunchtime we stopped at the punchbowl shelter for a midday break before pushing on. When we got to the Pedlar Dam, Firefly stopped and went swimming with locals again, much like the day before. The rest of us watched. We then pushed on to the shelter.

The gang wanted to stay at the shelter. Wrong Way and I had a better idea. We were going to push on ahead to the highway down the trail and catch a ride into Buena Vista, where we would split a hotel bill. No one knew where Scout was and we waited for quite some time before we left.

The road to Buena Vista was about two more miles down the trail. We started out with just enough daylight to make it to the road. About halfway to the road the thunder started rolling in and it began to pour. My raingear was a poncho that was large enough to fit over my backpack, but when it was new it was not that great at repelling water, and now it was well worn.

By the time we got to the road, Wrong Way and I were both soaked and the temperature had dropped significantly. The road had very little traffic, it was after dark, and we were both visibly soaked. No one wanted to have anything to do with such rough-looking riff-raff. Our attempts at hitching a ride grew more desperate after the first hour and finally in desperation Wrong Way stopped putting out his thumb and instead was waving his arms in desperation.

Finally a nice local stopped and picked us up. Once at the hotel, we began the process of drying out our clothes and gear. I put on my raingear and went to a local fast food place for a sandwich and shake.

One of the reasons I needed to get to Buena Vista was to get some food. I had not been rationing my seven-day supply of food well and thought I might be short before I reached Waynesboro. The other reason was, I had no reception that evening on the trail and needed to talk to Marilyn about the coming weekend at Waynesboro. I found out that the plane trip was not going to work because of the flights, times, and other issues. So we came up with an idea that would give us more time together for less money. On Friday after work she would start toward me and meet me halfway. When I got to Waynesboro, I would rent a car and drive toward her. She liked the plan and so did I, and so we set it all up. It was a very productive trip to town.

When we checked into the hotel, the clerk informed us that there were some other hikers in one of the rooms. For just a moment I was curious as to who it might be when the clerk mentioned they were a rowdy bunch led by a guy with a funny accent—Team Australia! So when we were fed and cleaned up we snooped around looking for them only to find out they were in the room next to us. I went to their room to touch base with them. They came into town because they had heard that there was going to be heavy rain and they were also low on food. That night they must have been quite subdued because we never heard any commotion out of them.

While in town a strange thing happened—Wrong Way called home and talked for quite a while and when he hung up he explained to me he was getting off the trail and going home. It took me by surprise because he seemed delighted to have joined up with us. I understood and was supportive.

There is a phenomenon among thru-hikers known as the "Virginia blues." The theory as I have heard it is that the terrain in Virginia has so little variation and the state is so long that the hiker gets frustrated. Supposedly many hikers get off the trail in Virginia. What I have noticed from my own experience is that hikers are by now in unbelievable shape. The physical challenge is gone. It is all mental at that point. At the end of a twenty-plus day you do not seem to be any closer to the end and Katahdin seems an eternity away. And with most of us the mental challenge is much tougher than the physical. I was enjoying Virginia. It may have been my favorite state. But the thought that I was not halfway to Katahdin was still on my mind, and you cannot help but think of all the things you could be doing.

Because I had waited for Wrong Way to make so many phone calls before deciding to leave, I was getting out late. Now I was on my way back out to the trail by myself. I used the microwave in the fleabag to heat up some more breakfast and then I was off.

It was late in the morning before I caught a ride; it was with a farmer.

⋙•⋘

Once up on the ridge I was into heavy fog. I also had no idea where the rest of the gang was. They could have gotten an early start and crossed the road ahead of me, or they may still be behind me. This, coupled with the low visibility and the loss of Wrong Way, caused me some angst. I guessed they were already ahead of me and so I started up the trail intending to push hard. About an hour later I met a hiker going the opposite way and he wanted to know if I was "Blue Streak." He had met Scout up ahead and she sent word back. He thought she was about an hour ahead of me. It settled me to know where they all were. Looking at the map, I had a good idea which shelter they would head for. All morning and into the afternoon I walked in the low-lying clouds by myself. It was a strange sensation.

With the late morning breakfast wearing off, I was famished and sat on a log next to the trail to eat some peanut M&Ms. Through the eerie fog there was something moving and I watched it get closer. It was Feather and when she saw me sitting on the log eating my favorite snack, she let out her little laugh that meant she was glad to see me. I invited her to join me and she was delighted to.

"I know Scout is ahead of me, but where is Firefly?" I asked.

"He is with Scout. That was a wild storm last night. Did you get caught in it?"

"We got soaked and about froze to death. By the way, what happened to Scout yesterday that she was so long getting to the shelter?"

Feather explained, "She went the wrong way after lunch and added about three miles to her day."

"It happens to all of us. I hiked three extra miles in the Smokies on a steep trail. Speaking of all of us, there is one less. Wrongway threw in the towel. He was trying to find a way home when I left him."

"What? Why?"

"It was no longer fun. It lost its magic for him."

We talked more about the strain the trail takes on us and how important the friendships and camaraderie were to take the edge off the trail.

That night there were a lot of hikers at the Seely/Woodsworth Shelter. There was a hiking club out for a few days. The club members had all pitched their tents near the shelter. In the shelter, I met Robo. He was a section hiker from Grandville, Michigan, out using his vacation time. Every year he would hike two weeks during his vacation. He lived about a mile from the mall I take my grandson Elijah to play at. It was getting close to mushroom season in Michigan and we talked about morels for some time. I would end up seeing some on the trail but was always too tired to push the issue and, besides that, I did not have the ingredients it took to cook them. It was nice to talk to someone from Michigan again.

That night was one of those when I paid the price for the lighter sleeping bag. It had rained intermittently throughout the night and it was unusually cold. I did not sleep very well and would need to go over twenty miles in order to be in striking distance of Waynesboro. Another issue that I dealt with that day was an increase in the amount of pain on my right little piggy. It had been bothering me off and on for the last two weeks and it was now getting chronic. For the first time it was bad enough to force me to take Ibuprofen. Some hikers carry and take some form of anti-inflammatory for prevention of problems. Long-distance hikers refer to it as vitamin I. I did not subscribe to that, but I did carry it for those times when I got nagging pains. I had learned a few days ago that if it was wet, the pain did not bother me as much, so I had experimented with some triple antibiotic ointment for the lubrication. It had been working, but on that day it did not help.

⇒•⇐

The next day we would log another twenty-plus day. Feather and I got out in front of Firefly early and stayed out in front of them all morning and into the afternoon. We found a rock formation that afforded us a nice view that included a cattle farm. I could barely see the cattle from that vantage point, but I mentioned, "Those cattle down there look great. I am picturing a loin cut, or maybe a juicy T-bone."

"You are awful, Silver. You know I am a vegetarian."

"Yeah, but I am sure there is some kind of vegetation in that pasture you could eat. You would just have to make sure you cleaned off the manure."

"I wonder if any of those are dairy cows. I would not mind a shake!"

"Hmm! Burgers and a shake. Let's get going, maybe we can make the six o'clock seating."

We worked our way down off the ridge to the valley below and crossed Cripple Creek and the Tye River. Once over the footbridge on the little river, we stopped for a late lunch. Beside the river was a large, flat rock that had been warmed all day by the sun. I laid out on it, covered my eyes, and took a nap. I was just in the process of betting with myself that Firefly would go swimming in the river when he showed up. I won the bet and decided that I had bet a chocolate shake—a large chocolate shake. I told Feather about it and she wanted in on it. So we agreed that we would get to Waynesboro fast the next day and buy a shake as soon as we got there. We stayed there for over an hour soaking up the warm sun and enjoying the serenity.

Once we had eaten enough to get us up over the mountain ahead of us, it was time to pack up and head out. The climb was 3,000 feet up and over three peaks. Two months before it would have been a major accomplishment, but now we were in better shape and our bodies were lighter. By that time, I had lost about twenty-five pounds. When I met my wife that weekend I weighed the same as when she had married me.

Once at the shelter, Scout, Firefly, and Feather laughed as soon as they saw me come in because I apparently had a definite perkiness about me. It had been a long time since I saw my wife and I had noticed all the features on the map were seemingly taking the form of the female body.

⋙•⋘

The next morning I was first out the gate. I moved so fast I did not think anyone was going to catch me. I was wrong about that. In the early afternoon, Feather caught up with me and we walked together. She wanted to get that shake. We stopped around three for a quick snack without even sitting down. By 5:00 p.m. we had banged out over twenty-one miles and found our way to

Rockfish Gap and the road that would take us to town and our large shakes.

Within minutes we were sitting in a place called Tasty Freeze. We both ordered the largest shake on the menu and drank it down with only a few breaks to moan. Once we had satisfied our obsession, I called the car rental company and they came and picked me up. I then returned to Feather who had walked to the post office. While there I picked up my bounce box.

I took Feather to the hotel where the three of them were going to stay and I was off to meet Marilyn.

Almost exactly when I dropped Feather off, Marilyn was leaving work and heading to me. I had her head for Highway 77 in Ohio and I would drive in that direction also. Once we were close to each other, we would look for a good place to stay. We met at Marietta, Ohio, and checked into a nice hotel. It was eleven o'clock before we checked in.

THE FRIGHTFUL HITCH

Waynesboro to Thornton's Gap
Total miles hiked: 80 miles
Days hiked: 4

After a day off I was back on the trail energized. I arrived at the trail at about one and registered myself. In the park you must be registered, and the registration must be displayed on your pack much like the Smoky Mountains. The trail through the Shenandoah National Park would be rated more for beginners and there is abundant food sources. I was looking forward to the park for those reasons. I had no idea where the others were now, or even who the others would be. I hiked all day crossing the main road through the park many times. I saw no one all day.

I met a couple on the trail that were visiting the park, and they were hoping to get a chance to meet some thru-hikers. They were planning on hiking half the trail in a few years. They had lots of questions and I was glad to answer them. I remarked that the halfway plan was not a bad one. And I was serious. I would rather see someone attempt a one-thousand-mile hike than dream of a full thru-hike and never do it.

I had it in mind that the gang would end up at the Black Rock Shelter and that was my goal. It required me to push hard that day. When I was close to the shelter there was a sign warning that the spring at the shelter may not be producing. Heeding the warning, I went to a stream just off the trail for some water. It was while I was there that I heard a bear cub balling. In the spring of the second year of a cub, the sow runs the cub off so she can go in heat and start the reproductive cycle over again. I had hunted bear in northern Canada many times and had observed that ruckus before. The year-and-half cub does not take abandonment well. I recognized the sound and did not want to tarry, but instead got as far away from that as I could.

Minutes later, I was at the shelter where Firefly was sitting at the shelter's picnic table happily eating. We just laughed and that was all that needed to be said. He brought me up to speed on the ladies. They were somewhere behind us, and they had planned to get to that shelter.

Sure enough, Feather showed up. When she saw me she let out a loud squeal, "Ah, Silver," and then followed with a big time hug. "I thought I had seen the last of you."

I was rather puzzled that she would think that, but I was glad to know we were such good friends. "Why would you think that?"

"I knew how excited you were to see your wife and just thought you would go home."

"We had an unbelievable weekend and I was glad to see her, but I am in the best shape of my life and making good time. So for now I am here. Besides, I had to bring the car back. It was a one-way rental."

While we were catching up on the weekend events, Scout came rolling in. "Hey, Silver, when did you get on the trail?"

"Late morning. Maybe ten."

"Did you have a good time this weekend?"

"It was a great weekend. I was able to rest up and get refreshed."

"What time did you get on the trail?"

"About one. And you?"

"I got on at eleven. You must have passed me when I got off the trail for lunch. I saw Yahtzee in Waynesboro. He had an infected blister and is heading home to Massachusetts."

"It is a shame he got this far and then got blisters."

To this day I am not sure he ever got back on the trail and wonder if he finished. The trail takes its toll.

"I have a bad blister myself from the damage to the shoes back when Braveheart was drying them out. It is bothering me. I am not sure I can go on much more. I was hoping the day off would heal it up, but not so much."

That night Scout worked on dressing it and it looked scary.

⇒•⇐

The next day was another uneventful day. The rest the weekend before did little to settle my troubled toe. It now seemed that there was no relief from the various ointments that I put on it. I struggled all day. At the shelter that night we met two young men working as painters and using the shelter as free lodging. They showed up at the shelter with fresh trout and all the trimmings. They brought only enough for themselves, and I thought they were rather brave men to prepare that food in front of us. Scout and I privately agreed that it would not be very Christian to beat them up and take their food. So Scout ate her pasta and I ate my Mac and Cheese. Aside from their rude teasing of our senses, they were not bad guys, but I believe they may have thought us to be a little strange. But we were used to that.

Scout treated her foot as best she could. She had already planned on getting off the trail that weekend to go to a family event, so she made the decision to get off earlier. Scout used my phone to call her sister and make arrangements. She would hike to a campground down the trail and wait for her family to pick her up.

⇒•⇐

The next morning, Scout's foot was too bad to be of any use for hiking. She asked for and received a ride from the trout boys. She would take a ride to the Big Meadows campground and wait there for her sister to come pick her up. Her sister was not going to pick her up for a couple of days so she was planning on tenting at the campgrounds.

129

She took her ride and I was off. I had been on the trail about an hour and I met a trail volunteer by the trail name Cooker Hiker. He offered me some tips on the park and we talked. He was there to groom the portion of the trail he was assigned to. I would see him two more times on the trail. The Appalachian Trail is abounding with such generous souls.

❧•❦

It was now time for me to start eating my way through the park. Ten miles out from the shelter was a store that served a campground. I arrived there well ahead of Feather and Firefly and decided not to wait for them. The store had no shakes, which was a disappointment to me, but they had ice cream, so I bought a pint of vanilla ice cream and two twenty-ounce root beers. The store threw in a large paper cup. I sat in the front lawn of the store and made a root beer float that was as good as any I had ever had. I was a sight. Picture a trail-worn middle-aged man sitting on the grass eating a float with a big grin on his face.

As I hiked that day I watched a forest fire across the valley to the west. It had been going on for over a day and was a rather large forest fire. The fire was many miles away, but I could tell they were having a hard time fighting it. Firefly and Feather were somewhere behind me and I did not see them all day. I found a small restaurant and had a burger and onion rings. Later that evening, we would all find each other, and I ended up having a salad at a classy restaurant. I had started with dessert at the store, dinner, followed by a salad. It was a backward day.

Scout had paid for a campsite that was large enough for all of us to pitch a tent, so we set up for the night. There were coin-operated showers at the campground so we all went to bed that night clean and well fed. I liked Shenandoah Park. The trails in the park were also some of the most gentle we had been on. I can only remember one bolder field we had to cross in the entire park. It was the kind of hiking an old man could get used to.

≫•≪

With camp packed up, we had breakfast at the lodge. Lunch would be at another campground eight miles away. Firefly and I walked on to the next meal and Scout hitched a ride to stay off her blister. Feather went with her because she had a nasty blister and did not want to get the kind of infection Scout had on her foot. Scout could now barely walk.

The walk to the next campground, Skyland, was torturous. My little toe was in such pain that two Ibuprofen did not help. Nothing I could do would give me any comfort. It is hard to believe how much attention one little toe can command. By the time I arrived at my destination, I was in shock. I was in such bad shape that Scout and Feather knew something was wrong with me as soon as they saw me. I took my time eating and weighed my options.

A long lunch gave me time to compose myself and let a couple of Ibuprofen do their work. I left the campground with every intention to get to the next shelter and hope that I could get the rest of the way through the park. It was less than ten miles and I decided I would be brave about it. I left well ahead of Firefly and Feather, knowing I might have to stop more than once.

That weekend my daughter Rachel and daughter-in-law Marcia were running in the Flying Pig Marathon and I was wishing I could be there. So I decided I would head back to Michigan, see my doctor, and take in the race. If I could get my foot taken care of I would get back to the trail.

At Thornton Gap, Highway 211 dissects the park. To the east a long way off was Washington, DC, and to the west was Luray. About the time I reached Skyline drive, so did Firefly and Feather. I informed them of my predicament and we said our farewells. I assured them I was going to pick up the trail where they were in a few days. I left information with both of them on how to keep me informed of their whereabouts so I could get back to hike with them.

While we were talking, another hiker came out of the trail. His trail name was Dreamer. I did not know it at the time but I would do some hiking with him soon.

After a touching speech about how enjoyable it was to hike with them, they took leave and I started to hitch a ride. I am sure they thought they would never see me again.

A volunteer working on the trail seen me and offered a ride. On the way to town, my ride wanted to stop at a diner and get something to eat. He gave me my options to consider. What I learned was that I had few options. There was no bus service in the Shenandoah Valley. There were three people in the area who offered shuttles to hikers and he was one of them. He could not give me a ride. He also knew one of the others was out of town. He gave me the phone number of the third one. My best option was to get to Harpers Ferry and catch the Amtrak home.

Once at the hotel I called the third shuttle driver. He was not available until late in the day, and by then I would have missed my train, and it only leaves Harpers Ferry heading west once a day. He suggested I hitchhike. I rejected that without another thought. It was seventy miles and there was no direct route, which meant it might take several hitches to get there. Hiking to and from the trail was accepted practice. I had gotten used to that. But I would not be going out to the trail. I would be hiking on major roads. Besides, I was not sure how much my foot would tolerate. I went to sleep not knowing how I would get to Harpers Ferry. I did make the call to inform Marilyn that I was on my way home.

It seemed that I had no choice. I searched for a rental car that would be one-way. There was no such arraignment available. I walked north through town to the outskirts and stuck out my thumb. It took me a while but hitch number one was secured. He was a building contractor that was on his way to Front Royal and stopped to give me a ride. He let me out on the south end of town and I started walking and hitching. The road through Front

Royal was busy and there was not a lot of room for drivers to pull over so I walked mostly, but I did have my thumb out some of the time as I walked. I walked over three miles through town to the north end without getting a ride. At the north end, a driver pulled over and offered me a ride to Inwood, West Virginia. That was hitch number two

Past Inwood it became interesting. It was a very hot and sunny day and there was no shade in the road. Again I walked with my thumb out. The national office of the Appalachian Trail Conservancy was at Harpers Ferry. I had their number in my guidebook.

At that point I was close enough to Harpers Ferry that I could have called the office and asked for the number of a shuttle, or at worst a cab. The problem was I had no signal on my phone. I walked for what seemed over an hour with no one even looking like they were going to stop. It was now getting late enough in the day that I knew if I did not get a ride soon I would miss the train. And the sun was beginning to get to me. I was out of water and very thirsty. To make matters worse, the pain in my toe was unbearable.

Finally two young men stopped and offered me a ride. They lived close by but would be glad to take me to the train station. The driver asked me if he could stop at his house to get some smokes, as if he needed permission. I was in no position to offer another suggestion. The driver ran in his house and while there a brawl took place between him and his live-in girlfriend. He backed his way out of the house, shouting every kind of obscenity in triplicate and was foaming-at-the-mouth mad. He slammed the door of the car and started out the driveway.

As quickly as I could, I inquired if I was the reason he got into the "spat." His explanation was that the B#&$%^ was just not very grateful for being allowed to have his baby and she was in need of learning some respect. I was glad that was settled.

Once down the road, he got out his "smokes." I noticed they were home rolled and hoped it was not what I thought it was. He did not seem like the type who would roll his own cigarettes. He lit up one of them, took a long drag and passed it to his passenger. He then turned and offered me one of my own. I politely refused. By now the smell confirmed my worst suspicions. And if that did not worry me enough, he decided he wanted to "go airborne." The road he was on was more like a roller coaster. The traffic at that time was quite heavy and it was slowing him down so he could not get the speed up to hit the top of a hill fast enough. His goal was to go over the top with enough speed to leave the ground. I surmised he had already left the ground. His solution was to slow down and get some distance between him and the car ahead of him. The difficulty with that was the car behind him now wanted to pass him so he was straddling the median to block the car behind him until the oncoming traffic would force him back over. He was getting quite frustrated because it was not working out. He kept hollering, "I want to go airborne." I kept praying, "I want to get to the train alive."

What kept going through my mind was what the accident report would look like. I always preached against drugs and alcohol to my kids. And my poor wife would have to face our Baptist friends and try to explain why her husband died in the backseat of a car in the back hills of West Virginia with drugged-out kids when he was supposed to be hiking the Appalachian Trail. And I could hear my Rotary friends I sit with at the table—"I knew there was something not quite right with Wally." All these things and more went through my mind in a very brief time. I grabbed my backpack and turned the softer side toward me, thinking it might serve as something like an airbag. But soon the road leveled out and the traffic was heavy enough to slow the driver down to a speed that was more in line with his ability to think. I considered that I was out of danger.

Strange as the boys were, they did deliver me to the train station, and early enough that I visited a local restaurant in the historical district. I ate a much-deserved burger with fries and had a much needed glass of Cabernet. As I sat in the restaurant, I wondered if our country was in trouble. If those two were the typical young person that would some day lead our country then we certainly were in miserable shape. Hopefully there are more Fireflies and Feather than there are those two. It did not seem real until that moment, but I was finally on my way home.

MOONSCAPE

Harrisburg, Pennsylvania to Culver's Gap, New Jersey
Hiking days: 10
Miles traveled: 192 miles

I was able to get a doctor's appointment to have my toe checked out, but I could not get in until Wednesday. Since I had to wait for the appointment, I decided I would stay for Mother's Day. The doctor turned out to be a nurse practitioner. I had wanted to get an appointment with a podiatrist, but I was more likely to get in to see the president. And I think the president would have been as helpful. The nurse practitioner looked at it, nodded her head, and told me to soak it in Epson salts. So I soaked my foot every chance I had. It proved to be futile.

Because of the delays, I did not leave until the traditional Sunday afternoon Mother's Day dinner. I left at about four in the afternoon and drove a one-way rental car to Harrisburg, Pennsylvania. From there I took a cab to Highway 11. I was leaving behind 188 miles south that would have to be filled in later. I wanted to find my friends and I was sure I was close.

The cab driver was a hunter who knew the area I was going to be hiking and gave me counsel. "There are some mean patches of rocks along that ridge. They are no fun to walk through."

"I have heard of those rocks."

"There are some good places to camp along the way and I believe there are a couple of shelters you could stay in tonight."

"I was planning to stay at the Doyle Hotel in Duncannon tonight."

The cabbie laughed and said, "You might make it there sometime tomorrow, but that hotel has to be at least sixteen miles." Actually it was eighteen miles. But I was not going to make it an issue. I was confident I would make my goal.

I stepped out of the cab and into a pouring rain. It was 11:30 a.m. by that time and so I pushed hard, knowing that I was not about to let the cab driver be right. I am not sure how far I walked before I came to the infamous Pennsylvania rocks.

Pennsylvania is known among hikers for the pesky little rocks. The rocks are not constant from border to border or people may not hike in Pennsylvania. There are stretches of the rocks that go on for miles, but they are scattered at different points on the trail. They came on me quite suddenly and they were every bit as horrendous as advertised. The rocks vary in size from a baseball to a softball or larger and the shapes vary as well. The rocks are continuous and there is no dirt between them. Walking on them is not hard, but it is not relaxing either. And if you step wrong you could end up with a sprained or broken ankle. I had met an older man who had attempted a thru-hike and it ended when he broke his ankle in Pennsylvania. Seldom during one of those stretches of rocks does your entire boot touch the dirt. The terrain in Pennsylvania is very moderate and would be such a pleasure were it not for the rocks.

As abruptly as the rocks began, they ended. I would estimate that they stretched for two miles. Aside from the rock gauntlet, the walk was a pleasure. Part of the day was spent hiking through pastures with tall grass and along rural roads.

When I had crossed a fence into one of those pastures I saw some artwork in the mud. It was a heart with an arrow through it. I knew from that that Scout, Feather, or Zama were ahead—or maybe even all three. Zama had started the tradition of leaving her mark that way and Scout picked up the practice. The markings were fresh enough that I knew they were made that day. It was an encouraging sign.

I stopped in at the Darlington Shelter for a rest and to check the register. I was delighted to see that Firefly and Feather had been there ahead of me and that they were going to be in Duncannon that night. I had guessed right. But there was no mention of Scout. I suspected she may have been just behind me all afternoon. I did not tarry because I had an appointment with a burger at the Doyle Hotel. I wrote something corny in the register, packed up, and was off on the trail, arriving at the Doyle Hotel at about 7:00 p.m.

The sun was out and it had been bright when I walked through the door into the dimly lit bar that served as the hotel office. My sight was momentarily lost when I walked through the door. Before I could regain my sight, someone came running at me with a blood-curdling squeal "Silver." It was Feather. She ran up and gave me a giant bear hug and was jumping up and down. There were several men sitting at a table by the door watching this touching scene with interest. I turned to them and said, "I get that with women a lot." They thought that was funny and so did Firefly.

We were by the door talking for a minute or two and the door opened again and a guy walked through. Again, Feather let out another squeal and ran and gave the new arrival a big hug with even greater enthusiasm. It was Gunter, who Feather had hiked with the year before and he was just dropping by. I watched that scene for a minute and turned to the guys sitting and watching all this and said, "Easy come easy go." Again they had another chuckle.

Firefly and Feather had given up on me. They thought they would never see me again, and my appearance at the Doyle was unexpected. They thought that I would get home, get comfortable, and lose all interest in the trail. They were right on two out of the three. The truth is I only lost interest in the trail when I was on it. Until I finished the trail, it always bothered me when I was not hiking. The human condition seems to be that we are always happy somewhere else until we get there. Happy is the person who can "live in the moment." But at that time I was content to be at the Doyle ordering food and talking with my hiking friends.

After all the excitement of our reunion, Firefly brought me up-to-date on the events of the last two weeks. "A lot has happened since you left, Silver."

"Where are Zama, Lug, and Scout?"

"Scout is right behind us but will not be in tonight. She got a terrible rash from the antibiotic she was taking for the infection on her foot. The infection is better now and she is still getting over the rash. We are getting reports that Zama and Lug are just behind us and working hard to catch up. How is your foot?"

"I am not sure. I was not able to get to a podiatrist, but I was told by a nurse practitioner to soak my foot with Epson Salts. I am not so sure that will help, but I am doing it every chance I get. Have you eaten? I am starving."

"I had the BBQ pulled pork sandwich. It was great."

I ordered the same meal and Firefly could not resist so he ordered another one.

Once the meal was ordered, he continued, "We have been hiking with Dreamer since you left. You may remember him from Virginia when you got off the trail."

"I remember him. I believe he is about my age."

"He is. We felt like we needed an old man to slow us down so we adopted him."

"So, now what are you going to do with two old men?"

"We may have to put one of you up for adoption. I heard Team Australia is close by. Maybe we could trade one of you for a couple of broken hiking poles or a leaky water bottle."

"Have you heard anything from Braveheart?"

"He is off the trail with Planter Fasciitis, the same thing that sent Tank home. We have been hiking lately with a section hiker who helped out Scout. He is with her now but is getting off the trail. He says he cannot keep up with us 'thoroughbreds.'"

We talked some more and ate. The hotel has good food at reasonable costs. It is an older hotel that is not much more than a bar and hostel. But I guessed it had some great history but its best days were behind it.

❧•❦

In the morning I joined Firefly and Feather for a huge combination of flour, eggs, meat, and grease and washed it down with some decaf coffee. We talked about options for the days ahead. Gunter had offered to take Feather, Firefly, and whoever was interested to Trail Days. Trail Days is a weekend event that is organized by the Southwest Virginia town of Damascus. The affair is always the weekend after Mother's Day. The event is attended by hikers from all over the country who have experienced the Appalachian Trail. To some it is a reunion and to others it is just an excuse to get drunk for an entire weekend. Feather and Firefly saw it as an opportunity to get away from the trail for a few days. They were unsure, so Feather set up a meeting place along the trail for Friday morning, at which time they could go if they chose to.

Their more immediate plan was to go four miles on that day to the first shelter north of town. They needed to stay in town to do laundry and shop and had planned to wait for Scout. I had just returned to the trail and was in no mood to rest for half a day. I needed to regain my trail legs and log some miles. I would have went nuts sitting around town. My plan was to go to the second shelter eleven miles away. So I left Feather and Firefly with my itinerary and headed out of town. On the way out, I bought my customary sport drink and a small orange juice. When in town I always tried to leave with some orange juice because of the nutrients it contains. The sports drink was for the bottle, which served as my water bottles.

It was late in the morning when I crossed the Susquehanna River on the bustling highway bridge and climbed up to the mountain and leveled off on the ridge for a beautiful hike. I had mixed emotions. I was eager to get some miles logged, but I was also leaving the people behind I had went to great measures to be with. I assured myself that they would catch up to me in no time. They always did. I also suspected I would need to regain my trail legs, and I was right. Easing back into the trail was a good plan.

There was a threat of thunderstorms most of the day. I pulled into the first shelter and had lunch with Dreamer. I was now not the only one on the trail with silver hair. He was from Erie, Pennsylvania, and was thru-hiking. We compared notes on things we had, such as aches and pains, abandoned wives, and what it was like to hike with the next generation. He was a pleasant person to talk to and I enjoyed hiking with him. He had hiked some with Scout in my absence and knew most of the people I had hiked with. He also knew about our long miles we sometimes did. He told me that he could not walk twenty-five miles in a day, but that he could drive that far. After lunch we both pressed on to the next shelter. Along the way I ran into another stretch of the atrocious rocks.

⧑•⧒

At the shelter, I was hurting that night. I had gotten out of trail shape during my leave of absence. To make it worse, I had mailed my hiking shoes to a town thirty miles into New Jersey. I had heard about the Pennsylvania rocks and how they tore up hiking shoes. Knowing that, I had reverted to my boots and sent my hiking shoes on ahead to New Jersey. I had been told by other hikers that the rocks persisted for a day or two into New Jersey, so I picked a town far enough into the Garden State. The result of the change in footwear was that I was wearing a much heavier boot now and it was affecting my legs.

At the shelter were two new guys. They were Spiritual Pilgrim and Stretch. Stretch was long and lanky—thus, his trail name. Spiritual Pilgrim was a retired Air Force man. Pilgrim and I had something in common because I had done a stint in the Air

Force fresh out of high school. We got acquainted while we fixed supper, did the dishes, and got our bed ready.

⇛·⇚

The next morning I noticed how unusual it was to me to not have a lady in the camp. I had hiked most of the trail with Scout and a lot of it with Feather. I decided that there were not enough women on the trail because they added something to the experience. Maybe they keep the men from being such pigs. I believe the ratio is close to ten men for every woman. I was hoping that the gang would catch up with me and was feeling a little guilty that I had pushed so hard.

That morning Air Force A-10 Warthogs were in the area. The high-pitched whine of jets' engines could be heard just above the trees. The trees had leafed out by then, obscuring the view of the planes, but the whine was unmistakable. They certainly were not the prettiest planes in the sky. They were famous for their ability to destroy tanks. During the first Gulf War they wreaked havoc on Iraqi armor. I could tell they were maneuvering for attack runs. When I was in the Air Force I was part of a two-man forward air control party. Our job was to direct attack aircraft into targets on the ground. Every day was an air show. Mixed in with the jets overhead was the distant sound of sporadic automatic gunfire from what sounded like fifty-caliber machine gunfire and M-16. It brought back memories, and I enjoyed it as I hiked.

Later in the day it became obvious what the aircraft were doing. I was close enough to hear the "burp" of the 30-millimeter Gatling guns on the A-10s. It is the primary weapon of the Warthog. The guns fire at a cyclical rate of sixty rounds per second. At that rate they do not make the familiar roar of a gun or rat-tat-tat of a machine gun. They were going in for target practice and then pulling out with a roar. Immediately after the A-10 would fire its main weapon, you could hear the thud of the rounds hitting the ground. I may only have imagined it, but I thought I also felt the ground shake when the rounds hit.

During lunch with Dreamer and Spiritual Pilgrim a trout fisherman came by and stopped to talk. It was trout season and he warned us that it was also rattlesnake season. He had seen a couple that day. I think he enjoyed telling us that as if it was going to worry us.

The Appalachian Trail has rattlesnakes almost the entire 2,175 miles. I saw a dead one in New Jersey, apparently killed for its skin. I also heard one underneath some rocks rattling at me in the hills in New York. I had researched the snake problem before I started on the trail enough to not be worried about it. I never did carry a snakebite kit, but Dreamer carried one. I decided that it might not be a bad idea to carry one.

After just less than eighteen miles, I settled into the Rausch Shelter and hoped that the gang would make it there that night. There were two locals, along with Dreamer, Pilgrim, and Stretch. It was going to be a crowded shelter. I fixed my ration of macaroni and cheese and decided it was time to splurge. I broke out the package of tuna fish I had been saving. While I was finishing my supper, Firefly and Feather rolled in together, both with their cheesy grin that I had grown accustomed to. They told me that Scout was coming in and warned me that she would be wiped from a twenty-four-mile day. Sure enough, late in the evening she came in quite tired. Since the shelter was crowded, Feather and Firefly volunteered to pitch their tents. Still it was crowded.

The next morning Firefly and Feather decided they were going to go to Trail Days. This was the morning that Gunter was going to meet them and they had a three-mile walk out to the road where they were going to be picked up. I headed out early with the intention of stopping at the road crossing where they were going to be picked up. I would say my good-byes there. But soon after leaving camp I missed a turn in the trail and went about a quarter-mile off the trail before I realized it. Apparently while I was off the trail they had passed me and I missed them. It would be much too quiet without Firefly, who provided our entertainment.

There was another stretch of the Pennsylvania rocks to walk over. My right foot was bothering me because of the toe, and the rocks gave me some relief from the pain. With some Ibuprofen, rests, and an occasional coating with salve, I was managing the pain so that long days were still possible. The more immediate concern was that my knee was giving me problems. The meniscus was swelling again on my left knee again and there was some pain. My left leg was out of position again. I would have to get to a chiropractor when I arrived at Delaware Water Gap.

Lunch that day was with Scout, Dreamer, and Spiritual Pilgrim. Stretch was long gone. There was much excitement about the shelter ahead. The shelter at Highway 501 was only a couple hundred yards off the trail and you can call in a pizza order from there. The day ended with a happy grin on my face.

⇒•⇐

The next day's distance was dictated more by shelter than ability. That is often the case. There was a shelter at fourteen miles and a town at twenty-four. For various reasons, we were off to a late start, but the trail was fairly easy and we pushed on to the shelter at fourteen miles. Scout sent me the quarter-mile off the trail to the shelter to make sure that Dreamer and Pilgrim were not there. We were also in need of water for the afternoon. They were not there and I returned with plenty of water.

We had lunch on the trail while we played with the options. It was getting late in the day and there was ten miles to go to get to Port Clinton. The forecast was for rain that night and hikers do not like to pack up wet tents in the morning. The decision was easy for me. Did I want Ramen noodles or real food? I decided I was going to Port Clinton and Scout was sure the others would also.

Most of Pennsylvania is the typical green tunnel, but occasionally there is an opening and you get a view of the countryside and it is beautiful. That day I saw the splendid beauty of Pennsylvania mountain country and it was something to behold. The far ridge spread as far as you could see with smaller ridges radiating from it. Nestled in the side of the mountain was a small town. You could see very little of the houses, but the church steeple proudly stood out against the dark green mountain. Below you could make out a river running through it. I stood there for several minutes taking it in.

I ended up behind everyone the rest of the day.

A church in Port Clinton has made their pavilion available to thru-hikers staying the night. By the time I arrived at the pavilion it was dark and no one was around. I set up camp in the pavilion and wondered where everyone was. A hiker I did not know came by and told me the rest of my party was at the hotel getting supper and gave me the directions.

The Port Clinton Hotel has a restaurant and a bar. Hikers are not allowed in the restaurant because of the hiker stench. We had all gotten used to most people treating us like humans and tolerating the smell quite graciously, but not at this place. We were instructed to take a seat at the bar. For whatever reason, the bartender treated us rudely. He would not take our orders at all so a waitress had to come in and take our food orders. The bartender would not even look at us except to give us a hateful stare. As rude as the bartender was, the waitress was every bit the opposite. She took care of us with great interest. It took us forever but we all got our food, and it was worth the wait. It included one of the biggest burgers on the trail and fries that were almost more than I could eat. We were all so hungry that all we could do was laugh when the food came. The feast was a fitting end to a day that covered over twenty-four miles.

Dreamer had a special visitor with him. His wife had driven from Eire to spend some time with him. Dreamer was planning on taking a couple of days off.

❧•❧

After a great breakfast, I was in for some extremely hard walking because of the rocks. They must have gone on for five miles and they wore me out. It was spring and the weather was gorgeous that day. And because it was the weekend, many people were out in the mountains. There was a campground close by and so I must have seen fifty day-hikers along the trail. They were friendly and added to the day's hike. Once the rocks ended, the hike was very easy again and since I was not going far I took a nice slow pace.

When I was within half a mile of the shelter, I stumbled forward downhill and fell hard. It hurt badly and I lay there for a few minutes to recover. I was badly torn up and took a minute to bandage the worst of it. Adding to that, I misunderstood the trail guide and went past the shelter about half a mile. Once I realized what I had done, I backtracked to the road. The reason I had been confused was because I did not realize the shelter was actually the garage of an old house right on the road. It was the only shelter of its kind at the AT. The house was owned by the forest service, and the caretaker lived in the house in exchange for keeping an eye on the shelter.

The shelter had running water and a shower house with a solar shower. The solar shower was just a hose run on the ground, and the sun would heat up the water. The gamble with the shower was that if you got all lathered up and ran out of hot water, you would have to rinse in cold water. As much as I wanted and needed a shower, I was not willing to take the chance of going into cardiac arrest and have some EMTs haul me out naked. I do not know of anyone else brave enough either.

At the shelter were GI Jane and Moses—two hikers I had never met. Moses was moving fast and would soon be way ahead of us. There were also some section hikers from Michigan, including the daughter of the doctor who had treated Scout earlier for the rash. The conversation was lively and the shelter was very comfortable. I impressed those in the shelter with my swollen meniscus. It was as large and hard as it had ever been. It looked like a golf ball had been inserted into my leg. It looked scary, but it was not giving me a lot of pain except at night. It also was somewhat of a problem when I had to sleep in a sleeping bag. There was not a lot of room to spread my leg in the bag and my knees ended up together, which was quite uncomfortable.

Overnight the spiders stretched hundreds of webs across the trail. It was my job as the first one on the trail to break up the webs. By early morning, I had a white coat of web covering me. After about two hours of breaking up webs, Moses passed me and took over the responsibility of clearing the trail.

The four of us spent the day playing leapfrog and we all ended up at the Knife Edge at the same time. The knife edge is a stretch of large rocks that form the peak of a very steep ridge. There is nothing dangerous about it if you are careful. You don't walk across it, you hop from rock to rock carefully. It takes time and it wears you out. We all crossed it with no real problems and pushed on to the town of Palmerton.

We got out to the road at 8:00 p.m, just before dark. The day ended up being just shy of twenty-five miles. Scout and I had gotten ahead of Spiritual Pilgrim and when we were off the ridge, we debated on whether to wait for him. While we were on the side of the road debating, a man pulled up and offered us a ride.

The man who offered us a ride was named Earl. He and his wife had been out to dinner and were on their way home. I believe they were in their late sixties. Earl's brother had walked the trail years before and Earl was a big fan of thru-hikers. They gave us a ride into town, which was about three miles away.

Once in town, they drove us around town showing us all the landmarks and telling their stories. It was as if we had our own tour bus operator. They let us off at the town hall and insisted on the pleasure of taking us back out to the trail. We set a time to meet and they were off, excited that they could take us back out to the trail.

Before we checked in at the shelter, we hit a pizza place. The "jailhouse shelter" presented a different set of circumstances. Once you are in you cannot leave except by an emergency exit.

The procedure to get into the shelter was to flag down a police officer and they would take it from there. In order to stay at the hostel, they must perform a lien check on you so the officer asked for our licenses. Once through with that, he "locked us in" for the night. Once we were in we took care of the showering and were off to a great night's sleep. Pilgrim was with us, but Moses decided to stay up on the ridge.

⇾•⇽

The next morning we had allowed ourselves plenty of time before Earl would pick us up. We used that time to take in a great breakfast at the same diner we had eaten at the night before. I took care of some business at home and went to the drug store. Pilgrim was still suffering from the effects of the extremely long day and decided to hang back and stay the night in Palmerton so he could watch the hockey championship.

Earl was where he said he would be at the appointed hour and joyfully took us out to the trail. He had brought along some chocolate chip cookies for us to take with us. We said our good-byes and headed up Blue Mountain. The climb up out of Lehigh Gap was reminiscent of the White Mountains. In places, it was climbing with both hands.

Some time that year a hiker was killed climbing up the trail at that point. I do not believe he was a thru-hiker. There are places on the Appalachian Trail that demand caution. They are not dangerous and most anyone can climb them, but getting in a hurry is not a good idea in places.

Once we climbed out of the valley and onto the ridge, we were not prepared for what we saw. The ridge is downwind from an old zinc smelting plant that has long since been shut down. The plume of waste from the smoke condensed enough to deposit chemicals along the ridge that killed all the vegetation

149

and contaminated the area. All that was left on the ridge was the underlying rock and tree trunks that had long been dead. With no roots to hold the dirt in place, it had all washed away over the years. I can only describe it as a "moonscape." I could not believe what I was seeing.

Along the center of the ridge a narrow ribbon of uncontaminated dirt had been brought in to support vegetation. That area had small trees and grass growing in contrast to the rest of the ridge that was completely barren. The government had made several attempts to get vegetation started. Crop dusters had flown over the area spreading seed and fertilizer, but to no avail. Their latest attempt was that very morning. It was so disturbing that even though I was hungry I had no desire to eat there.

≫·≪

The farther east we walked, the greener it became. By late afternoon we were able to clear our heads of the disgusting sight enough to eat a late lunch. Soon after lunch we had to tiptoe through another rock field. My knee was bothering me now enough that it made me forget my little toe. The rocks were particularly hard on the knee. It slowed me enough that I was glad to settle for a sixteen-mile day and set up at the Leroy Smith Shelter. It would leave me within striking distance of the Delaware Water Gap.

Scout and I both felt we had a day off coming and the next town would be the best opportunity. And we were both missing Firefly and Feather. Our hope was that a day off would give them time to catch up to us. I would use the down time to track down a chiropractor and get my knee adjusted.

Moses was at the shelter, as well as our old friends Team Australia. They had rejoined the trail that day after taking some time off to go to Trail Days in Damascus. I had not seen them since the little town of Buena Vista in Virginia. They had plenty of stories for us, including how Firefly had managed to kill a lot of brain cells that weekend via John Barleycorn.

While we were catching up on the trail gossip, a local came by. He was a savant. Someone made the mistake of asking him about the moonscape called Blue Mountain. He went on endlessly quoting publications word-for-word. They were things he had read, and once a savant reads something he never forgets it. We were not able to make much sense of what he was saying because he was quoting technical reports. Finally, I, in my own delicate way, let him know we needed to get some rest and he reluctantly left.

⇻•⇺

That night it was cold. It was the Monday before Memorial Day and I was so cold I did not get much sleep that night at all.

I left the shelter first and was down the trail an hour before Scout caught up. She informed me that Pilgrim did not stay in Palmerton. He had stealth camped short of the shelter and was in trouble. He was out of water and had nothing to make coffee with. Most hikers do not drink coffee on the trail, but Pilgrim was a retired Air Force man and they never get far from a coffee pot.

Later he passed me up heading for water without saying a word. He was in withdrawal.

There were more rocks again that day, but nothing I could not stand. The ridge followed a highway for a couple of miles before there was an opening in the trees so I could get a view. The ridge overlooked a river. It was the Delaware River and on the other side of the river was New Jersey—finally, a new state.

It was strange the way I had hiked the trail to that point. I was closing in on eleven hundred miles and had only scratched off two of the fourteen states the AT goes through. The twenty-five miles near Erwin meant that I had both Tennessee and North Carolina to finish and the one hundred eighty-eight miles from Luray, Virginia, to Harrisburg included the states of Virginia, West Virginia, Maryland, and Pennsylvania had to be finished. But none of that mattered. What mattered was getting my knee fixed and rest for my little toe. And then I was going to cross the river into the Garden State.

❧•❦

That night I arrived in Delaware Water Gap with plenty of daylight left. The trail goes through the town and there is a hostel operated by a church there. Scout and Pilgrim arrived ahead of me because I was slowed by my bum knee and a sore toe.

Scout knew a friend of a friend who was hosting her for a couple of days. She seemed to always have someone willing to put her up. She would end up spending the next thirty six hours in the lap of luxury. As for me, I checked into a fairly clean hotel room for two nights of rest. Pilgrim went off to find a bar and watch hockey.

Pilgrim would head off the next day to get to Vernon, New Jersey, before the weekend to get a package at the post office. I would never see him again. I did see Jolly Green Giant in town. I had not seen him since Erwin, Tennessee, in late March. He was still going strong. He was now sporting a kilt. I knew of a few other hikers who wore kilts on the trail. At least he called it a kilt; I called it a mini-skirt.

❧•❦

After only one day of rest, I was ready to move on. A chiropractor had taken care of my knee and I was rested up. Scout's plan was to go a few miles to a hostel on the trail. My plan was to get at least twenty miles so I would be in position to get to Branchville the next day. I had sent my hiking shoes ahead of me to that town. The boots I was wearing were great for walking over the rocks, but they were heavy. I would send home my boots when I picked up the shoes and it would make the hiking more pleasurable.

The crossing of the Delaware River is by means of a guarded walkway on the road bridge. At the trailhead I had mixed emotions. There was a part of me that wanted to turn around and head back into town, check into the hostel, and wait for Firefly and Feather. I was also excited about a new state. In retrospect that is what I should have done. I actually sat on a bench and debated both ideas. I had been on the trail for three months and was nearly halfway done. But in the end the practical won over. I was away from my family and business to hike the trail and every day that I spent on the trail was another day away from both. So with a sense of resignation, I put all the doubt behind me and found the trail.

Once on the trail I ran into dozens of high school-age kids backpacking. Every third person asked how far it was to the road, many with a look of desperation on their face that was comical.

It was the Thursday before Memorial Day weekend, and I was curious what these young people were doing out on the trail when school was in session. I finally asked an adult who seemed to be traveling with one of the groups. They were the senior class of a private New Jersey high school. In order to graduate from that high school seniors had to successfully hike with their class from Bear Mountain, New York, to the Delaware Water Gap. What a great school! I applauded that and told the adults who I was talking with what I thought of it.

I found out some time that day that I was walking on a rattlesnake preserve. Now why would anyone want to establish a rattlesnake preserve is beyond my comprehension?

That day I would see four black snakes and one rattlesnake. I almost stepped on the rattlesnake before I saw it. Fortunately it was dead. Someone had killed it and taken half the skin. I had been walking with my iPod in my ear, marching to country music all day. Rattlesnakes are named such because of the distinctive rattle they use to warn would-be-intruders to back off. In order to take advantage of that warning you have to hear the rattle. So the iPod found its way to the bottom of my bag.

⇒•⇐

I was pleasantly surprised at the beauty of the Garden State. The ridge had several openings in the tree cover so I could see the valley below and the little neighborhoods. When I had thought of New Jersey I imagined smelly factories and dead bodies in rivers. There may be parts of the state like that, but the part I saw was clean and wholesome. Whoever named it the Garden State must have been walking that ridge.

There was a hostel just off the trail about ten miles from the river. It is operated by the AMC club that also operates the huts in the White Mountains of New Hampshire. I stopped in to get a cold drink and check it out. I signed the register and noticed that Blue Bird and Abandon had stopped there the night before. I had not seen them for weeks, and I thought they were several days ahead of me. I noticed also that Pilgrim had stopped there. The hostel looked inviting, but I still had a lot of miles left in me. I was sure that Scout would be delighted to stay there.

It was hard to believe that three nights before I struggled to stay warm. It was hot that day and I had to conscientiously push the water. But the terrain was not steep and the miles were easy. When I arrived at the YMCA camp I was planning to stay at, I found a hand water pump and enjoyed some sweet cold water and it was just in time.

It turned out that the camp was not open yet and there was no one around. It is a large camp located beside a lake. There were many buildings, but I was able to figure out which building was the shelter. The shelter was actually a small cabin and the beds were cots with mattresses. What a delight. Four walls and soft beds was more than I had expected. I settled in and cooked a hot supper. It was one of the few nights I was alone on the trail.

After supper, I tried to call home about some business issues but there was no cell phone reception so I settled into my cot and tried to get some music on my radio, but there was no reception. I was in New Jersey, only an hour from New York City, and I could not get cell phone reception or a radio station.

❧•❦

Once back on the trail, it started to rain early. There were flat rocks that were slippery and I fell twice. Late in the morning Scout caught up with me. I stopped for an early lunch and found six deer ticks on my legs. Deer ticks are small, red ticks. They are not much larger than the head of a pin, but they can be a real problem. The deer ticks carry Lyme's disease. Hikers are wise to check themselves regularly and carefully for the ticks. It takes more than twenty-four hours for the tick to infect the host so if you find one on you, you do not need to panic, but you should check yourself carefully a couple of times a day.

During my lunch break, I called the office and was confronted with some issues that were going to need my attention. The more I walked and thought about it, the more it bothered me. On that day I was losing the mental battle. My knee was still sore, but my toe was really bothering me. Two hard falls from the slick rocks and the ticks did not help. I was missing my family. My grandson Elijah was a real delight to me and I was missing him. Slowly our gang had been busted up. But in part my separation from them was because I pushed hard every day with very little rest so that I could get home to my family. To say I was conflicted would be an understatement.

Early that afternoon I crossed the halfway point of my hike. I stopped and celebrated with a toast to myself with my water bottle. Mostly I was struggling with the future of my hike. I had talked with Scout and others for days about the possibility of leaving the trail. And the circumstances were working against me. With about two miles to go to Culver's Gap, I decided I was going to head home. Once I came to that conclusion, there was little doubt that I was going to leave. There were a couple of times on the trail when I struggled with going home. When I left Troutville, Virginia, I struggled, and when I was leaving my family in southern Virginia I wanted to go home.

Soon after I decided I was on my way home, Scout caught up with me. I informed her that I was getting off the trail at the road up ahead. We decided to go to a bar at Culver's Gap and have lunch before I headed out. At the bar I order a burger and a glass of Cabernet to mark the occasion. While there we me three ridge runners preparing for a weekend on the trail, educating hikers on bear safety.

After lunch they offered to take me into Branchville to pick up my shoes and start my journey home. Scout and I said our farewells and just like that I was off. Except for an occasional tinge of regret, I was fully committed to heading home.

Mostly I was excited about getting home. The ridge runners dropped me off at the post office, where I picked up my shoes. I found my way to the library. On the AT's official website I found the number for an AT shuttle driver named George Lightcap and arranged for him to pick me up along the road. Within an hour, he picked me up and took me to his house. Soon I was in a rented care heading home.

MONGA JOINS THE TRAIL

Thornton Gap, Virginia to Harrisburg, Pennsylvania
Total miles hiked: 187
Days hiked: 10

I had hardly unpacked my backpack and I was missing the trail. I left the trail without reservations or regrets, but when all my business was taken care of at the office I was gnawing to go back to the trail. Within a week I had devised a plan. We had friends from California who would be visiting Washington, DC, in late June. Marilyn had planned for months to visit them while I was hiking. I devised a plan to leave by train more than a week ahead of her. Amtrak stops in Harpers Ferry. I would get off at Harpers Ferry and hike north the one hundred and five miles to Highway 11 near Harrisburg. That was the northern end of the gap I had left in the trail.

At Harrisburg, Marilyn would meet me and we would drive down to Shenandoah and hike north to Harpers Ferry. By doing that, I would have accomplished a couple of things. I would fill in that entire gap and get my wife involved in a little hiking, which she seemed interested in.

It was a brilliant plan that would combine my hike with our visit with friends. After that, Marilyn was going to take me up to where the gang was and I would finish my hike with them, assuming I could find them. It was summer now and the heat and bugs would be a factor. Aside from that, I was quite excited that I had found a way to finish my hike that year.

❧•❧

While home, I tried to get an appointment with my podiatrist, but the soonest I could get an appointment was in late July. I took a chance and made the appointment, not knowing what the future held. My toe had not been bothering me, but the problem was still there. When I started hiking it would no doubt become irritated again. One thing was definite; soaking it in Epson salts was futile.

After fifteen days at home, my wife took me to the train station at Waterloo, Indiana. I was very disappointed that I had not been able to see the podiatrist. It was now June 12th. It was getting warm and the days were getting long. I learned before I left that Scout had gotten off the trail already to go back to Seattle to work. Feather had gotten off the trail with foot problems and would not return. I had no idea where Zama and Lug were because Zama seldom updated her journal on the Internet. I also had no way to track down Firefly. He did not take the time to post a journal on the Internet; in fact, I was not sure he ever kept a journal.

The train left Waterloo late at night and I rode all night and arrived in Harpers Ferry around noon. I headed north into Maryland. It was hot and I stopped to take the legs off my convertible pants. That is when I noticed a red spot about the size of a quarter with a black dot in the middle. I thought it may have been a spider bite and resolved to keep my eye on it. There was no pain or soreness with it, but it did look scary. I assumed I must have gotten it at home or on the train and did not think it was my worst fear, Lyme's Disease.

The trail was up and down, but nothing extreme. In the late afternoon, I came to Gathland State Park. I watered up there and was leaving when I noticed something going on at one of the pavilions. It was trail magic. There was a sign inviting thru-hikers and so I ambled over and made myself comfortable. Right away I recognized the trail angel from Shenandoah Park. He was Cooker Hiker. We had met on the trail and talked for a few minutes and then moved on. That was more than two weeks and a couple hundred miles away. Now he was serving food in the park. He served me a burger with all the trimmings, some chips, pop, and cake. We talked for a while and then it was time for me to go. I said good-bye to him and left the park quite sated. It was getting late and I had a schedule to keep. I would see Cooker Hiker a third time hiking in Vermont, and I recognized him on site. Of all the brief meetings on the trail, he has always been the most memorable.

Just before dark I strolled into the Dahlgren Backpacker Campground and it was delightful. There was a large area for pitching tents, some picnic tables, fire rings, and the most important—a shower building that was fairly nice. There was no shelter there. I met several hikers, including Rematch. He was a tall, redheaded hiker. I would see him again at the foot of Mount Katahdin the night before he was to summit. I went to bed that night tired but satisfied that I was on the trail again and doing well. I had traveled almost eighteen miles since 12:30 p.m. that afternoon.

❧•❦

The next day while hiking I came across a hiker doing the four-state-challenge. The challenge is to go from the northern point of Virginia to Pennsylvania in one day. The states you cross over are Virginia, West Virginia, Maryland, and Pennsylvania. That is fifty-eight miles in one stint. From all I could gather, few try it and even fewer accomplish it. I was a man in my fifties hiking with kids in their twenties. I decided to leave the heroics to the young and foolish. I had actually walked forty-five miles in one twenty-four hour period at home when I was participating in Relay for Life. It was on flat ground with no pack and I was hurting after that. But fifty-eight miles is not even imaginable to me. I always considered the trail enough of a challenge.

I was hiking with people I did not know. To them I was a section hiker—to me I was starting over. The rest of the trail would be like that. The rest of the trail was hiked by me in a patchwork that did not give me much time to establish friendships. It was different hiking and not as enjoyable. I can tell you that section hikers are at a great disadvantage when trying to finish the trail. I am sure that had I hiked along with the people I was hiking with on that day I would have enjoyed their company, but I was only going to be on the trail a short time and did not make a big effort.

There was an interesting trail angel on that day. I came out of the woods and into a small subdivision. The trail was approaching Interstate Highway 70. You could hear the highway from the woods. The trail led between a house and an empty lot. At that point the trail was just a path between the lot and the house. On the side of the trail were a couple of coolers with a note inviting thru-hikers to enjoy. I stopped there and sat on one of the benches provided and helped myself to some chips and pop. While I was there, one of the hikers I had been leapfrogging with that day came by and joined me. We were enjoying the treat when the lady of the house came out and visited with us. We talked like we were family and had a great conversation. She loved the hikers and had lot of fun visiting with them. We talked for quite some time and then I signed her register and said good-bye.

Once cleared of her house, the trail led out to the highway. There was a footbridge over the four-lane interstate. There are several such dedicated steel footbridges over major highways. Other highways are crossed by using underpasses or overpasses at highway crossings. I have since gone by that bridge while driving on Highway 70, always with a smile.

⤜•⤛

On the second day back on the trail I had hoped to make it to Pennsylvania by the end of the day. My itinerary called for five days of hiking a distance of one hundred and five miles to get to Harrisburg to meet Marilyn. To make it, I would have to average twenty-one miles. I decided to stop at the Devil's Racecourse Shelter, which was only a little over eighteen miles. With the day before factored in, I was six miles behind schedule and would have to make it up. But it was getting late and the next shelter area was too far away. The shelter was full so I pitched my tent at the top of the hill with some Boy Scouts. The Boy Scouts were great. They were well behaved and respectful. Part of the reason they were so well behaved is that they had hiked eight miles that day and they were exhausted, and few things please us older generation than worn-out boys.

The sore on my knee had doubled in size and was fevered. It also seemed to have swelled around the red area. It did not hurt, but there was a reason to be concerned. Whatever it was, it had to have happened while I was at home or on the train, and I convinced myself it was not a recluse spider bite. I had no other physical symptoms than the localized swelling and redness. I decided that I was not going to fret about it.

Early the following day I came to a wonderful park called PenMar Park. It is a city park that overlooks the valley below, and it is near the Maryland/Pennsylvania border. It was a good time to take a lunch with the other hikers. One of the hikers there had a sore on his back that was atrocious. It had all the markings of a recluse spider bite. The kid was pale and quite sick. He found out that a nurse visited the park once a week and would be there soon. I considered waiting for the nurse to have her check out the red swelling on my knee. It was getting worse every day. By the third day, it was at least three inches in diameter and was raised about a half-inch. After I had eaten and visited with the other hikers, I decided to push on. So I left the other hikers and headed for Pennsylvania and the Mason-Dixon Line.

I had noticed the hikers the last few days were making Yankee and Rebel remarks. They were approaching the Mason-Dixon Line as if it was a guarded crossing and passports would be necessary.

It seems everyone on the trail was either a rebel or yank. It was all in good humor. There was one person for whom it was not so funny. I met a hiker in a hostel weeks earlier called Blackbeard. He told me he had hiked the trail two other times. Both times he hiked to the Mason-Dixon Line and waited there. He waited there until he could conjure up a BM and then he would cross over into Pennsylvania and make his deposit and leave it there unburied and head back south to Springer Mountain. He hated Yankees. Blackbeard was still fighting the Civil War. I knew there were people in the south still fighting that war. Now I can say I have met one. One other time Blackbeard told me that the water from Pennsylvania north was heavily infested with Guardia and that I would need to boil it and treat it. He was strange.

I crossed over into Pennsylvania without ceremony and found a way to laugh about Blackbeard. I was in the land of contaminated water and unsweetened tea. I also decided to watch where I stepped. I celebrated what was only the second state scratched off in almost twelve hundred miles. Georgia was the first one after only one week on the trail.

That day I had dallied around some and found myself behind my schedule for the day. I had hoped to go the twenty miles that day to the Rocky Mountain Shelter. I needed to get that far to make my goal for the five days. I had gotten reports from people on the trail that thunderstorms were expected in the area. With about two hours of daylight left, a deluge hit. There were high winds and strong rain accompanied by some lighting. I picked up the pace almost to run and did not stop even though I was hungry. With only a few minutes of daylight left, I found the shelter, which was a half-mile off the trail. I was soaked and exhausted but the gear in my pack was dry and all was well. I slipped into the dry clothes and went to sleep that night contemplating my itinerary. In the next two days I would have to hike fifty miles to get to the meeting place I had set up with Marilyn, but I was confident that if there were not a lot of the rock fields in the way I would get there.

⇒•⇐

The next morning I scurried down the trail with the confidence that comes from being in good shape. I had to put on wet clothes but the heat generated from physical exertion soon dried off the clothes. I had consulted my trail guide and found that at Caledonia State Park there was a concession stand at the pool in the park. The concession stand was reported to serve burgers, fries, hot dogs, and other health food. I was disappointed when I arrived at the park and found out that it was not going to open for two hours. I had skipped breakfast so I could eat there. Having been thwarted, I fire up my stove and had some hot oatmeal at the park and headed off into the woods dejected.

One of the strangest encounters in all my hiking on the AT happened that day. I had stopped in at a shelter about lunchtime to take a break and eat some lunch. At the shelter was a group of clean and groomed young men laying around. That is unusual on the trail. Before settling in, I asked one of them what organization they were with and the young man, almost afraid to answer or acknowledge my presence, told me they were from a local military school. Apparently they were out on bivouac and I had happened upon them while they were taking a break. I had not even got settled in and one of the would-be-soldiers shouted out with military firmness "twelve minutes." It may have been the longest twelve minutes of my life. I picked a spot on a picnic bench that was occupied by a couple of the group and was confident that I was not going to interfere with their respite. The rest of them were lying around on the ground or in the shelter. They were so lifeless that it looked like a mortar round had gotten all of them.

At the other end of the picnic bench was a scary man. He was a couple of inches short of six feet and must have weighed two hundred and fifty pounds, and I would venture there was no fat on him. His hands were so beefy I suspected he could not hold an ink pin, which was probably okay because I doubt he could write anyway. He had a burred haircut that suggested military. His tattoos had tattoos. His muscles were not well defined like a chiseled weightlifter, but his skin was stretched tight from the bulging mass. I was sure he had killed people before. He had a look in his eye that betrayed a complete contempt for mankind, or at least me. Once over the fear of the experience, I would try to imagine how he killed his victims. Did he do them in by breaking their necks? Was he a knife man? Or did he pick his victims off from long range with a rifle. I rejected the last one, feeling that would be too impersonal and thus not very fulfilling. I decided he was a neck breaker.

But none of that scared me. What scared me was the way he stared at me. From the time I sat down at the only picnic table, he did not take his eyes off me. The stare was one of complete disdain. I have since tried to imagine what would have so incited this man. The leading theory is that he had not killed anyone for a while and was overdue. He was searching for his next victim and I just happened along. I am not the kind of person who is intimidated easily. If it was most anyone else I would have stared back at that person and asked what his problem was. But not this guy. From the beginning of this incident, I was glad there were so many of the students. Surely he was not going to kill me with all of these witnesses around.

I did take some comfort in a couple of things. He did not seem to be in charge. There was one other adult there who seemed to be in control of the group. And if I would venture a guess, this man was the kind of person who did what he was told to do. And I could only hope he was under direct orders not to kill anyone that day. My other consolation was that they were not going to be there long. The probie in charge of keeping the time would shout out every couple of minutes the time left. When the "one-minute" was shouted, I started to breath again and felt like I could make it through this. By that time I had opened my food bag and peered in to choose my fare for lunch.

When the one-minute was up the leader stood up and a synchronous rustle was initiated by all of the students. In one blink of an eye, they came back to life. They quickly slung their overweight backpacks over their shoulders and strapped down. They seemed to have established an order and manner in how they prepared for departure. They were well trained. And with one last look of disgust, the scary man picked up his pack and fell into line at the rear, but not without looking back one last time as if to say, "There will be plenty of time to get you."

Fortunately they were heading south and so I would not have to worry about being jumped by him further down the trail. As they walked away out of sight I was left to myself and my wonderment of what just happened. I do not remember a scarier person in all my days and I had been a juror in the trial of Samuel Hawkins—a serial killer from the Texas Panhandle.

Late in the day I stopped at Tom's Run Shelter for a rest. While I was there an attractive ridge runner with brilliant red hair stopped in the shelter. I approached with caution because she had her dog with her. She asked, "Are you going to stay the night here."

"No, I am going to Pine Grove. Are you staying?"

"Yes, we are. This is Rosco. I am Veggy. Where did you come from?"

"The Rocky Mountain Shelter."

"Oh my, you are going to have a long day. Are you a thru hiker?"

"Yes, I am. Do you know much about the store at the park ahead? I am looking for a burger."

"I do not think they have burgers there, but I may be wrong. They close soon. If you are going to get there before they close you should hurry."

I had been wondering if I was going to make it in time. After getting some water I was on my way at flank speed.

After about twenty minutes of walking, I came to the well-marked halfway point on the trail. It meant little to me because I had crossed the halfway point in New Jersey two weeks before.

The best part of the park that day was the store. It is the store that sells the half-gallon containers of ice cream to hikers as part of the celebration. The half-gallon challenge is an event recorded by the store keep. The record for the fastest downing of the ice cream is each hiker's goal. As of this date, the record is a matter of seconds, not minutes, but I was not the least interested in participating in that tradition. I was delighted to find out the store did have a short order menu that included hamburgers and fries. I had a quick supper and headed for the hostel.

The Iron Master's Hostel is the old mansion of the Iron Master that operated the furnace. It had been converted into a hostel to serve the hiking community. I got settled in for the night after a twenty three mile day. I looked forward to meeting my wife the next day.

⇒•⇐

I awoke early in the morning intending to make it to Highway 11. After a light breakfast, I quietly snuck out and called my wife to confirm our plans. She was just getting ready to leave the house in Michigan. It would be a long drive for her and a long walk for me. Once I was sure the plan was coming together, I struck out for Harrisburg with a particular bounce in my step. I knew from my trail guide that there was a restaurant a half-mile off the trail and decided I would need a good breakfast to cover twenty eight trail miles. It would take almost two hours to get there.

At the restaurant I placed my order with the waitress. "I will have the bacon and eggs, over medium, with hash browns and make the toast whole wheat. I will also have three blueberry pancakes with blueberry topping. I will have one of those cinnamon rolls I noticed when I came in. Could you bring the roll with coffee?"

The waitress's doubtful look was noticeable. Months of hiking had me almost skinny. "Honey, are you sure you want me to bring all that food at once? That is a lot of food. Our pancakes are very large."

"I am sure I will be able to handle it."

As she handed the order through to the cook, she said something and he managed to sneak a look at me and laughed. When the last of the food was eaten, she came over and said, "I did not think you could eat all that."

"You must not get many hikers in here. I am hiking the Appalachian Trail and I never seem to have enough food."

"Honey, you send me as many as you can."

"I will be sure to. It was a great breakfast."

I made it a point to recount my most excellent breakfast in the register at the next shelter. From there I am sure news spread up and down the trail.

I had gone about four miles past the restaurant when a hiker informed me there was trail magic just ahead. I was still quite full from breakfast and was not interested, but the hiker said it was Rematch's girlfriend. I had met Rematch just after Harpers Ferry at the campground and liked him. I thought I would at least say hi. So I walked the quarter-mile up to the car and took a small part in the festivities. Rematch's girlfriend was named Kate and she was a very nice girl. She was visiting him on the trail for a couple of days. I did not eat much because I was quite full, but I did have some orange juice and a small snack to take. I did not stay long. Once back on the trail, I knew I had to keep moving.

I went up over a mountain with a lot of Maine-like rock formations and down the backside of the mountain. Once off the mountain and out in the clearing, I came to a series of farm fields, which was unusual for the AT. I thought I had missed a turn and ended up in Iowa. I walked for a couple of miles and found myself in Boiling Springs. I took advantage of a pizza place that was next to the trail and called my wife.

The rest of the trail that day was more flat walking, similar to the fields, but with some cover. I had eight miles to go when I left the restaurant. I pushed hard and crossed Interstate 76 on a road bridge. At that point I had only about a mile left and knew I was going to make it. I walked the last mile in the half-light and came out to the footbridge over the highway with dark setting in. It was about a quarter of a mile from the trail to the hotel we were staying at.

After a night at the hotel our mission for the day was to go to Front Royal, Virginia, and be in a position to get on the trail at the point I had gotten off in early May.

I had two problems that were plaguing me. One was my small toe. It bothered me a little more every day. I was going to have to find a podiatrist to fix the problem or learn to walk on my hands. But the more immediate problem was the swelling on my knee. It was now about four inches in diameter and hot. There was some pain, but mostly it was discomfort from the skin being pulled tight. The swelling was noticeable. I was confident it was not a recluse spider bite, but I was concerned about the possibility that it might be Lyme's Disease. One of the symptoms of Lyme's Disease is a rash. But that did not make sense because I had developed it at home or on the train to Harpers Ferry. My wife was not near as stoic as I was about it. She was quite concerned about it.

Once I was in front of a nurse, she looked at it and pronounced the diagnosis immediately. It was Cellulitis infection. She qualified the diagnosis with a warning that the doctor would have to verify it, but that she was sure that was what it was. The doctor informed me that it was as the nurse had guessed and prescribed an antibiotic. He assured me that if it did happen to be Lyme's Disease the antibiotic would also treat it. I had a bout of Cellulitis Infection a year before on my left ankle and it was so severe that it had damaged the nerves in my ankle and it bothered me for months.

❧❦

The next day Marilyn drove me to Thornton's Gap. We entered Shenandoah Park on the North end and drove Skyline Drive to get there. We had not been in the park ten minutes when we saw a bear crossing the road. The only other bear I encountered on the trail was the night visitor in Georgia.

The drive was enjoyable and Marilyn was impressed with the park. She let me off at Thornton's Gap and returned to Front Royal. When hikers do a day hike they take a small backpack filled with lunch, water, and little else. Some hikers disapprove of this practice, which they refer to as "slack packing." Call it what you may, it was nice now and then to get some of the weight off.

The easy terrain of the park and the light pack were blessings to me. I sailed through most of the day. In the early afternoon, I came to a deer on the trail. It would not move, but just stared at me. I thought I was going to have to push her out of the way to get by, but she finally moved enough to let me by. There were a lot of park visitors on the trail that day. I saw dozens of tourists who were walking for a mile or two from their car. It was a nice change. I stopped and talked to many of them. We were late enough in the year that there were very few thru-hikers on the trail, but I would still see a few of them over the next few days. I was able to hike with Marilyn that day. She had parked at the road and walked in to meet me. I enjoyed that.

That day I came to the conclusion I was going to have to slow way down or do something with my foot. The burning in my knee from the Cellulitis was subsiding already, and I was now taking greater notice of my little toe. That day I hiked another twenty-eight-mile day and by the end of the day the pain was overwhelming.

Each day when I started out there would be very little trouble with the toe, but as the day wore on it got worse. But some days it would not bother me at all. I resolved that I would hold off any decision on what to do until I got to Harpers Ferry. It was only June 18th, which gave me plenty of time to finish the trail if I decided to go up north and pick up the trail. But I had to do something about my foot. I had made calls to local podiatrists, but it was impossible to get an appointment.

After breakfast we headed out for a four-day hike to Harpers Ferry. Marilyn was given the trail name Monga by me. Our eighteen-month-old grandson made a valiant attempt to talk, but the best he could do was call grandma Monga. She was proud of the name and was glad when people asked her how she got her name. It gave her an excuse to talk about her grandson and pull out some pictures.

Monga's backpack was like mine—lightweight. I bought her a lighter version of my backpack that only weighed seven ounces empty. I carried the stove, cook set, two-person tent, cell phone, first aid kit, cooking fuel, and trail guide. She needed only to carry her sleeping bag, rain gear, water, and, of course, some of the chemicals that women need. She carried some food, but for the most part I carried the bulk of the food. My intention was to make the hike over the next three days as painless as possible for her.

The forecast for the next three days was to be in the nineties. Our intention was to hike early and late and take long breaks in the heat of the day.

Monga started out ahead of me while I went back to the drug store for some last-minute items. When she crossed the road and disappeared into the woods, I could not believe she was doing this. My concern at the time was how she would hold up for the next four days. I was impressed at how well she did that first day. It took me two hours to catch up to her.

Once I caught up with her, we stopped in at a shelter and met two thru-hikers. They were Mercury and Minnesota Smith. I would see Mercury one other time on the trail in New Hampshire. Monga was very interested in their story. I thought how well she would have enjoyed the social aspect of the trail.

Most of the day was typical trail drudgery. The trail that day was quite boring. Sometimes the trail can be like that. We did see a black snake and watched if for a few minutes. It was strange how aggressive it was toward us. We had trouble getting by it on the narrow trail, but finally I had to get rough with it. The last hour of the day was rainy and we got quite wet. Monga began to develop blisters on her feet. We had planned to walk until we felt like stopping and then pitch the tent and stealth camp, but the rain and the blisters forced us to stop earlier at the next shelter. It would only be an eleven-mile day. I know Monga could have walked more otherwise, and I was pleased with her effort.

We checked into the Manassas Gap Shelter late in the day and found Minnesota Smith already there. Monga would get her first taste of shelter life. Since I had hiked hundreds of miles ahead of Minnesota, he wanted to know about good places to eat at and good ones to stay away from. We talked food for a while and he took notes in his journal. I treated Monga's blisters and decided we would watch them.

At home I am lazy when it comes to food. I have been spoiled by a good cook who enjoys cooking. When it comes to cooking, I limit myself to such things as oatmeal and other dishes that are easy to prepare. Occasionally when forced to I can make a mean pot of chili. I openly admit I am shamelessly spoiled. So I could imagine how Monga felt when I did all the cooking and cleaning that night on the trail. I fixed her some Ramen noodles, hot chocolate, and we snacked on nuts and bars. To this day when she talks about her experience on the trail, she emphasizes that she did not have to do any cooking or cleaning.

There was reported to be a rattlesnake around the shelter. The trail is interesting when it comes to reports. They fly up and down the trail with amazing efficiency. The news is talked about when hikers meet on the trail and stop to talk. It is reported in the hostels and the shelter registers. Usually the news is quite accurate given the primitive way it spreads. The truth is there are rattlesnakes all along the trail; they just stay out of our way. Nonetheless I was a little slower and more cautious when I went down to the spring to get water. It was my hope that if there was a snake it had been keeping the mouse population down. That was not the case. One ran over Monga's bag in the middle of the night and woke her up. I thought that to be strange because a train wreck cannot wake her. She got very little sleep after that.

⇒•⇐

Monga had not slept well and had lost much of her zeal for hiking. We took our time getting away to let the trail dry out from the heavy rain the night before. There was some discussion about getting Monga off the trail by retracing our steps from the previous afternoon. I have seen what blisters can get like if not taken care of or ignored. I did not want Monga's hiking experience to traumatize her against future hiking. I was surprised she had problems with blisters because she had done a lot of walking in the boots she was wearing to toughen up her feet. It was most likely because her feet had gotten wet in the rain the day before and that makes your feet vulnerable to blisters.

When we finally were on the trail, we decided to stop and check them periodically. If they were to get worse we would get off at the next road.

That day something happened that really impressed Monga. The trail emptied onto an old overgrown forest road later in the day. Sometimes when the trail gets on one of those, I miss the trail when it leaves the road and returns to a narrow trail. It happened that day. We had been talking and walked right by the turn in the trail. We had only went about three hundred yards when we came to a gravel road that I was not expecting. I drew out my trail guide to clear the confusion. At the intersection of the road was a man in an SUV talking on the phone.

I was consulting the trail guide and checking the surroundings when the driver got off the phone and asked me, "Do you need some help?"

"Do you know what the name of this road is?"

"No, I do not. Are you lost?"

"Well, not really, but I think I got off the trail recently. I am hiking the Appalachian Trail. I am Silver and this is Monga. I am guessing we will just need to backtrack a few hundred yards."

"How long have you been on the trail?"

"I have been on the trail since March 1st. Monga has been on it a couple of days."

"Are you going all the way?"

"I hope to."

"So you camp and cook on the trail?"

"Yes. I carry an alcohol stove and a tent and there are shelters on the trail."

"I have heard of you guys. My wife would love to talk to both of you. We are having a family reunion this evening and we would very much love to have you. If you call me at six tonight, I will come and get you wherever you are."

Monga chimed in, "Thank you, that is so sweet. How many people are going to be there?

"Maybe forty." He assured us, "We have BBQ and some great food and would love to have you."

He wanted to know much more about my experiences and we talked for a few minutes. As we closed out the conversation, he said while offering me a piece of paper, "Here is my number. Do you have a cell phone with you?"

I responded, "Yes, I do."

"At five you call me and let me know where you are, and I or someone else will come and get you and take you to our house. We would love to have you."

We backtracked the short distance to get on the trail and walked with a renewed vigor because of the amazing experience we had just been through. Monga still talks about that experience. I could tell he was not just being nice, but that he really wanted us to come. Were it not early in the day, we may well have went, but it was only about ten in the morning and we had a lot a miles we wanted to do that day. And the day would take another turn later.

The rest of the day was not so good. With every mile, Monga's feet became worse. I remembered the infected blisters of Scout and Yahtzee. They were frightful. It was early afternoon when we arrived at Ashby Gap. Monga was not in extreme pain, but my bigger concern was whether she could make it the next thirty-four miles to Harpers Ferry. We discussed our options. Hiking is supposed to be an enjoyable pastime, and I was sure she was headed for some major discomfort. We decided to walk down to a restaurant that was just down the road and give it more thought. I was anticipating that in the comfort of a restaurant it would be easier to decide on heading back to Front Royal. That was what I thought we needed to do, but I wanted Monga to come to the same conclusion. A Rueben sandwich with fries sealed the deal.

Sometime during our time there, I struck up a conversation with a local who was at the counter for an early supper. He was curious about the strange lot known as thru-hikers and had a lot of questions. We talked for a while and in the conversation our dilemma was brought up. We needed a ride back to Front Royal to get our car and he had just the solution. He had to get back to work, but his mother, who lived nearby, was available. I let him use my cell phone to call his mom. She was glad to and asked only that I give her some money for gas. Just like that, we had a ride the twenty miles back to our car.

She arrived and we loaded up. Somewhere between the restaurant and our car, she fell in love with us. Again, it was southern hospitality. She felt bad about asking for money, but I knew she was not well off and I was glad to pay her for the ride. I think she was ready to adopt us by the time we said good-bye and she wanted to give us a good-bye hug. It was the only time on the trail that anyone accepted money for a ride. Most would have nothing to do with taking money.

Back in Front Royal, we checked back into the hotel we had stayed in before. It was actually working out perfectly. Our friends from California were arriving in DC. Marilyn would drop me off back at Ashby Gap. I would hike the fourteen miles to Snicker's Gap at Highway 7 and Marilyn and our friends would pick me up. That would leave the last twenty miles to do into Harpers Ferry. After that, I would take a day off and do something with our friends.

After taking me out to the trail, Marilyn spent the rest of the day with our friends. For my part, I was somewhat glad she was not going to hike that day because the forecast was for temperatures in the midnineties and high humidity. I had also planned an early start to avoid hiking in the heat of the day.

My first challenge on the trail that day was the Roller Coaster, which started a few miles in from the road. It is a term that describes the terrain. When you look at the profile maps it looks somewhat like a roller coaster. It is a series of short but intense ups and downs in immediate succession. It was more hype than reality. However the heat took some of the starch out of me.

With about five miles to go, I came to a spring with cold, running water. I took the time to eat a lunch and rehydrate my body. There was a couple from Philadelphia who had stopped at the shelter for lunch. I visited with them and in the conversation it came up that I had done all of Pennsylvania. They were curious about the famous rocks. I told them that taken together the Pennsylvania experience was not all that bad. The ridges are long and flat with relatively gentle grades and there were some nice towns along the way. I ate lunch while we talked. I did counsel them not to get too confident when in the rocks because that would invite a broken ankle.

Later that day, I met four men from my home state of Michigan who were section hikers. It was always great to see Michigan folks on the trail and we compared notes for a brief time.

I was looking forward to knocking off two states—Virginia and West Virginia. It rained hard in the morning. During my six months on the trail, I was fortunate to not have a hike that was continually plagued by rain. Most of the time when it rained I did not even bother to put on my poncho, which also fit over my backpack. The body generates unbelievable calories backpacking. Only when the rain was exceptionally hard or it was cold did I bother with the poncho. On one occasion I had walked in the rain up a mountain and stopped at a shelter. The heat from my body combined with the water-soaked clothing and generated vapor. The vapor rose from my body like a steam machine. After just a couple of minutes, there was a cloud that had gathered along the ceiling of the shelter. It then condensed and began to form water on the ceiling and the condensation began to drop as rain.

The day before it had been in the midnineties and I struggled with the heat. So the rain was welcome. I knew it was going to rain, but I did not bother to bring rain gear, choosing to travel as light as I could. With no concern for overheating or dehydrating in the morning, I pushed hard and walked fast. At some point early in the day I said my good-bye to the Old Dominion and scratched off Virginia. I celebrated it with a tear-n-share bag of Peanut M & M's and a pint of V-8.

The trail was quite easy that day, and I had little problem other than my right foot. It was one of those days. Some days my toe flared up and I would be extremely distracted, and on others I could forget it was even there and move on. On that particular day, the pain was agonizing. I look back on that day and am thankful I did not carry a knife, because I may have amputated it.

Marilyn and I had an ongoing conversation about the possibility of her taking me to New Jersey and resuming my adventure from Culver's Gap. But that day I made the decision on my own. I was going to go home with my wife and keep my appointment with the podiatrist.

Toward the end of the day, I dropped off the ridge that the trail had been on and down into the Shenandoah River Valley. By that time the sun had come out and it was hot. I came out of the edge of the woods and into the hot sun. The trail crosses the river on a bridge, and I walked for quite some time in the open sun. By the time I reached wooded cover, the sun had me scorched and dehydrated. I was desperately thirsty when I reached the AT headquarters and everyone at the building knew by looking at me that I was in frantic need of water. I occupied the water cooler for a while, slugging down water till I was convinced I was going to live.

The Appalachian Trail Conservancy Headquarters is located in Harpers Ferry. It is staffed by a group of great people whose job, among other things, is to make thru-hikers feel important. And they do a good job of that.

I would soon be on my way home to begin plotting my next move to get to Katahdin before the mountain closed in October.

THE BIG MISTAKE

Hanover to Gorham
Miles traveled: 110
Days hiked: 8

The hike that had started in Northern Georgia was no longer what I had hoped when I left for Georgia. There was a struggle between my commitment to hiking the entire trail in one year and the draw of home and family. By now Feather had been forced to drop off the trail, Scout had to go home for the summer to work, and no one had any idea where Firefly was. I had not heard from Zama and Lug for several weeks. The trail companions were split up and the hike would never to be the same, but I was still going to go back. I was also about to make the biggest mistake of my Appalachian Trail experience.

My visit to the podiatrist finally came. I was excited at the thought of discovering what was going on down there. The doctor took one look at it and declared it a soft corn. I had experienced corns before and was able to treat them myself, but I had never heard of a soft corn. The doctor took a scalpel in hand and in a matter of five minutes scraped away much of the deformed toe and built up skin. I walked out of the doctor's office a new hiker, ready to take on the worst the trail could offer, not knowing he had not fixed the real problem.

When I pointed my hybrid car home in late June, Marilyn knew that it was quite likely I was not done and that I would return to the trail. I had not even unpacked my food bag and I was considering my next move. There was something about finishing the trail as a thru-hike that had a lock on me. I had set out to hike the entire trail in one year and that is what I intended to do. I had talked to many section hikers and I felt bad for them. They get out on the trail for one or two weeks, maybe more, and then they would have to go home only to return the next year. One of the great feelings I had on the trail was the feeling of my body operating on all eight cylinders. The section hiker never develops the level of physical conditioning that comes with a thru-hike. I had lost a lot of the conditioning sitting at home for just two weeks, but the section hiker typically only goes out once a year for a couple of weeks.

When I started the trail I had one date in mind. August 22nd was the NASCAR race in Michigan. My oldest son Garrett and I looked forward all year to sharing the event, but it was not the race that was important. I had been in the area when other Cup Series races were in the area. Bristol, Martinsville, Pocono, and others were close when I was on the trail. What was important was that it was something my son and I shared every year, and I was not going to miss it.

When I left for Georgia on March 1st, I had hoped to finish by August 1st. That was no longer possible. That was decided when I headed home for Memorial Day. So I needed to come up with a plan that would still get me across the finish line that year. By the time I had my toe treated, it was late-July. I had some business to take care of at the office before I left, which kept me in Michigan. I studied my trail guide and the maps to come up with an estimate of where to start and where I would end up. One of the main criteria had to do with the White Mountains. I knew enough about the Whites to know it was going to be a rough stretch. I also knew that I did not want to be hiking there in the fall. It only made sense to start at the Whites in the middle of summer and do the northern part of the trail while it was hot.

❧⋅❧

So with August right around the corner, I left home again. A plane ride and two bus rides later I was in a hostel in Woodstock, New Hampshire. After breakfast, I hitched a ride out to Kinsman's Notch. It was there that Marilyn and I hiked with our daughter and son-in-law. We hiked south about thirty-five miles over Mount Moosilauke and beyond. It brought back memories. That little torturous stretch of trail is what got me hooked on backpacking. I walked into the woods on the trail until I found the warning sign and took a picture of it again. The warning sign tells you this mountain is not for beginners, which we were at the time. We can laugh about that now.

It was late in the morning when I crossed the highway from the parking lot and headed up the ridge. It was raining quite hard by then, which would normally not bother me, but the terrain that day was not the kind you wanted to hike in the rain. In New Hampshire and Maine there is a lot of granite slabs. And there are a lot of steep grades. The two combine for some nightmarish experiences even when it is not raining. The rock formations are smooth and the hikers have long since worn the soil away. What you are left with is a slick, steep surface that has been slowly wearing away. The erosion from the weather and hikers leaves a crumbly surface. Getting good footing is a challenge in places. When it is raining, it is even worse. On more than one occasion I looked at the situation and said out loud to myself, "You have got to be kidding!"

That day I was working my way downhill on one of the slabs of greasy, crumbly rock formations and my feet went out from under me. It is unbelievable how quick a six-foot man can get to the ground. I landed on my butt and both forearms and it hurt. I also slid several feet. The sandy surface tore away a fair amount of the skin on my arms. It took me a minute to gather myself and make sure nothing was broken. The scrapes in my skin would bleed hard, but I was able to get the bleeding stopped shortly so that my hiking clothes were not bloody. That kind of fall would happen twice before the day was over.

Except for the falls, most of the day was quite enjoyable. It was certainly hard work. There were a lot of places where you were doing more climbing that hiking. That day I hiked just under fourteen miles. I was quite excited about being on the trail and attacking some of the most treacherous stretches on the trail while I was fresh and rested. It was early, but my goal of getting to Katahdin seemed reasonable and that was exciting. If I could get to Katahdin before going home to watch the race, I would just have to finish from Northern New Jersey through Vermont and I would be done. The thought of hiking Vermont in the leaf season appealed to me. It was a good plan, and I was determined to make it happen.

After fourteen miles of brutal hiking, I was ready for my first hut. There are no lean-to shelters in the White Mountains. The Appalachian Mountain Club is a private organization that operates a series of huts for hikers. The huts are always full and reservations are needed well in advance. The buildings have heat, kitchens, restrooms, and most of the conveniences except showers. It is expensive and most thru-hikers just do not have that kind of money. Furthermore, thru-hikers do not hike with a tightly planned itinerary and thus scheduling stays in huts is impractical. Since there are no other shelters and stealth camping is both illegal and impractical, thru-hikers have little choice but to stay at the huts.

Most huts operate on the work-for-stay arrangements for thru-hikers. Hikers report to the hut and request a work-for-stay opportunity. It is at the discretion of the manager. They can simply say no. The manager assigns you some small task, such as sweeping, dishes, or other tasks. In exchange for that, you get a supper and breakfast of whatever is left over after the paying guests are finished eating. For the most part it is a great deal for the hikers, but it is a little humiliating sitting around waiting for fifty people to get done eating so you can eat leftovers. But it is hot food and it is good food. I enjoyed my stays at the huts.

Another drawback to the huts is the sleeping arrangements. Thru-hikers staying for free must sleep in the dining hall on the floor. The paying guests sleep in soft beds in a bunkhouse area. Many of the evening activities take place in the dining hall and can last up till 9:00 or 10:00 p.m. That is well past a thru-hikers bedtime. Once everyone else is in bed, you can pitch your sleeping bag on the floor or tables and go to sleep. Then around five in the morning the breakfast crew shows up, turns on the lights, and starts banging around. I did not sleep well in the White Mountains and that may have been part of my downfall.

I was fascinated by the way the huts were managed. Each hut has solar collectors and a small wind generator with battery storage capacity. They also have a backup generator for when the renewable energy is not enough. They use propane for cooking and lights. They are not hooked to the electrical grid. Each year, propane, canned goods, and other dry storage food are hauled up by helicopter. Throughout the year the drones, mostly college students working for the summer, act as Sherpa. They use pack frames to haul loads of fresh food up to the huts, which are remote from any road. Menus are coordinated among all the camps so their clients do not end up eating the same foods. There is a radio for communication among huts and a home base to deal with problems.

The club offers to their customers a soft bed, food, and water, as well as some education and entertainment. It is big business. The paying guests do not have to pack stoves, food, tents, and other supplies. It is a great deal for them. The hut system gets hikers into the White Mountains who might not otherwise go. I saw lots of families in the huts and can see their value.

There is a full range of feelings among thru-hikers. For the most part I understood their role, but I wished the thru-hiker had more options. I loved the food. I took one full day's meal, a couple more lunches, and some snacks into the Whites for the seven days I hiked. Still, I carried food out.

My first hut was the Lonesome Lake Hut. I arrived soaked from a downpour and muddy from another fall. My arms were both skinned up badly and I had a lot of blood on me. I was greeted at the door by the manager. Her name was Erica and she treated me very well. Supper had already begun, and she urged me to get cleaned up and get dried off so I could eat. Within minutes, I returned with dry clothes on. The fare that night was ham, salad, peas, rice, and pineapple cake. There was plenty to eat and she encouraged me to eat till I was full. I complied with little protest. I met a south bounder named Stretch and we compared notes on what was ahead.

That night my knees were bothering me a little so I took some Ibuprofen. The biggest drawback of the huts surfaced on the first night. There were a couple of teenage girls and several horny teenage boys to chase them. Lights out was at ten and so I was bedded down on the dining room floor by 10:30 p.m. The teenagers spent the next hour and a half doing what teenagers do best—annoy adults. The noise was often enough and loud enough that it distracted me. It would be sometime after midnight before I would finally fall asleep.

About 5:00 a.m., the gaslights were lit and the pots and pans were banging. Once awaken to that degree, I do not usually go to sleep.

After breakfast I earned my keep by doing the dishes. Stretch and I had one last word before he left. Most of the visitors at the hut had avoided us like we were HIV positive, but Erica and her crew were very friendly. They sent me off with a ham sandwich, which I thought was a nice touch. To this day I think very kindly of Erica.

By 9:00 a.m. I was off to Franconia Ridge. I had needed to call my wife that day to deal with some personal business. All morning as I worked my way down to Franconia Notch I checked my cell phone, but there was no reception. At the highway I was forced to walk over a mile to a visitor's center called The Flume. There I used the pay phone to make my call. After that it was back to the trail. I was quite frustrated that I had to add two extra miles to my day. It would only get worse.

Once back at the trail, I headed up to the ridge. My goal was the Galewood Hut, which seemed possible. Down at the highway the woods were old growth forest. The surroundings changed to subalpine scrub and finally alpine as I climbed higher.

By the time I had cleared the vegetation, I was in the clouds walking on tundra. Visibility was less than one hundred feet and it had now turned cold. I had not walked far on the ridge and it started to rain. With each step, the wind picked up velocity and the rain came down harder. Before I reached the peak of Mount Lincoln, the wind had picked up to the point that walking was difficult. The wind was blowing from left to right and I saw something I would never have believed. The wind gusts pushing up the side of the mountain were blowing upward so hard that the driving rain was going up. I had to use my hiking poles extended out to my right just to stay upright.

Just on the other side of the peak was the turn off to Greenleaf Hut. I lingered at the junction for a minute, struggling with the decision to push on or drop the mile down to the closer hut. I studied my trail guide and considered my options. To get to Galewood Hut, I would have to cross another exposed ridge at Garfield Mountain and I was beginning to shiver from the cold and extreme wind. What made it so difficult to decide was Greenleaf Hut was over a mile off the trail and it was a steep decent. Galewood, on the other hand, was right on the trail. I had read enough about the White Mountains weather that I knew the safe play was to head down to Greenleaf and get off the ridge. So with a dejected resignation, I headed down the trail to the hut and comfort.

My day ended up with little more than nine miles logged. But counting the round trip to The Flume and the trip off the ridge to the hut, it was well over twelve miles. I spent the next couple of days second-guessing my decision not to press on. It turned out that Garfield Peak would have had plenty of cover to keep the wind off me.

At the hut I met Black Fly—a southbound thru hiker. They are referred to as SOBO's. She was given that trail name because she had a lot of black fly bites in Maine when she started. I have always thought one method of enhanced interrogation could be black flies.

That night after lights out, two campers at the hut decided they were not finished playing cards. They played for over an hour with their headlamps on, talking loudly as they played. It would be another night that it took me till after midnight to get to sleep. Like clockwork, the cooks were up by 5:00 a.m. So I got up and had some coffee and worked on my journal.

I had planned an early exit, but the next morning my clothes were still wet and the clouds and wind created a depressing atmosphere. Therefore I decided to stay for breakfast. Once breakfast was over, I would change out of my dry clothes and into my wet ones. I headed out and onto the trail, wet clothes and all. It was a bitter pill to swallow having to hike the mile up the mountain to get to the trail.

I was hiking in the clouds all morning, but the rain and the wind had dissipated. The trail went down from Lafayette Mountain and then back up Garfield Mountain. By the time I had peaked Garfield, the weather had cleared and I could see back to Lafayette. It was beautiful. I tried to take a nap on a rock but was interrupted by a father and son who had arrived. They were peak baggers. They were working on every peak in New Hampshire over four thousand feet. The boy seemed to be genuinely proud of what he was accomplishing.

I worked my way the thousand feet down Garfield and across a bog to the Galewood Hut, which was my goal the night before.

I stopped in for some lemonade. For a dollar thru-hikers can have all the lemonade they can drink. The drink has sugar and hikers are always looking for calories to burn. There were a lot of paying guests there already and most had settled in for the night. I had miles to go so I snuck out and headed up Twin Peaks.

I had hiked for over thirteen hundred miles without a blister and now I had developed blisters on both my feet. They were caused from all the rain I had hiked through. Wet shoes soften the skin and soon it rubs a blister. I had treated several hikers' blisters over the last few months and had used up my supply of blister treatment. While I had my feet out of my shoes examining them, a couple from Ottawa, Ontario, happened by and saw my dilemma. They offered some moleskin and second skin and I accepted. I spent a few minutes treating my feet and then pushed on. My goal had been campsites past Zeeland Falls Hut, but the lateness of the day and my generally exhausted condition forced me to reconsider. I checked in at Zeeland Falls Hut and they were glad to see me. There were no thru-hikers and some of the guests were very interested in these strange people they knew little about. Some of the guests approached me with questions. I had done almost thirteen miles that day, plus the mile getting back to the trail from the previous hut. I was unbelievably tired that night.

That night I slept in the dining hall on the floor and all the guests staying there had to walk past me to get to the restroom. Several times in the night I was disturbed by old men with even older bladders. But what kept me up most were my knees. They were burning. The trail in New Hampshire is mostly rock and there is a lot of hopping and jumping down. The constant, unforgiving pounding on my knees was developing into tendonitis. It is a malady I am quite prone to. I had hiked twenty-plus miles a day for quite some time early in the trail, but most of the trail to the south was dirt. Most of the hiking in the Whites was over rock.

In the middle of the night I maxed out on Ibuprofen and hoped my knees would settle down. There was a burning sensation and they were starting to pop and crack a lot. I decided that the next day would be a light day and I might have to take a day off at Gorham.

⇛·⇚

The trail north of the hut was an old railroad bed and I was excited to get some level and hopefully softer trail that would calm my troubled knees. The railroad bed had not been a railroad for quite some time. The mountain was in the process of reclaiming the valley. There were deep washouts in places. There were also huge piles of boulders, some as big as refrigerators. There was a mountain wall to my left going straight up. The boulders were shed from the steep cliffs above the trail over the years, forming a series of obstacle courses. Man had come through to clear out and level a base for the train tracks. When they were done with the tracks, they removed them. The mountain was in the process of returning the valley to its wilderness nature, and was doing a fine job of it.

Later in the day, I came to Crawford's Notch. It was the anniversary of our first date and I needed to call my wife and wish her happy anniversary. The restaurant was set deep in a valley with a steep wall almost straight up. I looked with amazement at the cliffs far above, not knowing that I was going to be up there soon. With lunch and the phone call out of the way, I returned the one mile back to the trail and resumed my long day.

The trail started off gently with some switchbacks, but it did not take long for the trail to get steep. I was working my way up to Webster's Cliffs. At one point I stopped and said out loud "You have got to be kidding!" I paused at the top and looked over the valley I had just come from. The restaurant was twenty eight hundred feet below. At the cliffs I encountered a lot of families and young people. They were the tenants at Mizpah Hut, my destination.

I checked in at Mizpah Hut in the middle of the afternoon. The manager asked, "I am only a substitute manager and I do not have a program for the guests. If you would be interested, you could do your work for stay by presenting a program about your thru hike to the guests."

"I would be glad to. I just met Jump Start outside and he is a thru hiker looking for a work-for-stay. Would you like me to include him in the program also?"

"Sure. And you guys can eat with the regular guests as well. There will be plenty of food. And you can have all the lemonade you want, no charge."

"What time is the program?"

"Seven o'clock. Until then you can get settled in and we are glad you are here."

The substitute manager considered us celebrities and we were allowed to eat with the guests. At supper it was announced that the program would be put on by Silver Streak and Jump Start, and they were going to talk about their experiences on the Appalachian Trail. Jump Start and I expected that a few of the guests would be somewhat interested.

Later that evening, the word was sent out to those who were outside that the program was about to begin. To my amazement even the teenagers suspended their mating rituals to come in. Jump Start and I were in for an interesting night. Everyone, including all the help, stopped what they were doing to listen in. There must have been sixty in the audience. We were the center of attention.

I have done a lot of public speaking in my years, and so I was very comfortable taking the lead and Jump Start was glad to let me.

Once I had given them a thumbnail sketch of our experience, I opened it up for questions. The questions seemed endless. Almost everyone had at least one question. There was every question imaginable. I answered most of the questions and referred some to Jump Start to see if he had anything to add to the answer. The program went on for almost two hours before finally the manager had to step in and close out the program. After the program, others came up and talked further. Later I received visits from some of the guests thanking me for the program. Truly it was a memorable experience and one that I treasured.

The Mizpah Hut had much better sleeping arrangements than any of the other huts. There were bunks in an upstairs storage room where they stored the canned good and other items. That meant Jump Start and I were isolated from the noise of the kitchen and the intrusion of the guests. While talking to Jump Start I found out that Firefly was only about two days behind me. I was elated and began anticipating seeing him. I decided I would wait for him in Gorham.

❧·❦

I enjoyed my first good sleep since being in the Whites. I headed out for my goal, Madison Hut, as soon as breakfast was over. The previous day I had covered sixteen and a half miles, including the two-mile round trip to the restaurant. At the time it did not seem like much, but I was sorry by morning. My knees needed a break badly, or at least to slow down. I decided I would continue my pace through the Whites until I got to Gorham and then take a day off. With that in mind, I completely dismissed the idea of stopping short of the Madison Hut. After all, it was less than twelve miles and I could do that on my hands. It turns out I should have.

The morning hike led me to the Lake of the Clouds Hut. I stopped there for some lemonade and a chat with the staff. After leaving the hut, I crossed paths with more of the help at the hut on the trail. They had their pack frames loaded with about fifty pounds each of fresh food and other items destined for the hut. The next stop was at the top of Mount Washington. There was a visitor's center at its peak.

The visitor's center was a hub of activity that day. The center could be reached by car and there were lots of tourists there. They served food there so I ended up having a couple of hot dogs.

Jump Start was there and we ate together and watched the humans with the same curiosity that a fourth grader would watch animals at the zoo. That was my fifth day on the trail and I was in need of a shower so I steered clear of the visitors as much as I could.

When I arrived at the visitor's center, the top of the mountain was enshrouded in clouds. By the time I left, it was clear and you could see for miles. The view was incredible. The only thing spoiling the setting was the annoying train that chugs its way up the mountain. It is an old steam engine and it pulls a load of tourists, spewing pollution as it goes and blowing an annoying whistle. There is an age-old tradition on the trail concerning the train. Hikers are expected to moon the train as it goes by. Most traditions on the trail have some sort of skewed reason and I could certainly understand that one. However, seeing an old man's butt would be quite traumatic for young kids, so I refrained.

❧·❦

The hike down from the top of Mount Washington is burned into my memory. That entire stretch was one big boulder field. And the boulders were large ones. You do not step from one bolder to another; you must hop. They are large enough that you cannot get any stride. So for several miles down the mountain, I hopped from one rock to another. My knees were already bothering me and the experience that afternoon was the worse on the trail. The physical struggle was not the only problem. It was unnerving because one missed step and you would end up with a broken leg.

Midway through the stretch, I met up with four women who were out on a two-day excursion. They were in a mood to flirt so I let them have their fun and played along with them. It lightened up my day. They were headed to the Madison Hut also.

I arrived just before dinnertime and found that a work-for-stay was available.

That night my chore was to head up a group for the program doing pretty much what I did the night before. But there was not as much interest with this group, and there were other program options. Still, there was a small group of about eight, including one of the flirting ladies. We talked in the small group about the AT experience. For those who only hike the Whites from hut to hut, it would be hard to envision what the real experience was for the thru-hiker.

It would be my last night in the huts. That night I met Power Stroke at the hut. Power Stroke started his hike at Key West, Florida. From there he hiked to Springer Mountain to start the trail. Once he had arrived at Katahdin, he would then continue on through the rest of Maine and end up in Canada on the seven trails that are referred to as the Eastern Continental Trail. That is a lot of hiking—over four thousand miles. I would guess Power Stroke to be in his fifties, so age has nothing to do with it. Hiking is for all ages.

That night I took the maximum Ibuprofen and went to bed, but I could not sleep. Crossing the boulder field was much too traumatic on my knees and tendonitis was setting in. I was carrying an over-the-counter sleep aid and used it as well. It was less than twelve miles, but it was the worse stretch on the trail.

I had two more full days into Gorham and then I would have to take a day off. In the morning I had some more fun with the four ladies I had met on the trail the night before. They flirted some more and before I left they all wanted a picture with me. They said I looked like Paul Newman and they wanted a memory of the night they spent with Paul Newman. I obliged them and we had some fun with it. I said good-bye to the ladies and to the huts. In total, I looked upon the huts as a good experience. But I also wonder if the lack of sleep in the Whites contributed to the deterioration of my knees.

❖•❖

The hike down was particularly difficult because downhill is torment on the knees. For some reason that morning the pain was not as bad as I had anticipated, considering the pain I was in the day before I kept reminding myself that this was supposed to be fun. From there I pushed on up Wildcat Mountain, which lived up to its name.

That night I got to a point when my knees would not allow me to go any farther. I found an area just flat enough, soft enough, and large enough to pitch my tent and crashed. It was a long night, because I was not sure if I was going to be able to hike past Gorham and that bothered me.

❖•❖

I had not slept much the night before but now the trail was considerably more gentle. But the damage had been done. I came out of the woods to the highway and was relieved to be done with that stretch of trail. I had gone ninety-one miles in the White Mountains in seven days. That was thirteen miles average per day. Added to that was six more miles off the trail. The biggest mistake of my hike to that point was hurrying through the Whites. I had been hiking twenty-mile days up through Pennsylvania without any sign of tendonitis, and now it had flared up so bad that I could hardly walk. My knees were making noise when I walked and the burning was there even when I rested.

Instead of a hostel I checked into a nice inn with an ice machine. Once checked into the hotel, I ordered a pizza— delivered so I did not have to leave the inn. I packed my knees in ice as much as I could stand, and pushed the Ibuprofen to the max. I had everything to treat my vexed knees but time. And that is what is most needed with tendonitis. Complete rest is the best medicine.

My only theory was that the hard surfaces of the Granite State had been the culprit. I had hiked considerably longer and harder days early on the trail. My two theories were that the last week I had done a lot of hopping and other pounding motions on my knees. The other thought was the lack of sleep I had experienced in the huts. My body was not able to sufficiently heal itself every night. The information that I had on the next few days to the north in the Mahoosucs was that I would have a similar experience. I went to sleep that night at the inn not knowing what I was going to do and that bothered me.

The next day was a day off for me. I went into town and bought Ben-Gay for my knees. Later that day I checked out of the inn and into the Hiker's Paradise Hostel. By the time I had checked out, I had come to a brilliant conclusion. I would make my way back south to the Dartmouth ski lift access near Hanover. I would then hike south past Hanover and into Vermont. The trail in Vermont would be much gentler according to all I could gather from talking to hikers. I would continue south until it was time to return to Michigan to go to the races with Garrett. With a little luck, I could make it all the way to New Jersey. After the race, I would return rested and ready to resume the hike, finishing off New Hampshire and Maine. With the day off and the day of travel, the next day my knees could recover enough to hopefully get back on the trail at a slower pace for a couple of days. I liked the plan.

The next morning I was intending to take a couple of buses to get to Hanover to execute my plan. I passed on the complimentary breakfast at the hostel and went to a local restaurant that had an AYCE breakfast bar. I sat in a booth that was next to a middle-age couple. Fred and Marsha were their names. They introduced themselves and had a lot of questions for me. It was obvious I was a thru-hiker and they wanted to know a lot more. They invited me to join them and I was very glad to sit in the booth with them. I put on my best manners and moved my plate. The usual questions were such things as what we ate, where we slept, what did we carry in our packs, etc. I think they thought if they asked enough of those questions they could figure out the answer to the most important question that people seldom are bold enough to ask: "Why are you doing this?" This couple was genuinely friendly and was most interested in how my wife and I handled the separation. That one was not so easy to answer.

As we talked I recounted to them my recent history with my knees and the decision I had made to get south of the Whites and hike toward New Jersey. Fred and Marsha just happened to be from Vermont and were heading home that day from visiting Mount Washington. They knew of the place on the trail where I needed to get to and offered to take me there. It was not far out of their way. I believe in divine providence and that was nothing short of God's hand. My stay at hiker's paradise included breakfast, but I had opted to pay for this breakfast because I had heard from hikers I had talked to that it was excellent. Of all the places I could have sat, I took the booth next to them. To this day that experience amazes me.

They took me back to the hostel and I picked up my gear and was off. The drive to my drop-off point was full of conversation about hiking, and Fred was a hunter. They had both run marathons and so I told them about my daughter and daughter-in-law. The trip went fast with all the talk of common interests. By the time we got there, I felt I had known them all my life. When we departed, I asked them to visit my journal and leave a message for me on my website so I would have information on how to contact them and let them know how my hike went. I assured them they would love to meet Marilyn and we would have to visit them when we were in New England. They never did contact me, and I do not know to this day how to contact them. I sometimes wonder if they were real angels who had been sent to help me. In retrospect the experience almost seems unreal.

If Fred and Marsha were angels, I should have had them perform divine healing, because by the afternoon my knees were on fire and were popping and crackling like a bowl of Rice Krispies. The trail was not all that bad but my knees were as bad if not worse than they were two days before. It made me miss the pain in my toe.

With a couple of hours left in the day, I pitched my tent for the night and called it quits a few miles short of Hanover. It would be a rough night. I took the maximum dose of Ibuprofen and a sleep aid but still I had trouble sleeping with my knees bothering me and the inevitable decision that needed to be made about my knees. I needed several days or even a couple of weeks to get my knees back in hiking shape. And to push on would only compound the trouble.

❖❖❖

After a distressful night, I walked the last five miles into Hanover suffering with each step. I found the bus station and took a bus to Boston. Within hours I was in a rental car heading home.

THE WILDERNESS

Mount Katahdin to Caratunk
Miles: 152
Days hiked: 8

We all have strengths and weaknesses. My strength is my tireless ability to pursue an endeavor. I hiked over twenty miles numerous days. In Virginia, I hiked 139 miles in seven days. My muscles and my psyche can hold up to those kinds of days. My weakness is my tendons. I have been prone to tendonitis for years and have to be careful about it.

I would spend twenty-seven days at home nursing my knees and spending time with my family. There was little at the office for me to do. I was able to play with my grandchildren during my rest.

When I left Hanover dejected, I knew there was a small chance I would get back on the trail and try to finish it. I monitored the progress on my knees and after about ten days I decided they were going to be in good enough shape to finish the trail. My toe was not bothering me yet. The toe problem would surface again later and would be a problem until the real cause was diagnosed and addressed.

I now was facing a deadline of sorts—the weather. I figured that I had almost two months to finish the trail, and that was adequate time. By then I had just less than 1400 miles completed and 775 miles left to finish. Of that, approximately three hundred were in Maine and New Hampshire, which is very demanding. But Vermont south to New Jersey would be fairly easy. I was confident that I could finish that year if my knees held up.

I had heard little from Scout, Feather, Zama, or Lug. I only knew that Zama and Lug had finished the trail and Feather had retreated to Georgia to heal up her feet. Eventually I heard from Scout and she gave me her itinerary for her return to the trail. She was going to hike from Monson Maine north through the one-hundred-mile wilderness to Katahdin. Once she had finished her climb up Baxter Peak, she would then find a ride back down to Monson and hike south from there to finish the trail. She asked me to join her. Her itinerary made no sense to me. Getting around on the trail can be difficult and that was one more shuttle than was necessary. She was also starting a week later than I was going to start. Scout wanted me to wait for her, but I was concerned about the weather and I was getting itchy to get back on the trail. Also, bowhunting season was coming and I had a date with a big buck that fall. So I made my own plans and I liked them. It was great hiking with her and the rest of the gang, but this would be different. It would not be proper for me, a married man, to hike with Scout alone. And I was not expecting many hikers to be southbound that time of year to accompany us. And so I accepted the fact that I would spend the rest of the trail by myself.

On August 26th, I said good-bye to my wife and flew to Boston. A plane, rented car, and bus and I was in Millinocket. Ronnie, one of the owners of the Bed and Breakfast, was there waiting for me when the bus arrived. The bed and breakfast was perfect. However, Ronnie explained to my dismay and amazement how Baxter Park works.

Each day the park lets in a limited number of people. And only so many people can climb Mount Katahdin on any given day. That is if they let anybody up the mountain at all. If the weather is bad, they close the mountain and no one is allowed to go up. I am aware of at least one day they did not let anyone go up because the rescue teams were exhausted. They had performed four rescues the day before and the rescue teams had simply worn themselves out to the point that rescues might be dangerous. So in cases like that, they close the mountain. Ronnie explained to me that the only way to be sure you can get into the park is to be there early in the morning. And by early, I mean 5:30 a.m.

The rangers work hard to keep track of who is on the mountain because it is so dangerous. People attempt climbs up the mountain, not realizing how difficult the climb is. Common rescue scenarios are exhaustion, dehydration, and injury. Approximately 50,000 people go up Katahdin each year. Many are simply not up to the challenge of the mile-high mountain. The rangers are there to make sure that if 50,000 people go up the mountain in a season that 50,000 come down alive. I am sure that it is a daunting task. Mountain rescues that require a stretcher take twelve to twenty-four hours and require up to sixty people to affect the rescue.

The park itself is also tightly controlled. There are a limited number of campsites and you have to have reservations well in advance of your visit. The one exception is the thru-hiker. There is a shelter/campground near the base of the mountain called the Birches, which is reserved for thru-hikers. To be considered a thru-hiker you have to come into the park through the hundred-mile wilderness at Abol Bridge. For that reason I would not be considered a thru-hiker and would not be allowed to stay at the Birches. The park posts a Ridge Runner at Abol Bridge to monitor and report thru-hikers who come into the park from the wilderness. That left me with a dilemma. If I entered the park as a visitor and had no campsite reserved, I would have to leave the park by nightfall. I attempted to reserve a campground but the campsites were booked weeks in advance. I was left with two choices. I could go into the park, hike to the peak, and go back to Millinocket for the night. I would then have to return to the park, wait at the gate for hours, and then hike out of the park and on my way through the wilderness. The other choice was to get into the park early, get up and down Katahdin, and hike out of the park to the wilderness in one day. It would be a trying day, if at all possible. It was either an extremely long day (twenty miles) or an extremely short day.

My solution to the dilemma was to prepare for both options. With that in mind, I made my reservation for two nights at the bed and breakfast. On the first day, I was up bright and early and ate a quick breakfast. Ronnie wanted to be at the gate by 5:30 a.m. to assure us that I would get into the park. When we arrived at the park, we were about thirty cars back from the front gate. We patiently waited our turn to plead for entry. The ranger had some questions and then explained that I would have to be out of the park by dark. Once the ranger was satisfied that I was going to be out by dark, she let us through. Ronnie took me to the ranger's office at the base of the mountain where I requested permission to climb the mountain. I left my backpack there and the ranger loaned me a daypack for the climb.

Once the red tape was out of the way, I started up the five-mile trail that would lead me to the summit. I was beside myself with excitement and I was not even finishing the trail. I can only imagine the hiker's feelings finishing the trail on that mountain. For me it was just another mountain and yet I was visibly excited. The first couple of miles were the usual woodland and then subalpine cover. Farther up, you begin scrambling through rocks. At one point the trail levels off briefly and you can see half way up the mountain and the sight is overwhelming. It looks like you will be going straight up. There is nothing about the climb that should be dangerous if you are careful. There are places where rebar is anchored into the rock to give you footing. But mostly you just have to be cautious and not get in a hurry. There were points on the way up where I stopped and wondered how I was going to get down, but I decided I would deal with that on the way down.

About two-thirds of the way up, the grade changed from extremely steep to a fairly gentle grade the rest of the way up to the peak. At that point I could see there were dozens of people on the mountain. I pushed on to the top easily and arrived at the famous sign that so many thru-hikers had celebrated at, including Zama, Lug, Pilgrim, and Dreamer. Three weeks earlier Zama and Lug had celebrated in an interesting way. Lug presented Zama with an engagement ring. Scout and I knew that was going to happen well ahead of time because Lug had clued us in. It was great to read Zama's report of it on her posted journal. I wish I could have been there.

At the top there were many day hikers who were celebrating their accomplishment. As I was waiting my turn at the sign, I started up a conversation with a couple of ladies who were also waiting. They assumed I was a thru-hiker and I explained my situation to them. One of them offered to take my picture and the other one insisted she be in the picture, and I was glad to have her in the picture. So my summit picture was with some model-type gal whose name I did not know. One more thing to explain to my wife!

Once I had taken some pictures and eaten lunch, I headed down the mountain. The climb down was harder than the climb up. There were places where I had to slide on my butt down the rocks, but I was now on my way south. I was heading for Gorham, New Hampshire, logging miles and I was excited. Once off the mountain, I checked back into the ranger's office to let him know I was off the mountain and was hiking out of the park walking south. He questioned me at length about the reality and wisdom of the plan, but I assured him I was up to the occasion.

My intention was to hike the ten miles out of the park to Abol Bridge. Before I did, I stopped in at the Birches Shelter to find out who was there. Some of the guys I met in Pennsylvania were there, including Rematch. Also, there was Power Stroke, who I met in the White Mountains. He had a problem with an infection in his leg and it had affected him enough that he was not going past Katahdin. All those at the Birches were planning on summiting the next day, and they were excited. They had lots of questions about the mountain, and I assured them it was duck soup for anybody who had been through what they had.

After a brief visit, I departed south out of the park. The rest of the hike was easy compared to the ten-mile round-trip up and down the mountains. But the entire hike that day was over twenty miles and I was genuinely whipped by the time I arrived at the store at Abol Bridge. I reported to the Ridge Runner who I was and that I was now out of the park. It was a relief that I was not going to have to go through the red tape to get back into the park. So far my plan had worked well. It did not take me long to get a ride back into town. The Ridge Runner knew someone who was going to town and he tracked them down and secured a ride for me. My ride was a local who had been visiting someone at the campgrounds. He mentioned that he was returning the next day late in the morning and offered to give me a ride back. I gladly accepted and offered to buy him some gas, but he would not have it.

⇒•⇐

The next day my hostess, Mary Lou, put together a marvelous breakfast and I visited with some guests who I had seen the day before on the mountain. I had planned a late start because I wanted the full breakfast. I sat and visited with the other guests, drank coffee, and thoroughly enjoyed myself. After breakfast I met my ride who would take me back out to Abol Bridge. And then without ceremony I walked into the woods heading south and disappeared into the wilderness.

The hundred-mile wilderness is neither a hundred miles nor wilderness. It is a little short of one hundred miles and well short of being a wilderness. Nonetheless, getting off the trail is difficult. It is more mental than anything else. I actually had my best trail magic halfway through the hundred-mile wilderness.

The first day I circled Rainbow Lake, and negotiated numerous mud bogs, exposed roots and rocks. Fifteen miles later I was at the Rainbow Stream Shelter just about dark. The rustling stream and gently falling rain lulled me to sleep that night.

Morning brought more of the same. The difference is that it had rained the night before and everything was wet. The organically rich mud in the bogs makes everything black. Several times I thought I was stepping on solid ground only to have my feet sink a foot into the rich, black muck. At one point there was a service road near a lake and I noticed a truck and an SUV near the lake. The lakes caused me to think about my two boys, Garrett and Brian. We have done some fishing in our time and I thought about how we needed to get out and do some fishing again. I missed them.

All day I pushed hard so I could keep my options open later in the day. There is a hostel one and a half miles off the trail called White House Landing. It is a fish and bear hunting camp that also houses hikers. They serve a famous one-pound burger and I never miss a chance on the trail to get a monster burger. The camp is accessible by an old logging road for the owners or by boat for the guests. The round trip off the trail amounts to three wasted miles and so I was planning to make the decision when I got to the turn off. The other option was to keep on the trail and stay at a shelter and eat trail food. I got to the junction with plenty of time. I stood at the junction debating with myself for a few minutes, but ultimately my vision of a one-pound burger dripping ketchup and some salty fries was more than I could stand.

The access to the camp from the AT is by boat. There is a dock lakeside that you walk out on and wait for the pickup. You sound an air horn and then wait for the owner to come and get you. There is a sign that said only sound the horn once and then wait. While waiting I was second guessing my decision, but I would soon be glad.

There were four thru-hikers there. Gator Goat, Mystic, Marley, and Chill had been there two days eating burgers and drinking beer. They had built up quite a tab. They were in a festive mood, anticipating the end of the trail. I had met a few others heading for Katahdin and it was impossible to miss the excitement they were experiencing. Bill and his wife fixed me up for the night with a soft bed and I enjoyed a warm shower.

❧•❧

The next morning I had an unbelievable breakfast before getting out to the trail at 10:00 a.m. I had planned a long day and was frustrated by the late start, but then the pancakes sloshing around in my belly reminded me it was worth it. It was perfect terrain for getting in a lot of miles that day. It was a flat, dry, and wide trail with no meaningful obstacles. I was able to get up to a good cruising speed all day.

During my hike that day, I met two hikers from Muskegon, Michigan—Stitches and Upload. I stopped and visited with them for a few minutes. The wilderness is popular for local hikers. I met many hikers who were out for a couple of days, and several of them who had planned to get off halfway through the wilderness.

Later in the afternoon I had decided to eat my supper at a shelter and then push on to try to get across the East Branch of the Pleasant River before dark. I stopped at the shelter to eat supper. I was just getting set up to fix supper when some thru-hikers came into the shelter and we started talking. "Where you coming from?"

"I stayed at the White House Landing last night."

"How was it?"

"It was nice, but I am not sure it was worth the extra three miles."

"You staying here tonight?"

"No, I am going on to the next shelter."

"Hmm. You may want to wait on supper. If you hurry you can get trail magic. And I do not mean some Kool-Aid and candy bar. I mean a seven course meal including beer."

"Where is it at?"

"Clark Lake Road. About seven miles down the trail. Nice people. If they are still serving it would be worth pushing on."

I checked the time and consulted my guidebook, then asked, "How late are they going to be there?"

"I cannot tell you that, but I can tell you it is worth the try."

With one continuous motion, I packed my bag, strapped it on, and was off down the trail at warp speed. I arrived out at the Clark Lake Road and found the angels waiting.

At the road there were two pickups parked right in the road. There were five people my age—four men and one woman. They started out the trail in 2003 individually and met each on the trail and hiked together the entire way. They go back to Maine every year to serve the hikers meals in the wilderness. One of the hikers was Old Corpus. I had read his trail journals on the Internet during my preparation stage and I remembered him.

They sat me down in a lawn chair and fixed me up with two cheeseburgers, cantaloupe, corn-on-the-cob, chips, a banana, ice cream, and a beer. I was dumbfounded! There I was in the one hundred-mile wilderness eating a picnic lunch and visiting with five wonderful people. We talked for quite some time and I really liked visiting with them. After I had eaten and the conversation had started to die down, I excused myself because it was getting late and I needed to get to the shelter. To this day I think about the trail angels who added so much to the hike.

After leaving the trail angels, I pushed hard to get to the shelter, but it was getting late. I arrived at the river after dark. The river was quite rapid and I decided it would be better to cross it in the light of day, so I backtracked about one hundred yards and found a small area for a stealth camp. Once the tent was pitched, I reviewed my day and decided it had been an excellent day.

⇉•⇇

I was glad I had not tried to cross the raging river in the dark. It was difficult even in the daylight. That day may have been the hardest fifteen miles I had done on the trail yet. The trail was a big part of it. There were steep ups and downs, boulder fields, and it seems there was not one stretch that was easy. But besides the terrain, there was the residual effect of the twenty-plus miles the day before.

On the way up there were some special vistas. I could see Katahdin from that peak. As I was taking out my camera, a huge gust of wind blew me just as I got it out and almost knocked me over. I dropped my camera and it broke. Fortunately I did not loose any of the data, which includes the Katahdin pictures. The rest of the day was a series of severe ups and downs similar to the Whites but not quite as prolonged. I was out of trail shape. The weeks off in August had not been good on my conditioning.

What a time not to have a camera. I met a moose on the trail a few hours later. It was a bull, probably two and a half years old. It stood in the trail twenty feet from me and refused to move. It just stood there with a stupid look on its face. I had been pushing to get to the West Branch before dark and now I had a moose that would not move. The vegetation was thick enough on either side of the trail that I could not get past him. I hollered, banged my poles together, waved my arms, and did about everything. Finally I took a step toward him and he walked backward down the trail a few feet and stood there again. Several times I took steps toward him again, but he would not move off of the traill. After a few more minutes of this standoff, he turned his body enough and stepped forward into the bush to eat some vegetation. Now his butt was even with the edge of the trail and I decided to try to get by. When I walked past him, I could have hit him with my hiking poles on the hindquarters. He just kept eating and looked at me as I walked by. It was strange.

That night I camped just north of the West Branch of the Pleasant River. It was a seventeen-mile day and I was hurting. I decided I would try to take it easy the next day.

⇒•⇐

The West Branch river was an easy ford. The trail that day was lot of small ups and downs and some rock scrambles. My knees hurt for a while. I did not worry too much about it though and stopped again for a long supper. I decided I would push on past the next shelter and stealth camp. I had grown accustomed to tenting as opposed to sleeping in the shelter. So I stopped and fixed supper at about 6:00 p.m. With supper taken care of, I continued down off the Barren-Chairback range and down to the plateau leading into Monson. There I pitched my tent along a stream and finished up a seventeen-mile day with a hot supper and big helping of chocolate-covered raisins. I went to sleep with the promise that I would have a big plate of bacon and eggs. I was only fourteen trail miles from Monson.

That night I woke in the middle of the night with my knees burning. The pain was such that I could not get to sleep. So at the crack of dawn I packed up and headed for Monson. There was a famous hostel there and I would get a private room and take a nap to make up for the sleep lost. I walked all morning hoping that my knees were not going to be a problem and contemplated a day off in Monson to settle the knees down. But all during the walk that day out to the road my knees did not bother me.

Off in the distance I could hear dogs on the scent. It was September 1st, the first day of bear season. Late in the morning of day five in the ninety-nine-mile wilderness, I busted out onto the road and caught a ride to Monson.

Once in town I headed for the restaurant, but to my dismay it was closed. I stopped a mailman and asked where I could get a plate of bacon and eggs and he said there was no such place. I headed to the hostel and checked in. I paid the extra cost for a private room so I could take a nap.

Awake from my nap, I went to a small restaurant with an outside picnic table. It was a beautiful September day and I opted for a burger and fries. I had drowned it in ketchup and half eaten it when Scout appeared. She had her backpack on and looked like she had been hiking. When she saw me, all she could do was laugh because I was quite wrapped up in my burger. A hug was in order and then she went to the window and ordered food. We visited for quite some time.

Scout had decided to get on the trail at Caratunk instead of Monson because it was easier to get to. She had been hiking north the last two days. The rest of the day was just catching up on what we had been up to. She was a week behind me and there was not much chance she would be able to catch up so this would be the last time we would see each other.

Back at the lounge area in the hostel, Scout brought up something interesting. "Silver, I learned a few minutes ago that there was going to be a bluegrass festival tonight."

"Where at?"

"The store we ate lunch at."

"No way. That store is too small."

"They have one every Friday night and the store owner told me I could sit in tonight. He is tracking down a banjo for me right now."

"You will fit right in with that, being an old North Carolina gal."

"Are you going to come?"

"Sure. If nothing else I will be able to see how they have a festival in that small store. Besides, I do love that music in small doses."

"The store owner says it is very informal and you never know who is going to show up, but he is making sure that there will be enough to have a band tonight."

The only general store in town was a small store that sold everything a local would need to get by until they could get a major market. The building itself is small. The band sits in one corner, jammed into a small space. The audience stands in the aisles, some not even able to see the band. The store stays open during the event, so in addition to the ten to twenty in the audience, there are people coming in for a loaf of bread or some cornstarch. The audience also changes every fifteen minutes as people come and go. The music is as good as you could expect given the lack of continuity with the band.

I arrived at the hoe down and was amazed. I have been to concerts before with the Oak Ridge Boys and Alabama. They were a lot of fun, but they were nothing compared to the fun that night. I grew up watching Hee Haw every Saturday night and one of the parts I remembered was "pick'n n grinnin'." And that is the best way to describe that night. I am not sure who was having more fun, the singers or me. I particularly liked the gospel bluegrass that night. There were some teenage thru-hikers from the hostel that came by. They were mesmerized by the experience and went back to get their other hiker friends to experience the music. More than once I had to step outside to make room for someone else. I shall always remember that quaint little store and the music festival.

After the festival, Scout and I and some other hikers went to the new pub in town and had a mini-feast and rehashed the best and worst of the trail.

After a fantastic breakfast I said good-bye to Scout for the last time. She headed north into the wilderness and I headed south to Caratunk. I had hiked over a thousand miles with her and she had been a great hiking companion. Together with Firefly, Feather, and the others, the trail had been a much better experience, and now I was going off hiking by myself and she by herself.

The hike that day was a very easy hike, mostly along a river and mostly flat, and it ended after eighteen miles. During the day I ran into Sourdough and Sidewider. I met them at the hostel in Hot Springs, North Carolina. They were a father and son combination. I also ran into other northbound hikers who informed me that the latest hurricane Ernesto would be bringing several days of rain to Maine. That news did not bother me because I hiked very well in the rain. Rain kept me from getting too hot and I liked it better when there was more water available for drinking. I arrived at Moxie Bald Shelter at 5:30 p.m. and wanted to push on but my knees were aching. I took two Ibuprofen and ate a big supper.

I had not slept well because of the pain. I got up early and headed out with some concern about my knees. I went up and over Moxie Bald and was in considerable pain by the time I got to the other side. The combination of steep downhill terrain and the hard surfaces took their toll on my knees.

That day I watched a huge bull moose feed for about fifteen minutes before he winded me and bounced off in a hurry. The rest of the day would build up to the extreme descent from Pleasant Pond Mountain. The downhill experience made it plain to me I was in trouble. I had noticed over the past three days that my knees had gotten progressively worse and the pain was familiar. The Whites had severely affected my knees and I apparently had not had enough time to get over the tendonitis.

Once out to the highway, I hitched a ride to the Northern Outdoor Center and signed up for a tent. It was Sunday and it was Labor Day weekend. The place was hopping with campers and rafters, but they had a tent available for me. For less than ten dollars, I received a tent with a cot, linens, and a towel for a shower. I took a nap that evening and then went to the clubhouse to watch the California 500. There was quite a party going on. I was rather conspicuous with my hiker clothing on and my silver hair. A table full of young girls invited me to come over to their table and I joined them for a while. They wanted to know my story and I was glad to tell them, even though it was tough to hear over the live band.

Once the race was over and the girls' curiosity satisfied, I crashed for the night. But it would be a sleepless night. The campground was full of loud drunks who were not interested in sleep. I am not sure why alcohol causes a person to talk so much louder.

A night with very little sleep is not good for hiking. I headed out late with enough food to get me to Stranton. I reached the trail at 10:00 a.m. with my knees burning. The trail takes you down to the Kennebec River and a canoe operator is there to take you across the river. It is the only such crossing on the AT. Were it not for the canoe, the trail would have to be rerouted to lead hikers to a bridge crossing. The canoe is provided by a local hiker named Steve Longley, who organizes it. There is a hydroelectric dam upriver that releases water without notice. When a computer in Massachusetts decides the grid needs more power, it opens the dam. The computer neither knows nor cares if a hiker is going to cross the river. The river can be shallow enough to ford one minute and rise rapidly without notice.

In 1985 a thru-hiker named Alice Ferrence was drowned when she was caught in a release. The canoe is available for a limited timeframe so hikers have to plan their hike around the crossing times. There have been close to 20,000 hikers ferried across the Kennebec since it went into operation.

Once across the river, I started south. But it was clear with every step that the knees were just not going to last. I would have to take a couple of days off and then go slow. Hiking like that I would never make it to New Jersey that year. I had gone about three miles, and with each mile I was further convinced that it was time to pull the plug on 2006.

After several miles, I sat and took a break for about an hour while I deliberated the situation. I turned around and headed back to the canoe crossing. It was a hard walk to make.

Once back across the Kennebec, I went straight to the road and caught a ride in a matter of minutes. From there I took a bus to the Portland airport. I rented a car one-way and before I knew it I was driving home. The ride home gave me a lot of time to think about the year's hike. I knew separation from my wife and family would be a problem when I started. If I had it to do over again, I would have approached the return to the trail in late July so that I did not trash me knees going through New Hampshire. It would be a long winter. I had hiked almost sixteen hundred miles. Eleven hundred of that was nonstop, followed by some sections during the summer.

HOLLY AND AMANDA

Culver's Gap, New Jersey to Dalton, Massachusetts
Total miles: 247
Hiking days: 13

During the winter, the soft corn on my toe developed again. My visit to a different podiatrist would reveal the real problem. I had a bone spur on the inside of my little toe. That bone spur was causing the soft corn to develop. The treatment was an outpatient appointment to open the toe and grind the bone spur down. It was discovered and treated early enough that I was able to completely recover before I was going to return to the trail. I asked the doctor what would cause the bone spur and he suggested several things, trauma being one of them. When I asked him if walking twenty miles a day would cause trauma to a little toe, he only smiled and shook his head. By his expression I surmised that it was a stupid question.

❧•❧

The first hike of the year was during the month of April 2007. My wife and I traveled to South Carolina for spring break with our grandson Elijah. Along the way we stopped in Tennessee long enough for me to complete the twenty-five miles along the border of Tennessee and North Carolina.

Part of my hike was going over Big Bald. Most of my crossing over balds on the AT were not enjoyable events. This one was no different. The wind was howling and the temperature dropped to just above freezing. I moved quickly across the mountaintop. It was still better than it was when I would have crossed it a year earlier. Then there was about three feet of snow, high winds, and bitter temperatures. While in the area I stopped and visited with Miss Janet in Erwin and was able to introduce her to my wife and our little traveling companion.

Before resuming our travel, we delivered some trail magic to a point on the trail where the interstate highway crosses the trail. We saw several hikers and passed out some fruit and donuts. While there, Elijah, age two and a half, was interested in the trail. He took off up the mountain and went almost two miles on the trail. He was quite excited about the trail and we were quite amused at his eagerness. For such a little guy, he went up the mountain fast. He was so small that when he came to water rods in the trail, he had to crawl over them. It was a memory that we will treasure for the rest of our lives. It was the second spring break in a row that he hiked on the Appalachian Trail. The next spring break we took Elijah to the Smokies and he ended up hiking again around Clingman's Dome.

❧ • ❧

During the month of April I had been in contact with my old hiking partners just to keep them informed. Feather had gotten a job working as a guide in the mountains out west. During the summer of 2007, Feather would hike the Pacific Crest Trail. She kept me informed about her progress occasionally, and she did end up finishing that year.

My plan was to finish the trail in two separate hikes. The first one would be in the month of May. I would hike from Culver's Gap, New Jersey, to Hanover, New Hampshire, thus finishing the southern section of the trail not finished. The distance would be four hundred twenty-four miles, most of it fairly easy. I wanted to do that portion of the trail while it was spring to avoid the heat of summer. But the hike in Maine would have to wait until the mountains had thawed out and dried up. One other concern was the black flies. For that reason I would wait until mid to late summer to finish the trail in Maine and New Hampshire. By waiting until summer, I could have the luxury of having my wife along with me.

So in mid-May of 2007, I left the house at 4:30 a.m. and headed for New Jersey. My son drove me to Bishop International in Flint, Michigan, and I caught a flight to Newark, New Jersey. From there I rented a car one-way to a small town not far from Culver's Gap. I was dumbfounded when I went to get gas and found that in New Jersey drivers cannot pump their own gas. I am in my early fifties and had never had someone pump my gas. When I had arrived at the trail, it was pouring down rain so I went into Elmer's Tavern. By the time I had polished off the bowl of chili, the rain had let up a little and I was in the mood for some walking.

By 3:00 p.m. I was on the trail. I was alone and the rain made the setting even more depressing. The trail that day was easy. There were not a lot of ups and downs and there were no Pennsylvania rocks by that point on the trail. With the gentle terrain, I made the fourteen miles to High Point Park just about dark. From my trail guide, I knew the number for an inn and called them. Within minutes the manager came by and picked me up. And so I had woken up in Michigan as Wally, traveled a thousand miles, hiked fourteen, and was sound asleep in New Jersey as Silver Streak. Other than a serious lack of sleep, I was in pretty good shape.

❖❖

The innkeeper drove me down the road to a diner so I could get a hot breakfast fit for a hiker. I had slept in to make up for the previous day. I met two section hikers from Michigan. They were a mother and daughter. We compared notes about Michigan and it was nice to visit with them. The mother's name was Patty, but I cannot remember the daughter's name. Then it was back on the trail by nine o'clock. I was determined to make it all the way to

Vernon, but I would have to keep up a good pace. I said good-bye to the gals from Michigan.

Later that day I crossed a bird sanctuary and then started up a hill to the Pochuck Mountain Shelter. At the shelter was Ed Ache. He was a man probably in his sixties. Ed was from Rhode Island and was heading south. We clued each other in on what was ahead. I spent about an hour resting my feet and eating a late lunch. Ed was already settled in for the night. At about 4:30, I said my farewell to Ed and was off. I was glad I had at least seen someone and I enjoyed our conversation. It was also the first time I had met someone from Rhode Island in my life. I crossed over Pochuck Mountain and eventually came out to a most remarkable walkway.

The Pochuck creek and adjoining wetlands were once bypassed on the trail by way of a road walk of over two miles. Through private and governmental cooperation, an amazing one-mile long boardwalk of remarkable quality was built. It was used heavily by locals for their evening walks. At the end of the boardwalk was a large suspension bridge over the Pochuck Creek. One cannot travel this without being amazed at the extent of the boardwalk and bridge. They were built by over 500 volunteers as well as state, local, and national agencies. The boardwalk is built a couple of feet above the wetlands (swamp) with treated wood and is supported by 874 piers. When I walked over it, there were several local residents out for their evening exercise. I applaud the accomplishment of those involved in the cooperative effort to enhance the trail and the community it passes through. It avoids a road walk, which hikers despise.

To me the Appalachian Trail is a testament to cooperation. It is a story in itself. The Pochuck Creek project is one of many examples of what volunteers can do when government enables the citizens and then gets out of the way. It begs the question that is far beyond the scope of my book. How many other problems can be solved in the country by volunteers? Everyone should see the walkway and bridge and contemplate the accomplishments. My hat is off to all who had a hand in it.

Once over the walkway and bridge, I crossed a field and was at a highway crossing to Vernon. I hitched into town and stayed at a local hotel. There I ordered a pizza and salad. Aside from Ed Ache, I had not seen any hikers all day. I had hiked twenty-one miles on my second day on the trail and I was tired. After supper, I took the remote control to bed and had a great night's sleep.

❧•❦

The next day I walked almost three miles before someone picked me up. I was no longer in the south and hospitality would not be as common. My goal that day was a reasonable fifteen miles to Glenwood, New York. The climb out of the valley was easy and I was beginning to settle in to hiking but the lack of any companionship was already getting depressing. A significant part of the day was spent walking on a ridge above Greenwood Lake, which I found quite pleasant. I would end up that day scratching another state off my list. I crossed the New Jersey/New York state line later that day. I stopped at the border marker long enough to celebrate with some peanut butter cups. I arrived in the little lakeside town of Greenwood Lake and checked into a small hotel. The terrain had not been very demanding and I was at a hotel with town food and a shower every night. The soft hiking was the consolation for having to hike alone.

❧•❦

I got a late start out of town and hiked a much more demanding trail. I now had three days' food and fuel. Getting a ride out to the trail was also difficult. I walked over a mile toward the trail while attempting to catch a ride. I arrived at the trail at 11:00 a.m., which I considered very late.

The first half of the day included continuous ups and downs that wore me out. I did not push hard because the need just was not there. I was in a funk all day and it affected my speed.

Later in the day I entered Harriman State Park. I arrived at the Fingerboard Shelter with enough daylight to fix my supper. The shelter was full and so I set up on the ground in front of the shelter and was very comfortable. It was nice to have other hikers in the shelter. All of them were local hikers out for a few days. That was a short day—only about fifteen miles.

❧•❦

The next day I came to the one place on the trail where you can see the Big Apple. It was too hazy that day to see that far, but I could see the Hudson River from there. I also saw the scariest thing I would see on the trail that day—a sign that said, "New York City 34." I saw a few local hikers that reported a rattlesnake on the trial. But the sign was the scarier of the two.

The climb up Bear Mountain was a road hike. It was a hot spring day and the bikers were out in force. The visitor's center at the top of the mountain was closed for remodel and so I pushed on over the top of the mountain and down toward the river.

At the base of the mountain the park is quite developed, with a huge inn that was also under renovation. There was also an area that had pavilions and refreshments and it was open. I stopped there and had a magnum soft drink and watched the locals at play. There was a family of three there with their little son. They reminded me of my daughter and her family. The little boy was my grandson's age and he reminded me of Elijah—not because he looked like him, but because he had all the energy, excitement, and curiosity he was supposed to have at that age. I watched them for a while then I became very concerned about the appearance. An old, smelly vagabond with a pack and a haggard appearance watching a little boy in a park is not a welcome site anywhere. I walked over to introduce myself and explain why I was watching them. They did not reveal it in any way, but I am sure they were relieved. They were very gracious and welcomed me to sit with them. I explained that I was just passing through hiking the AT. They were not even aware the trail passed through the area. They asked the same myriad of questions. When I had sufficiently satisfied their curiosity about the trail, I told them about my grandson Elijah and showed them a picture of him. I talked at length about the joys that he had brought to our life and how seeing their son at play had affected me. They talked about their son with typical pride and joy.

They were a young family with their first child and wanted everything to be right for their little boy. His name was Chad. I watched him at play with the other kids while we talked. Talking to them made me homesick. I had very little interaction with Chad, but he did have some questions about what was in my sack. When I mentioned the tent, his eyes tripled in size and he was excited. At the mention of the tent, he decided that he and his daddy should sleep in a tent that night. After a few seconds of talking to his parents and me, he bounced off to resume his play. At some point he decided he needed to swing and wanted his dad to give him an "underdog." Dad gave him a couple of underdogs while I talked with his mom.

After the enjoyable visit, I reluctantly began packing up to continue my journey for the day. The little boy saw that I was leaving and offered me half of a Popsicle he had coming to him. There was no way I could say no. That was a special moment on the trail for me. He was one sweet little boy. I graciously accepted and enjoyed it only because he had offered it to me. I thanked them for the moment they shared with me and moved on. There were so many people I had met on the trail and had a strong connection with and would never see again—like two ships passing in the night. But sweet little boys had become a part of my life as a new grandfather and I was quite touched. I hoped to myself that he had a grandpa and that the grandpa was taking an interest in his life and adding to it. I also wondered more than ever how anyone could in any way hurt a young child. No wonder Jesus promised a sure curse on anyone hurting a child.

The trail approaches the Bear Mountain Bridge through a small zoo. Hikers with backpacks are allowed to pass through the zoo without paying. The bridge is a suspension bridge that has a pedestrian lane for the AT that is protected by a steel guardrail. The crossing is about a half mile. Once across, the trail goes up over a ridge and then crosses a highway again. I had gone about twenty-two miles before I called it quits and pitched my tent. It was a long day and I did not see any sense in pushing on because there was not a shelter for quite some time. It had been a long day. I went to bed that day with mixed emotions over the event back at the park with Chad.

The beauty of long-distance hiking is in the simplicity of life on the trail. Your only responsibility is to find food, water, and a place to sleep. It does not get much simpler than that. The night before, I had been walking one minute and five minutes later my tent was set up and I was boiling water for some Mac and Cheese. I felt good about the pace I was making with little effect on my body. There is quite a difference hiking in the soft earth on flat ground in contrast to the trail in Maine and New Hampshire.

That day on the trail was pure drudgery. The trail had become less enjoyable with each stretch since I left the gang back in New Jersey the year before. The walking was easier since the Mid-Atlantic states were much flatter. But the trail was devoid of hikers and it was taking its toll on me. I stopped in the RPH Shelter and visited with a section hiker who had set up for supper. It was about six in the evening and I was not close to being ready to stop for the day, but I fixed supper while I visited with him and then I left him and pushed on. I toyed with staying at the shelter just to have some company. I walked again for another six miles and settled into another stealth camp. It was another twenty-two-mile day and I decided I would take it easy the next day.

I slept in a little and took my time getting prepared for the day. Because I was in a clearing, dew had settled on my tent and I wanted the morning sun to burn off some of the dew before I packed it up. While I was eating a Pop-Tart and craving some coffee, Hobbit came by. I recognized him from a picture on a trail journal posted on the Internet. We talked for a few minutes while I packed up. He was trying to reach the train at Pawling. There was a commuter train station right on the AT that could take hikers into New York City. He and Blue, a female hiker with him, were planning to go into New York so he could visit his daughter. I threw my stuff together and walked with them for a short time. I was low on water and had to stop but they kept going. I would never see them again.

It was another uneventful day—picking up feet and laying them down. That is what the trail had become. I was disappointed when I found out that Hobbit and Blue were leaving the trail. I was happy with the progress I was making, due as much to the flat terrain as anything. The one difficulty I was having was following the trail. The leaves from the fall of the year before had produced a blanket over the trail. The usual worn appearance of the trail was well hidden in places and the trail was hard to follow. It was early enough in the spring that few hikers had been on the trail to wear it down. Because of that, I had followed a false trail three times in the last few days, which added both miles and frustration to my day.

The next morning I walked out to a local diner for breakfast. After breakfast I was picked up by a section hiker named Nanny Goat and her husband. Her husband was providing vehicle support and they were going from hotel to hotel for her hike. She had also had a problem with following the trail because of the leaves and had gotten completely turned around for quite some time the night before. I was disappointed that Nanny Goat was not going to be hiking in the same direction as me. Once at the trail, we talked for about half an hour about some of her experiences.

We went our separate ways with a good-bye and good luck. Then, without ceremony, I mentally checked off another state. New York was behind me.

Connecticut is a short state, covering only fifty-two miles. It starts off like a kitty and ends up like a lion. The first half of the day was a walk along a river. When I left the river and started uphill, I ran into a section hiker whose name escapes me. He had a pack that an army ranger would struggle with. He was on his first hitch on the trail and had not yet learned the value of trimming weight. He was a cook by trade and I think he brought his kitchen and pantry along. His philosophy was that he was going to enjoy quality food while on the trail. I wished him good luck and I meant it. For every hiker there are criteria that they use to prioritize their hike. His was food.

I had used up my few ounces of fuel that I had bought at the other end of New York, and I decided I was going to have to go into Kent to get some denatured alcohol from the outfitter there. I had hoped to go past Kent by getting the food supply that I needed, but I had not been able to get more fuel at the last resupply. I found that New York and New Jersey were just not as hiker friendly in many ways compared to the previous states.

The walk into Kent was about a mile and it was a hot day. I went into the outfitter and was rudely told to come back later. I found an acceptable restaurant and wolfed down some food and rehydrated my body before returning. The outfitter had left and the other person would not have anything to do with me out of fear of her boss. I was told to come back in an hour.

While in town, I made a phone call to the office and found out about a major issue with a contract that needed serious attention. The project manager for my company needed me to be involved. There was a chance that I might have to hurry home to deal with it. With that in mind, I checked into a local inn and made calls to line up travel options should I have to get to an airport fast. My cell phone would get a lot of use and so I would need to be where I could recharge the battery. That day I spent a lot of time on the phone.

≫•≪

The next day more phone calls were necessary and we were able to resolve the issue sufficiently that I could confidently move on. The issue kept me in town until eleven o'clock. I got out on the trail with a vengeance. The days were long enough that I was sure that I could make good miles even with a late start. I had a great breakfast to carry me and was enjoying the hike, knowing that a major crisis seemed to have been averted.

I had planned on stopping at Salisbury the next day because of the famed Mrs. McCabe. At the road to Cornwall Bridge, a young couple had just stopped to take some pictures of the first hiker that came along. I happened to be the one. They were new to the area and wanted to send info about the kind of place they were now living and wanted some pictures of a hiker. They offered to take me into the town of Cornwall Bridge and I accepted. It was another extremely hot day and I was fully depleted. I decided an ice cold drink would bring me back to life.

They dropped me at a corner convenience store that had a picnic table on the front porch. I purchased a huge root beer and a small container of ice cream. The storeowner let me take a cup and so I sat on the front porch and fixed myself a root beer float. While I was there, two ladies about my age asked if they could sit with me. They were extremely friendly and I enjoyed talking to them. They were curious about what I was doing and I explained. They had many questions and I must have talked for half an hour about my experiences. I made sure early in the conversation to say how much I missed my wife, lest there be some kind of misunderstanding. What peeked their interest the most was the "trail angel," so I expanded my description of what they did. They had no interest in hiking the trail, but they were interested in

223

becoming trail angels. So I gave them some tips on how, when, and where to set up.

In town, I stopped in a local package store that was known to show considerable support for hikers. In return for signing their register, they offered some treat, but I cannot remember what it was. We talked about many things on the trail and the two men who operated the store were very interested in the hikers who passed through. During our conversation I mentioned that I had found three deer ticks on me that morning. They told me that the county I was in had the highest per capita occurrence of Lyme's Disease in the country. I had grown accustomed to checking myself regularly for the ticks and during the course of the trail I found at least twenty on me. Only about one in one hundred tick attacks end up transmitting the disease. The challenge is finding the little buggers. They are quite small.

While I was there a local they knew came in. They asked him to give me a ride back out to the trail and he was glad to. Just like that, I was back out on the trail energized by the root beer float.

The hike into the Pine Swamp Shelter was without event. I was pleased that despite all the delays getting out of Kent and the trip into Cornwall Bridge, I was still able to log seventeen miles. There was not a soul in the campsite or shelter.

⫷•⫸

The forecast was sunny with a high in the nineties. I had planned on getting up early to beat the heat of the day, and I was assisted in getting up early. The Lime Rock Race Track was just over the hill from the shelter and the drivers were out early practicing and so my wake-up call was the roar of engines and squeal of tires. I was on the trail banging out miles by 6:45 a.m. and enjoying it. It was as pleasant a hike as you get on the trail. There was a small road walk to get over the Housatonic River by bridge, and later an old one lane iron bridge, a beautiful waterfall, and a river walk. On the river walk I met a local out for a run and she stopped and talked for a minute. I told her I was stopping in Salisbury and she said, "So you can stay at Mrs. McCabe's?" I smiled and she told me she had talked to many hikers over the years who had stayed with her and they all had high praise for the lady.

It was a seventeen-mile hike to get into Salisbury by midafternoon. By the time I was in town, I seemed to have had all the juices cooked out of me. I found my way to a small bistro off the main road and went in. I was parched and exhausted. The heat of the day had taken all the sass out of me and I cared not the least where I ate. The bistro happened to be a very nice place where all the proper New England ladies went to talk about all the things that old ladies talk about. They were dressed such that I wondered if it was Easter again. To say I stuck out would be an understatement. The proper New England ladies made no attempt at hiding their curiosity about this strange sight in their hangout. Their stares did not bother me at all. There was one snobby old lady that watched me with obvious disapproval. I considered getting up and going over and sitting with her just to irritate her. I am sure it would have given her a heart attack. I downed several glasses of water, some lemonade, and a BLT with all the trimmings. The cold drink and the air conditioning got my body temperature down to a safe level and the food revived me.

Maria McCabe is a charming lady with quite a story. She was a teenager during World War II in Italy and saw Mussolini when he was hung upside down in Milan. She recounted some chilling stories of Nazi occupation. She met and married a U.S. serviceman and immigrated to the United States. She is now a widow who takes in hikers as much for her entertainment as for money. For thirty-five dollars, she does laundry, provides a shower, a soft bed with fresh linens, and breakfast. She also drove me to a local pizza house for supper and ate with me. I pumped as much history out of her as I could during my stay there and was quite fascinated with her. It took me a while to figure out why I liked her so much. She reminded me of my mother. She was about that age, she could be quite brassy, she had a wonderful sense of humor, and she was interested in helping people. One other thing reminded me of my mother—she washed my underwear and hung it on the clothesline to dry. I enjoyed my stay with her.

⇨•⇦

By prearrangement, I fixed myself a cold breakfast and saw myself out early. I wanted to get an early start because of the heat. I would be going up over Bear Mountain at the boundary of Massachusetts and as usual I wanted to avoid pushing hard in the middle of the day.

The early part of the day was spent on a ridge overlooking a valley below with a couple of lakes. The lakes looked inviting. When I arrived at the top of Bear Mountain there was a tower made from stacked rocks. I had planned on a long break at the mountain peak, but there were about ten noisy college kids who spoiled the tranquil setting. That day I also met a mother and three of her daughters hiking together. They were having fun on the ridge and my presence did not cool their enthusiasm at all.

I arrived at the Hemlocks Shelter with adjoining campgrounds late in the day. I stopped at the shelter to see if there were any thru-hikers I could visit with, but none had showed up yet. The mother was there with her daughters and they were gathering firewood for the evening. I planned on pitching a tent and so I moved off to a camping area farther away. In the camping area were several weekend hikers, who all tended to keep to themselves. I checked back at the shelter an hour before dark and only the mother and her daughters were there and they were having fun being silly. I visited with them for a few minutes and returned to my camp for an evening of sleeplessness. Holiday weekends are a great time for drunks and idiots to howl and so it was most of the night. The campsites were close enough to parking lots that coolers full of beer could be brought in and parties could be had. I would have picked up and moved down the trail and slept but stealth camping in Massachusetts is not allowed.

After a frustrating night I got off early, intending to check into a retreat area that night. The ridge continued for a couple of miles and I could see there was a long, flat valley below. I knew I was headed for that flat area. The thought of an extended hike without the ups and downs appealed to me. I had no idea what awaited me. There were places along the ridge where the drop was almost straight down. The sheer cliffs did not seem to fit with the surrounding area. One problem developed on the ridge. My left shoe came apart. The sole separated from the shoe starting at the toe. I duct-taped the front of the shoe together until I could get another pair ordered.

Once off the mountain I crossed a road and was met with a greeting party of mosquitoes such as I had never seen before. The build-up of the mosquitoes was not gradual. They pounced on me in a way that I was not prepared for. I carried repellant but did not put any on unless it was necessary and it usually was not. Even when I put it on the perspiration washed it off in no time.

I was in a low-lying area and decided to push on fast to get through the area. I thought that if I moved fast enough I could get past them or at least keep them off me. They were still managing to land on me and were eating me up. I stopped to spray myself and could not believe how many mosquitoes lit on me immediately. Bad idea. So I grabbed my gear and resumed my travel at a near run. Speed did not matter. I felt like I was in a Hitchcock movie. The mosquitoes were bouncing off my face and arms, and my hands were not free to swat at them because I was carrying my hiking poles. I was attempting to swat them as much as I could while keeping up my pace. And I dared not stop to stow my poles.

By then, I was breathing hard and practically running. At one point I looked back and there was a black cloud of mosquitoes. Several of them were swallowed during the next few miles. I had seen cartoons as a little kid of swarms of bees chasing people into lakes and I almost laughed at how real that seemed.

I was sure I had walked and jogged ten miles through the ordeal, but in fact I had only covered four miles. I came out of a brushy area to an open field adjacent to a highway. It was Memorial Day weekend and Great Barrington was having festivities.

At the edge of town two policemen were working traffic control. When they saw me running out of the bush with poles in my hand and attempting as best I could to swing at the insects, they laughed out loud. They knew what I was dealing with.

The farther I got into the clearing the more relief I got from the attack. The policemen did not say a word to me and I managed a smile and shook my head. Once out to the road I was able to stop and catch my breath. The ordeal had taken all of the energy out of me. I found a large rock to sit on and cooled off. The nightmare had left me soaked with sweat and trembling with exhaustion. There were still some mosquitoes, but nothing I could not manage. I sat there for twenty minutes cooling off and thinking about how thrilled I had been earlier that day to be walking on low and flat ground. I then applied a liberal amount of repellant and resumed my travel with an appreciation for those who lived in the area.

I crossed the valley and moved up onto the next ridge. I was glad I was back in the hills and out of the valley. Because it was Memorial Day weekend, there were plenty of people on the trail. Many were people who were going on the trail a few miles to say they had walked it. Some were the usual weekend hikers out enjoying the outdoors. None were very friendly that day.

After over sixteen miles that day, including the few I ran, I arrived at Highway 23. To the left one mile was the East Mountain Retreat Center. There had been little doubt all that day that I would take that one-mile trip to the center. When you are on the trail you are willing to walk an extra two miles each day for a shower and soft bed.

The retreat center is a silent retreat. That would be a welcomed change to the night before. Guests go there to contemplate and reflect. Silence is required of all guests, including hikers, who are strictly instructed not to speak to the guests, or to talk aloud in common areas. Once in the hiker area, we were free to talk all we wanted as long as it did not get loud. I checked into the retreat and paid my ten dollars. For that I received a shower, soft bed with clean linens, and a kitchen area for preparing food.

Once in the hiker's dorm area, I met Holly and Amanda. They were in their midtwenties. Amanda had a strong aversion to mosquitoes. For that reason they had bypassed the area I had just passed through because it was known for its mosquitoes. Their plan was to come back later and do that section when the bugs were not that bad. The operator of the outfitter in Cornwall Bridge, Connecticut, shuttled them up to that point. We hit it off right away and I enjoyed talking to them. Amanda was finishing her trail from a previous year and Holly was going along as her sidekick.

Amanda and Holly went to Great Barrington that night to eat pizza. I took advantage of the opportunity and took a short nap. When they returned they were in the mood to talk and we spent a lot of time visiting. They were aware of my shoe problem and had noticed there was an outfitters store in town. They checked and it was going to be open the next day, which was Memorial Day. We made plans to hitch a ride into town together and have breakfast together. They were going to take the next day off so I would eat with them, buy my shoes, and be off to the trail. I was disappointed they were not going on because I liked their company.

❧·❦

Once in town I said good-bye to the girls after breakfast. I went to the outfitter and bought a great pair of hiking sandals that were lightweight, and I loved them. The outfitter where I bought my shoes took it upon himself to find me a ride out to the trail from someone in the store who he knew was headed the same way. So by twelve o'clock I was on the trail. I had expected more people on the trail that day because it was the weekend, but I walked the entire day and only saw two weekenders. I did not make my goal of getting to Upper Goose Pond Shelter, so I ended up camping under the stars close to the trail.

The next morning had a depressing start to it. The hike the day before was just short of twenty miles and I was tired. The day's trail had just what I needed to cheer me up. The crossing at Highway 90 was a special event. It was a footbridge across the interstate. The bridge had a special meaning to me. I had driven under the walkway a few times and said then that I would be walking there one day. I took some pictures of the bridge and of the "Bershires" sign.

The rest of the day was drudgery. It was twenty-two miles into town, but it was not a particularly tough day. I met two section hikers who had a lot of questions. They were considering a push to get the last half of the trail done the next year. They were southbound and had come from Vermont, which was where I was headed. They were covered with black fly bites and were cursing the insects. They cautioned me about going into Vermont. This plagued me as I walked the rest of the day. What I saw when I walked into town I shall never forget.

When I turned down the main street running through town, there were half a dozen police cars spread along the main road through town with their lights on. I thought to myself there must be a big drug bust or a big heist or maybe even a hostage situation. Dalton is where all the paper for our paper money is made. I was sure I had walked into a piece of history by the sight of all the police cars. I walked slowly, observing my surroundings to make sure I was not going somewhere I was not supposed to go. The first car I passed by, the policeman was simply directing traffic. I slowed, expecting him to inform me I could not go any farther at this time, but he just kept directing traffic and ignored me. The next car was the same. And the next. They were all just directing traffic. I did know one thing for sure—I was going to find out what this was all about.

I stopped in the library to check my email and asked the lady at the desk what all the excitement was all about. She gave me a strange look and I had to explain to her that there were police cars lining the streets with their lights flashing.

"Oh that…" she said. "They are cleaning the storm sewers."

"I do not understand. What do they need the police for?"

"They direct traffic. It is a state law. Anytime someone is working in the streets a policeman must be there to protect the worker."

"What a waste. In Michigan we have barrels and signs. You do not have to pay them."

"I am not saying I like it, most people in this state do not like it either, but nothing ever seems to change. The policeman's lobby is very strong in this state."

⇒•⇐

When bear hunting in Canada, I experienced black flies, and they are horrendous. We returned from Canada with little to show for our hunting trip except dozens of bite scars that lasted about a month. I was not the least bit interested in hiking through black fly country. The season for them is in the spring and ends in early July when the heat and arid weather kills them off. I wanted to enjoy Vermont, a state I had always wanted to hike in.

I was at a good place on the trail to get off. I was not about to knowingly hike into black fly country. I had hiked 247 miles in thirteen days. Pittsford, which is just a few miles away, has an Amtrak station and the afternoon train heads west. If I did get into Vermont and found the bugs to be intolerable, I would have more trouble getting off the trail because transportation from the trail is not as easy there. I had always wanted to experience Vermont during leaf season so I accepted the fact that it was time to go home and save Vermont for the fall. It would end up being a good decision. The next day I was on the train and home.

THE NOTCH

Gorham to Caratunk
Miles hiked: 140
Days hiked: 10

One of my favorite movies is *The Outlaw Josie Wales*. Josie's Indian friend talks about his visit with a government dignitary. The man told the Indian to "endeavor to persevere" before shipping him off to a reservation to starve to death. I too was endeavoring to persevere. The many trips I had made to and from the trail did not bother me, but it was expensive. For a person who loves to walk so much, I sure was doing a lot of flying, driving, and riding trains and buses. The one foolish thing I had done was hurrying through the Whites the year before and allowing my knees to deteriorate. It cost me the opportunity to finish the trail the year before as a thru-hike. It also added to the number of trips I would end up making to the trail.

My wife and I had both hoped that she could do some hiking with me when I first left for Springer Mountain the year before. We had been to Maine before and she wanted to go back. I came up with a plan we were both comfortable with. I would leave ahead of her and do the cruelest part of the hike in those two states, the Mahousics. Marilyn would then join me at Rangeley and we would hike from Caratunk south to Stratton. If she could tolerate that stretch, we would both continue south and hike up over Sugarloaf and Saddleback Mountains to finish Maine. I liked the plan because it would allow me to bust out the difficult part without worrying about her, and she liked it because it was a time and distance that was reasonable for her. I would drive my car from home to Logan International and leave it there for her. She would wait five days and then fly to Logan, pick up the car, and meet me at the Rangeley Inn.

On July 20th I left late in the day to drive to Boston and by way of bus arrived at Hikers Paradise. I hung around til breakfast, even though I wanted to get an earlier start, and I was glad I did. In the little eating area at the hotel, I noticed a woman who was a little younger than me and who was obviously a hiker. I invited myself to join her and she gladly accepted. Her trail name was Slowly-but-Surely and she was a section hiker. She had finished the trail only the day before, twenty-five years after starting. She was going to finish her breakfast and start her journey back to St. Petersburg, Florida. I felt honored that I could join her in her celebration. Her husband had not accompanied her in the pursuit all these years, but he did support her in the endeavor. We talked until it was time for her to catch the bus to Boston. We compared notes about our most favorite and least favorite places on the trail, as well as many places and people. I could have talked with her all day. When it was time, she excused herself, grabbed her pack, and was gone. It was one of the most delightful breakfasts I had on the trail.

With breakfast taken care of, I caught a ride out to the trail and was off on a long day of hiking. The elevation changes that day seemed worse than the map suggested. I wanted to get past the border and into Maine before dark. Along the way I stopped at the Gentian Pond Shelter and talked to some section hikers. They had only Maine to do and they were finished. They had left Gorham the day before. They got almost to the Mahoosuc Notch and decided they did not need to finish the trail. They turned around and headed back to Gorham. They were cursing the trail, the people who planned it, and the people who hiked it. It was half good humor and half serious. They warned me to turn back. While we were talking, I told them about the couple of times I stood and said aloud to myself, "You've got to be kidding me!" One of them laughed and said he had done the same thing that very day. I told them where I came from and where I was headed and they assured me emphatically that there was no way that I could make it to the shelter before dark. Up til that time, I wondered if I could. I had considered cutting my goal short and staying at that shelter, but when they told me there was no way I could make it, I knew then I was going to make it. I politely said good-bye and was off with a new determination.

The last few miles were torturous and there was one point when it took some serious problem solving to figure out how I was going to get down a steep area near the border. I arrived exhausted at the Carlos Col Shelter with just enough daylight to pitch my tent. I was forced to fix supper by the light from my three-watt headlamp. I was sure glad New Hampshire was done.

❧•❦

The next morning I faced the challenge of tackling the toughest mile on the AT. I stopped at the shelter just before the Mahoosuc Notch to have an early lunch and get my mojo up for the notch. A south bounder was there who was recovering from the experience. He informed me there was a dead moose at the beginning of the one-mile gauntlet. It had been dead several days and had gotten quite ripe. I was glad for the warning. It is always good to have some time to get accustomed to a bad experience.

The drop down into the notch was its own punishment. I thought I would never get down the steep 1,000-foot decent. There were several local hikers who had walked in from a separate trail just to do a round-trip of the notch. The hike into and out of the notch was apparently known as a badge of courage among the locals. They were waiting for someone in their group who was way overdue. They were not quiet about their displeasure. They reiterated the warning of the moose ahead and suggested that

I hold my breath because it was bad. The moose was a calf that had been born that year. Apparently the cow had attempted to pass through the notch and the calf had slipped and jammed its leg in the rocks in such a way that it could not free itself. Other hikers had been forced to get past it while it struggled to get free and the slow death had been chronicled in shelter registers along the trail for several days. Attempts to get a game warden up to assist the moose had fallen on deaf ears—not that anyone probably could do anything for it except shoot it and put it out of its misery.

The Mahoosuc Notch is a jumble of rocks in a narrow valley between two sheer cliffs. The walls on either side had been shedding the huge rocks for generations. The rocks are mostly squared off shapes that range in size from refrigerators to small houses. Because of the steep sides and the narrow valley, there is no getting around the rocks. You must climb over them, around them, and in some cases under them. At one point you come to a rock that is so big and steep on the sides you must crawl under it, and the space is small enough that you must take your pack off and drag it behind you. Because you are in a valley, there is a stream. The stream can be heard flowing under the rocks you are crawling over and around. Northbound hikers are hiking slightly downhill, although you may never notice it. This natural obstacle course goes on for a mile and ends as abruptly as it begins.

There was nothing particularly difficult about the notch. It just took some time. I thought the bigger effort was getting down to the Notch and out of it. Before I knew it, I was finished. I stopped at the other end to celebrate with a peanut butter sandwich made with English muffins and a Snicker bar. I thought the notch was interesting.

Before I started up the mountain on the far side, it started to rain hard. That made the seemingly endless slabs of granite wet and treacherous, but I endeavored to persevere and soon I had topped the peak. Within an hour, I had found my way to the Speck Pond Shelter where I pitched my tent. I had gone 9.5 miles that day and was exhausted. Before I began to pitch my tent, I spent some time decompressing by working a Sudoku puzzle I had picked up at a shelter.

⋙·⋘

I awoke early, broke camp, and clamored out of the valley I was in and headed up to Old Speck Mountain. The last two days had been quite demanding and for some reason I had kept my appetite. Usually when I started on the trail I did not have much of an appetite for a few days. The previous two days I had consumed more trail food than I had planned and was sure that I would not have enough food to make it to Rangeley. I decided I would go into either Bethel or Andover to get some food.

At Highway 26 there is a trailhead parking lot. There had been a lot of activity on the trail from people who were just stopping for a small hike up the mountain. There I met a nice couple who wanted to know if I wanted a ride to Bethel. They did not live far from the trail and had thru-hiked the trail in a prior year. They had just dropped off some friends who were hiking for a couple of days. I accepted the ride and soon was in town. I ate at a Chinese restaurant and bought some groceries.

Getting back to the trail was not as easy as getting to Bethel. I had played with the idea of staying the night in Bethel, but the day was fairly young so I headed out of town walking and thumbing at the same time. After about forty-five minutes I caught a ride back to the trail. Out at the trail the daunting challenge of Baldplate Mountain faced me and I was tired, but I persevered and the climb of well over two thousand feet was eventually accomplished.

At the Hall Mountain Shelter I expected to be the only one there and I was right. Most hikers go into Andover for resupply and there are some good options for hikers to stay in town. I was too tired to make the push to get to the road so I dropped my gear and stayed for the night.

It would be another Maine marathon. There were two large descents and two tough climbs before the trail would level off some. I was not expecting Moody Mountain to be so tough.

At the Bemis Mountain lean-to I met a thru-hiker whose name I cannot remember. He, like me, was struggling with the decision to move on or stay at the shelter. It was early in the day, but I was tired. Maine was wearing me out fast. But in the end we both opted to get back on the trail and push on. Part of our trouble was we did not know if there was a place ahead to pitch a tent. In Maine so much of the terrain is rock or it is too steep to find a level place that is a comfortable place to pitch even a small tent. Our trail guide listed a stream and we decided to gamble. If we pushed hard we could make it by dark. And we arrived with enough light to pitch a tent in a nice camping area and fix supper. It was a seventeen-mile day and I was glad the next day would be a short one.

When I woke up, my hiking buddy was long gone, leaving only some tent stake holes in the ground. I was glad I had slept so well because the previous four days had beaten me down. After some Raisin Bran cereal with dried milk, I left the campsite and headed up to cross Highway 17 and work my way to Rangeley. I had some new pep in my step because I had a light day and Marilyn would join me that night. The heat that day was unbearable and I soon was out of water. I came to a pleasant shelter at a pond. It was called the Sabbath Day Pond Shelter and it was nice. There were canoes at the pond. The water source was a piped spring with ice-cold water. I spent some time at the shelter recovering from the heat and dehydration.

The rest of the day I was light on my feet. I was looking forward to getting to the inn and having dinner with my wife. When I arrived at the road there were a couple of locals who offered me a ride in the back of their truck. The one caveat was

I was going to have to share the back of the truck with his two Labradors. I knew I was going to be in the shower in a short time so I toughed it out. It was a ride I would just as soon forget. Once in town, I checked at the inn and waited for Marilyn. She arrived later that night and we began making plans.

I arranged for a shuttle to take us from Stratton to the Kennebec River. Our plan was to hike back to our car at Stratton. We arrived at the river soon enough to get across on the canoe ferry. We stopped at a beautiful waterfall and took pictures. Marilyn looked great in her hiking outfit with the mist rolling off of the beautiful waterfall. Our goal was to get as far as we could the first day out so we could make it to the Bigelow Mountain Shelter the next day. We put in about seven miles and then set up a stealth camp with the two-person tent I carried.

Monga handled everything well and seemed to be enjoying herself. We were both glad for the mosquito netting on the tent. The mosquitoes were swarming us while we set up tent. Once in the tent we spent a few minutes with our headlamps on killing mosquitoes trapped in the tent. We celebrated our great camping spot and a pile of dead mosquitoes with some nuts and chocolate-covered raisins, then we settled in for a good night's sleep.

⟫•⟪

Monga impressed me. She walked all day with a good pace and no problems. She commented on all the work done on the trail by volunteers. She was especially impressed by the boards installed through the swampy area. The care of the trail was something I had never taken for granted. We stopped at a shelter for lunch and a rest before we pushed on to the next shelter.

Later in the day the stream we had counted on for water was dry and we had to go on without resupply of water. It was anther hot day and we were parched. We were out of water but we were led to believe there would be a stream ahead. We met a thru-hiker heading north late in the day.

Once we had greeted each other, I asked, "Is there a stream ahead with water in it?"

"No, I don't think so." I may have a quart you can have"

"You will not get water until the shelter so you will need all you have. There are a couple of dry streams where you may think you are getting water. We are headed to the shelter up the mountain so we will be okay."

"There is a nice source of water there."

"You are sure there is not water in a stream ahead? It looks like a pretty good stream according to the map."

"I am sure there is not one. But it is only about four miles to the shelter for you."

Later we came to the large stream shown on the map and were able to get water. The hiker would have had to ford across the stream in knee deep water, and he did not remember any water in the stream. It is a common experience to plod along mindlessly when hiking and miss things you would otherwise notice.

After we spent some time drinking, we pushed on and we ran across the 2,000-mile mark for the trail. It really did not mean much to me because I was hiking the trail in sections. However, I was close to the 2,000 miles on my hike and would cross that point in two days on Saddleback Mountain. Before we walked up Bigelow, I gave Monga the choice to abort the hike at the road and find a way to our car. She saw no reason at the time to do that and so we headed up the base of the mountain to the shelter. It was another mile and a half and a fair climb. The long climb at the end of a seventeen-mile day was enough to leave me impressed with Monga.

At the shelter were several thru-hikers, including the hiker I had camped with a couple of nights before. Monga and I elected to stay in the shelter as long as the bugs did not bother us. We spread some DEET on and I fixed supper, did the dishes, and put things in order for the next day while Marilyn visited. There was a storm threatening, but it did not materialize. We did get some troublesome news from those who were northbound. There was no water on the mountain until the far side. And we knew the weather forecast for the next day was extremely hot. Monga and I talked about going back down to the road and ending her hike. We decided to sleep on it.

Monga is as social a person as there is and she enjoyed visiting with the hikers in the shelter. And they enjoyed her.

We were the last ones out of camp and just as we were to make the turn to proceed on, Monga decided it might be better to go down to the road and hitch a ride. I am sure I talked her into it. I was concerned about the complete lack of water on the way up on a day that was supposed to be in the nineties. We were carrying four quarts of water and I could go through that much myself on a hot day. I assured her it was not going to cost me any time because we were going to take two days going over the mountain and down the other side and I could do it in a day by myself. So we made the mile and half walk back down and hitched back to our car in Stratton. It took three hitches to get back to the car. We drove into Rangeley to stay the night. While we were sitting in a restaurant that afternoon, an unbelievably violent storm hit and we decided we had made the right decision. I would not have wanted her in that storm.

❖•❖

The next day Marilyn drove me back to the north side of Bigelow and let me off. We set a time to meet late in the day at the parking lot on the south side of the mountain. I was going to have to go almost eighteen miles so it gave her plenty of time to discover more of Maine. The storm the afternoon before did nothing to cool off the mountain or start the water flowing. I went in the mile and half up to the shelter, got three quarts of water, and was on my way up the mountain. The climb up was not that strenuous but it did take some time. There were places where I had to climb on all fours up, which made it a typical Maine mountain. I went through my water in no time. I topped the mountain in the midafternoon and took a break there to enjoy the view and reflect. The view was gorgeous and the weather was great for relaxing.

The rest of the day was fairly easy. There were a lot of people on the mountain that day. It was a great Saturday to conquer a mountain. I was able to get water about six that afternoon at a shelter. It took me a few minutes to replenish my dehydrated body.

The downhill was not all that difficult, but it was just a long way down. Once I was off the mountain, I crossed about two miles of lowland swamp and was within earshot of the highway when Marilyn met me. She was excited about the souvenirs she had bought and the shops that she had visited. I was glad to have crossed another Maine mountain. It was a win-win.

❦

It was Sunday and I decided to make it a light day. I checked the maps and decided I could do Crocker Mountain as a day hike and then spend the rest of the day taking it easy. That day's hike would only be ten miles and it would leave me with Saddleback and Sugarloaf Mountains and I would be done with Maine.

Marilyn drove me to the south side of the mountain and let me off. The climb was not hard by Maine standards. I met a husband and wife who were thru-hikers named Jitterbug and Hoover. They were from New Hampshire and were southbound. They were carrying extremely heavy packs. I tried to be subtle in my assessment of their packs. I thought as I left them that they would never make it unless they cut down their base weight. I would meet them a few weeks later in Vermont on the same day I finished the trail.

At the peak of Crocker I met a married couple who were "peak baggers." Peak baggers set goals of conquering peaks according to various criteria. I once met a peak bagger in Colorado who was working on "bagging" every peak in Colorado above 14,000 feet. I met one once that was bagging the highest point in every state in the continental U.S. These particular baggers were going after every peak above 4,000 feet in New England, of which Crocker was one.

At the parking lot, Marilyn was waiting and we went to an old hotel in Kingsfield. We enjoyed staying there and decided we should go back there some time to spend some quiet time in the fall.

❧⬥❧

I had a late start the next day. For a Monday there were a lot of people on the mountains. They were mostly locals out for a hike for the day. I saw very few with backpacks. From Saddleback I could see Sugarloaf and it seemed as if it was a three-day hike away. My plan would be to get to the Spaulding Mountain Shelter, which was almost to Sugarloaf. That would be a nineteen-mile day. A short hike the next day would finish off Maine. I ate lunch at the peak of Saddleback, took some pictures with a nice-looking young girl there, and was off. The hike that day was made interesting by some of the local characters I saw. It must have been a full moon because all the weird people were about and acting strange. But I took delight in knowing people were using their time for such outdoor adventures as hiking.

❧⬥❧

At the Poplar Ridge Shelter, I saw Jitterbug and Hoover again. The husband and wife team that I met on Crocker were a very nice couple that I would have enjoyed hiking with. They had checked in for the night, but I was only stopping by for some water and a peanut butter cup. They were a little confused as to why they were seeing me again heading north and I explained how I was hiking the trail with short hikes while my wife was with me so we could spend our evening together.

I wished them luck and happy hiking and was off. It was late enough in the day that I knew I would have to push hard to make the shelter by dark. I do not like hiking after dark.

From the Poplar Ridge Shelter it is a steep drop down to a stream and a long climb back up to the shelter. I walked as quickly as I could and made it with very little light left. There was no one at the shelter, which did not surprise me. There is a building at the top of Sugarloaf, which was nearby. Hikers are permitted to use it. It is popular with hikers because of the view. Sugarloaf is the second highest peak in Maine. From Sugarloaf you can see Mount Katahdin to the north and Mount Washington, New Hampshire, to the south. I did not have enough daylight to get to the Sugarloaf. I ended the day with a cold supper and was asleep in no time. I was pleased that I had gotten such a late start and was still able to get in nineteen miles. That night was one of the few times that I stayed in an AT shelter by myself.

In the morning I got out of the shelter earlier than I had planned and walked the last few miles to the road. Along the way there was a place high on the ridge where I took a wrong turn. It was around some semi-alpine scrub. I only went a few feet before something did not look right to me and I slowed down. What I thought was the trail had become loose rock at the steep edge of a cliff. I gingerly retraced my steps the few feet back to find out where the trail had gone. I recognized that as a precarious spot for any hiker. I took the time to tear off some scrub and make a pile that would block hikers from making the same mistake that I did. The cliff overlooked a drop off of about one thousand feet. A fall like that could ruin your whole day.

Marilyn was not due yet, so I walked almost to the highway before she arrived. She had packed and loaded the car for the trip home. Once Maine was done, I changed my mind about it. It is a beautiful state and I would go hiking there again. It still is not my favorite state, but I can see why Old Corpus and his gang would think so.

THE FINISH

Dalton, Massachusetts to Hanover, New Hampshire
Total Miles Hiked: 178
Days hiked: 10

It was now Labor Day weekend and I was leaving for the last trip to the trail. I had a few miles in Massachusetts and all of Vermont to do. Approximately one hundred seventy miles left. It was only fitting that my parents were visiting us that weekend. So on Saturday we had dinner together, I said my good-byes to them. I slipped out at 1:00 a.m. One plane ride and two bus rides later I was in Pittsford, Massachusetts. I walked from the bus stop all the way to the trail. It was a hot day and no one would stop and give me a ride, but that did not bother me at all. I had gotten so many rides from so many nice people, and I was on my way to the trail for the last time. I was so excited I could have walked on my hands.

I got to the trail at Dalton late in the day and my destination was Cheshire. There was a bed and breakfast there that I could stay in to launch my last push to Hanover, New Hampshire. The ten-mile hike to Cheshire was an easy one, and I arrived at the B & B just after dark.

I had arranged with the hostess to have a cold breakfast. I was out early in the day with the expectation of getting to the Seth Warne Shelter, which was on the other side of the Vermont border. I planned a lunch at the memorial on top of Mount Greylock.

The climb up the mountain was very gradual and did not pose any problem. The mountain was quiet because the road access was under construction. The only noise came from the construction workers who were working on the road. All the services, including the hostel at the top, were closed. I anticipated seeing some southbound hikers, but there were none all day.

At the top of the mountain I stopped for a long lunch break and made some phone calls. It was a beautiful sunny day so I tried to take a nap, but the thought of not making the shelter kept me from going to sleep.

The views from the peak were fabulous. Mount Greylock is the highest point in Massachusetts. From its peak you can see four other states: New York, Connecticut, Vermont, and New Hampshire. When open, there is a road that takes visitors to the top. Located on top is the Veterans War Memorial Tower. It is a seventy-foot tower dedicated to those who fought in all conflicts. There is also a building that houses a hostel for hikers and a snack shop when it is open. As is my custom, I paid respect to the servicemen represented by the memorial.

The hike down Greylock was not as easy. The last 1,000 feet down was very steep. At the bottom of the mountain, I crossed a small residential area and met a group of hikers from Princeton. They were out for an extended backpacking trip. The seniors were leading incoming freshmen on a hike for a few days. It was a form of orientation. I was impressed by the concept. The group seemed very cooperative and polite. I talked with some of them. But they seemed quite subdued and talking with them seemed to be off limits. It could be they were all exhausted by the demands of the trail. It is delightful when teenagers can be exhausted to the point that they are quiet.

Over the next few days I would see numerous groups from several colleges, all very well behaved and respectful. It was another example of the great variety on the Appalachian Trail.

I crossed a narrow corridor of houses and businesses lining the main highway and headed back up into the mountains.

Once in the forest I found a great little stream to have supper and rehydrate. While I was enjoying my supper of peanut butter and Fritos, the college students I had seen earlier came by. They seemed to have recovered and were in good enough spirits that a couple of girls flirted with me.

The climb up the mountain was not overly demanding and I was soon up on a ridge. After topping the ridge, I found what I was looking for—the state line. There was no war hoop or noisy celebration. I was too tired for that. I broke out the bag of Fritos and ate what was left of them while I sat there contemplating the next and last border one hundred and fifty miles away. Soon I was at the Seth Warner Shelter and ready for a good night's rest.

The good night's rest was not to be. There was a southbound hiker whose name I neither can remember, nor want to. He had tarried long over John Barleycorn and was suffering mightily. In the night he was moaning and vomiting. Several times in the night, I was awoken by his discomfort.

The twenty-two miles from the day before and the lack of sleep at the shelter were not enough to take the bounce out of my step. Back in Maine the year before I had met thru-hikers finishing their trail and tried to imagine then what they were feeling. Now I was experiencing that sensation. It was like being a senior in high school on the last week of school. I dropped down off the ridge and onto Highway 9 and gave no thought to going into Bennington. It was a town known for being very good to hikers, but I had plenty of food and was walking with purpose. I had also estimated my days and I needed to average around twenty miles per day in order to get to Manchester Center. I had planned on that being my last stop in town.

One of the reasons I needed to get to Manchester Center was I had shipped some items ahead that I had been doing without. One of them was my stove. Given the difficulties traveling on a plane, I did not leave Michigan with fuel for my stove. I was not sure TSA would take kindly to me packing a flammable liquid in my luggage. Since I was arriving in Vermont on Labor Day, getting fuel may have been a problem. So I sent some fuel along with my stove. I had been running a cold camp until I could get to Manchester. It would be another twenty-two-mile day.

Vermont is a great place to hike. I was almost wishing I had started a couple of weeks later so I could be in Vermont during the peak of leaf season. I was seeing some color but the peak would be later. The one problem I was having was water. It had not rained in a long time and many of the streams and springs had dried up. I carried extra water all during my hike in Vermont. When I arrived at the Goddard Shelter for the night, I loaded up on water from the trickling spring.

At the Goddard Shelter there were about eight hikers. They were all hiking the Long Trail. The Long Trail starts at the Vermont/Massachusetts border and follows the ridges of the Green Mountains all the way to Canada. The two hundred and seventy-mile trail is the oldest footpath in the U.S. It was established before the AT was even thought of. The first hundred miles of the Vermont AT is shared with the Long Trail until they split and the Long Trail continues north and the AT turns east. The name Vermont comes from is the French words *Verd Mont*, meaning Green Mountains.

⇒•⇐

The next morning I was glad that I had loaded up on water from the spring because it was dry when I was ready to leave. On the way I passed by a large encampment of college kids out for their orientation hikes. I left early because the days were getting shorter and so in order to get in twenty-plus miles you had to leave early. That morning I met a south bounder on the trail named Tits. His trail name was the result of a remark he had made early in his hike about the shape of the Maine mountains. I had to laugh because I noticed that after I had been on the trail for a while, everything took the form of a female body. We helped each other on locations and lack of locations of water, which was a growing concern for all who were on the trail. I also met a group of southbound hikers who referred to themselves as the "Samari." There were four of them and they were quite energetic.

My objective that day was the Stratton Pond Shelter. It was just under twenty miles. I came to a "stream" on the map. It was bone dry. Later I was barely able to get water at the East Branch of the Deerfield River. Tits told me of an apple tree near the river so I was able to water up and also get some fresh fiber. The apples were a welcome change to the food I had been eating, and I took a few extra.

I settled into the Stratton Pond Shelter just before dark. I had the place to myself that night. After dark, while I was working on getting to sleep, the Loons on the pond started singing. If you have never laid at night in the northern darkness and listened to Loons you have missed something special. Their cry is distinctive and leaves you wondering what they are saying. It is a melancholy kind of cry that causes you to think deep thoughts. I have spent a lot of time in the northern bush country where they are prevalent. It is no wonder Canada made the loon their national bird. I went to sleep at the sound of their crying, wishing Marilyn were there to take it in with me.

❧•❧

I awoke at the crack of dawn, intent on making it to Manchester Center by noon. I knew there was a Friendly's there and I was working on a calcium deficiency that was best treated with a large chocolate shake, which I would down in memory of Feather. But first I would have to negotiate twelve miles of Vermont trail. I must have been fixated on the town food because twice I missed the turn in the trail and all together added an extra mile to my day.

Midmorning I met and walked for some time with Stalker from Rochester. She was thru-hiking the Long Trail. We walked together until I met Cooker Hiker going in the opposite direction. I recognized him immediately from the year before. We had met briefly in Shenandoah Park and again in southern Pennsylvania where he was serving as a trail angel in a park. He was thru-hiking the Long Trail. I brought him up to speed on my hike. He was a section hiker that had finished the trail in 2005. It was as if God had put him there as a final encouragement to me, and I walked away from our visit with a new kinship.

I made it into town and filled up on town food. I then found the library to check my email. After that I went to the store to resupply and there met a couple who were section hikers named Needles and Pit Stop. They would play a part in the rest of my hike. From there I walked out of town to a hotel that had great hiker rates and a diner next door. Before I left Michigan, I purchased a ticket to the NASCAR race in New Hampshire. It would be a small reward for me, as well as an incentive to keep up a good pace so that I did not miss the race.

❖•❖

The next day I was off early for another twenty-mile day. I ran into Needles and Pit Stop taking a break and stopped and talked to them. They were from the city of New York. Needles was given his trail name because he was a brittle diabetic and required injections.

I also met a mother and daughter from Vermont who were out hiking for a few days. The mother was younger than me and seemed to be quite suspicious of me, as if I was after her daughter. Aside from that the trail was quiet, considering it was a weekend. I settled into the Lulu Tye Shelter and had a good night's sleep.

❖•❖

The morning brought rain. It was also quite cold that day and I kept walking fast just to keep warm. As it is with most hikers, my custom was to always look ahead, calculating so that I could figure where I might stay. I had heard good things about the inn at the Long Trail. It is a must for any hiker. From my estimates, I did not have to hurry that day. I could be there easily the next day.

So later in the day when I reached Highway 103, I walked a mile off the trail to the Whistle Stop Restaurant. I was in the mood for a BLT and a piece of pie. I missed out on a downpour while I ate a great late lunch and enjoyed some coffee. After that I was off to the Clarendon Shelter. There were several hikers at the shelter—it was good to have some company.

❧·❧

I awoke to the delight of walking sixteen miles. I was in ski country and most of the mountains were skiing mountains. I visited with a few south bounders and a man in his sixties with his daughter who were peak bagging all peaks in New England above 4,000 feet. That day I arrived late in a heavy rain at the Inn of the Long Trail. My feet had been wet most of the day and blisters were starting to form.

Before eating, I went and showered up and changed into my eveningwear. I then went to the bar and found Needles and Pit Stop and they welcomed me as if I was a long-lost relative. I joined them and ordered a Rueben. Between the Rueben and the forecast for heavy rain the next day, I resolved to take the next day off. Needles seconded the motion and the ayes had it. It was settled. We were all going to stay another day. I still had plenty of time to get to Hanover and was expecting the last forty-five miles to go easy and get there in two days.

❧·❧

After a much needed day off, I left Needles and Pitstop and did not see them again until Hanover. That morning I ran into a group of about twenty women who were out on a guided excursion. They seemed interested in the trail and its hikers. Once past all of them, I pushed hard all day with very little rest. Late in the day, I came to the Wintturi Shelter. There was a hiker there who was just out for a few days. He was in the army and had just come back from Iraq. We talked about hiking mostly, as I did not know if he wanted to talk about Iraq. He was in for the night and was getting ready to eat. I had a quick bite to eat, thanked him for his service, and was off.

I was able to do three more miles that day and ended up with about twenty-two miles that day. I rolled my sleeping bag out on my pad and slept under the stars that night, quite satisfied with my accomplishment over the last few days.

It was a great night for sleeping under the stars. I awoke at the crack of dawn and ate a cold breakfast, packed up, and was off. I had only about twenty-four miles to go and was determined to get to Hanover that night—not because I had to in order to meet my schedule, but just to be done with the trail. I crossed the highway leading to Woodstock and went up the ridge. The hike was not strenuous at any time that day. I was enjoying the hike. I met a local who was out for a few miles and he clued me in on a great place ahead for a burger, which is always welcomed information. The rain the two days before had eased the water situation.

Early in the afternoon I came across something I had never seen before. It was a cable or hose that went from tree to tree. I had spent a lot of time in the woods and never saw anything like that. I thought at first that it might be an electrical cord to something. Upon further study, I decided it was a hose and that the trees were tapped for maple syrup. I was in Vermont syrup country. I live not far from a town called Vermontville in Michigan and tapping trees and making syrup is a big thing, but they use buckets to catch the syrup and I had never seen hoses used. Vermont is the number one producer in the U.S. of maple syrup. I followed the tube as far as I could and it went to a small shack, where I presume they cook the liquid down. The entire incident made me hungry for a stack of pancakes.

With my geography lesson out of the way for the day, I continued on until I got to the general store at West Hartford. It was early afternoon and I was hungry. I stopped in for a burger and some rest. Back on the trail, I was headed up in the woods when I ran into Hoover and Jitterbug. They were still at it and seemed to be doing just fine. I had been expecting to see them if they were still on the trail. We talked for a little bit and I proudly explained to them I would be done with the entire trail by dark. After our visit, I topped Griggs Mountain and headed down. Just before dark I crossed over the Connecticut River and arrived at the center of Hanover. I was done with the trail. There was no fanfare. There was no one to celebrate with. I thought of Scout, Feather, Zama, Lug, Tank, and the others. I sorely wished they were there to share the moment, but I was heading home to my wife and that excited and pleased me. I checked into a local hotel and gladly made the phone calls.

❦

The next day I rented a car and took care of some business and stayed in Lebanon overnight again. I also went and found Needles and Pitstop and had breakfast with them. They needed to get to Pittsford and I was going on to Boston with my rented car. I offered to drive them to Pittsford, which was not that far out of the way for me. I enjoyed my time with the couple. After I let them off, I was on my way to the north side of Boston, where I had made hotel reservations. After treating myself to the NASCAR race at Loudon, I headed home.

CONCLUSION

My wife had me back. At home the family was waiting with a party, complete with gifts. The gifts were items purchased from the AT website that would remind me of my hike. Not that I needed reminded. One of them was a five-foot tall, framed map that hangs in my office to this day. I stop often and look at the map and reminisce. I look back on the experience as one of the highlights of my life.

One thing I learned on the trail was that you can find happiness and contentment in the simplest of things. Like the moment at the Stratton Pond Shelter when the loons started singing. And the trail has a way of simplifying life. You have three questions to answer everyday. What am I going to eat? Where am I going to get water to drink? Where am I going to sleep? I lost thirty pounds on the trail. I have since gained it back. But I look at life in simpler terms and find that I do not need as much to make me happy now. I find family and friends are what most delight me.

I often think with fondness of those who I hiked with and those who helped me on my way. I went by myself but found out hiking is not a walking thing but a people thing. And the myriad of locals that helped us hikers on our way has had an effect on me. My sense of accomplishment must be shared with them. My attitude toward my fellow man has changed. Certainly, alone is much better together.